ODYSSEY MOSCOW

ODYSSEY MOSCOW

ONE AMERICAN'S JOURNEY FROM RUSSIA OPTIMIST TO PRISONER OF THE STATE

MICHAEL CALVEY

The
History
Press

*For the men of cell 604. Your courage
and decency during the darkest of times
was, and remains, an inspiration.*

Jacket illustrations: Michael Calvey arrives for his hearing, 29 October 2019
(Maxim Shipenkov/EPA-EFE/Shutterstock); Red Square at sunrise (Mordolff/
iStockphoto).

First published 2025

The History Press
97 St George's Place, Cheltenham,
Gloucestershire, GL50 3QB
www.thehistorypress.co.uk

British Library Cataloguing in Publication Data.
A catalogue record for this book is available from the British Library.

ISBN 978 1 80399 730 8

Typesetting and origination by The History Press
Printed and bound in Great Britain by TJ Books Limited, Padstow, Cornwall.

MIX
Paper | Supporting
responsible forestry
FSC
www.fsc.org   FSC® C013056

Trees for Life

Contents

Preface

Thursday, 14 February 2019. Moscow

It is almost dawn when I hear the dull thudding through my earplugs. I have only recently arrived from London and the noise comes at me through a fog of semi-sleep. Thud. Thud. THUD. On it goes. I assume it is the neighbours. What the hell are they doing at this hour?

I sit up in bed and adjust my earplugs. That's when I work out that the noise is not coming through the wall. It is too clear and crisp for that. With growing anxiety, I realise it's coming from my front door. I get out of bed to investigate, wearing just a pair of shorts, but the view through the peephole in my front door is blocked by someone, or something. Then there is a new round of pounding from the other side, shaking the door with its force. I hear the muffled voices of several men directly beyond, standing just a few feet away. *Holy shit, they are here for me*. Now panicking, I rush to my bedroom to get dressed. Before I can get there, the door bursts open and ten or twelve men charge through, some with weapons drawn, screaming at me to freeze and raise my hands in the air. Shocked and disoriented, my hands shake with adrenaline.

When I went to bed just a few hours ago in my rented apartment in a 1990s block just off Moscow's central Tverskaya Street, my only concern was to be ready for my meeting later today. There has been an ongoing business dispute and the hope is we can negotiate some sort of resolution. Now I find myself literally staring down the barrel of a gun. A collection of them. The men wielding the firearms, I grasp, are operatives from Russia's FSB – the successor organisation to the old Soviet secret police, the KGB – and from the Investigative Committee, roughly equivalent to the American Federal Bureau of Investigation.

I grab yesterday's clothes from the floor – jeans and a button-up shirt – and try to put them on as one of the invaders shouts at me to keep my hands visible. He holds his gun with tension in both hands, pointed at the floor. Dazed, I do up the buttons of my shirt all wrong. When they can see that I am going to try to neither fight nor flee, they holster their weapons but keep their hands on them, just in case. From their muscular frames and abrasive commands, it is clear that these are hardened *operativniki* trained in combat. Two of them stand either side of me, one holding on to my arm, while the others fan out through the apartment to secure the location. They push me towards the sofa to sit down, while they remain standing.

With the search in full flow, one of the investigators engages with me. He is in his late 30s or early 40s, the only one who has no weapon. He also wears a different uniform from the black or camouflage outfits the others sport. He is passively aggressive and warily confident, rarely making eye contact as he takes in the apartment and considers his next steps. He presents me with a paper indicating the criminal accusations made against me. They relate to the business disagreement I have come here to try to settle. My company, Baring Vostok, includes in its portfolio a bank, the Vostochny Bank. Vostochny recently acquired shares in a group of promising fintech companies in lieu of a debt, but two minority shareholders at Vostochny recently raised questions about the deal. I immediately understand that this search must have been initiated by these shareholders, Artem Avetisyan and Sherzod Yusupov. I know their accusations are bogus and without substance. Yusupov even admitted a few months earlier that he had only raised questions about the deal because of a wider shareholder conflict in which his own actions were being investigated. But negotiations to resolve the dispute have been heated and recently reached an impasse. It was my hope that this evening's scheduled meeting might help us all find a new path through. A hope that now seems distant, to say the least.

My first impulse as my apartment is ransacked is to try to bring my racing heart rate down. The logical side of my mind dismisses the idea that this is the first step in a genuine criminal investigation, since there has been no crime. It is, I conclude, surely just a business tactic – a brutally delivered message from Avetisyan and Yusupov intended to intimidate me and to sway the flow of negotiations in their favour. I try to remain stoic and keep a poker face. I want to avoid showing any outward sign of the fear gnawing deep in my core.

They search my apartment for about four hours, during which time they confiscate my phone, iPad, and laptop, as well as old personal papers. I have no idea what they hope to find. They even carefully flip through a pile of business cards and very old photos – dating from pre-digital days when we still had film cameras – as if they think they might find some evidence of espionage. Mr Passive-Aggressive pauses at one photo in particular. It's of my first child, Mishuta, when he was about 4 years old. He has a black eye in the picture, the result of his typical rambunctiousness. The investigator gestures at it and gives me an accusatory look. He asks something like 'Are you also guilty of child abuse?' Like all my interactions with them, it is barked at me in Russian. I am so stunned that I can't tell if the question is a joke. 'Are you serious?!' I demand to know. He ultimately decides not to seize that photo and discards it, but he keeps several others for 'further investigation' – old family snaps and pictures from a friend's wedding, presumably to check out if I am in touch with American officials or any Russian opposition figures.

About halfway through the search, an advocate, Dmitry Kletochkin, arrives. I haven't met Dmitry before but his firm has done some work for Baring Vostok previously, and he has been scrambled on short notice to come and support me during the search. I have been forbidden to use my phone, but it turns out my office is also being raided, so the news has quickly got back to my colleagues and they immediately engaged Dmitry to come to my aid. Having lived in Moscow since the '90s, I can speak Russian fluently, which is how I have been able to communicate with my interrogators. But Dmitry speaks English. One of the first things he does is to pull me aside for a private word. 'Imagine that this is like the surprise attack on Pearl Harbor,' he says. 'It seems devastating right now, and we are obviously at a disadvantage since we weren't prepared for it. But there is a system to fight back, and in the end we can win.' I think that this simile is an apt one. In any event I take comfort from it.

After they finish their search, the lead investigator settles down weightily at my kitchen table to write up a report. As this takes him a couple of hours, the six or seven remaining FSB operatives mostly sprawl out on my sofas and take naps while I pace nervously around my kitchen. Once the report is printed and signed, everyone puts on their warm coats and I am led downstairs past the stunned concierge, a typical 70-year-old Russian grandmother, who still hasn't recovered from the shock of the morning raid. She watches on as I am stuffed into an unmarked car with a few FSB operatives flanking me closely on both sides. The engine revs up and I am driven away to the headquarters of Russia's Investigative Committee, a roughly fifteen-storey building set amid mostly Soviet-era residential apartments in the Basmanny district, just outside Moscow's Garden Ring Road.

In the course of a few surreal, terrifying hours I have morphed from one of the most successful Western businessmen in Russia into a prisoner of the state. Like Odysseus setting off to return to Ithaca after the long Trojan War, I have no idea what now awaits me. Or when I'll be back home.

SECTION 1

FEBRUARY 2019

1

The Accused

The Russian Investigative Committee headquarters are a cheaply constructed relic of the 1990s. Before we are allowed to enter, we have to pass through a temporary security checkpoint – a tiny, windowless kiosk outside the main entrance. Today the checkpoint is jam-packed with witnesses or detainees like me: about ten people, including a few FSB minders, standing shoulder-to-shoulder in the dim space while paperwork is checked. No one makes eye contact; the tension is palpable, and the suffocating room reeks with sweat. After fifteen or twenty minutes, my documents are approved and I am led inside the investigators' fortified compound, surrounded by high, concrete walls topped with barbed wire.

The main building is a dreary place, with long corridors of closed, silent offices. It reminds me of Orwell's Ministry of Truth. There is an atmosphere of plodding but irresistible force, the kind that can slowly grind a stone into powder. It's the sort of place that instils not exactly fear, but hopelessness.

By the time our arrival is 'processed', it is about 2 or 3 p.m. I am left with my advocates (Dmitry has now been joined by a colleague) in the office of a major – the same investigator who has led the search of my apartment – while he goes for a long lunch. It is a small, typically cluttered office of a mid-level bureaucrat, with dusty wooden filing cabinets stuffed with towering stacks of official papers, accented with random personal knick-knacks including, incongruously, miniature gnomes and tiny mammoth tusks.

I learn from Dmitry that the investigators have been busy this morning. Several of my Baring Vostok colleagues – Vagan Abgaryan, Philippe Delpal and Ivan Zyuzin – have also endured house searches, as have Maxim Vladimirov, the CEO of PKB (another company involved in the dispute), and Alexey Kordichev, the former CEO of Vostochny. They are now all being questioned elsewhere in this same Investigative Committee building.

I am told that, when the major returns, I will be interrogated and a formal statement taken. My advocates remind me of some facts around the business deal in question, which is helpful as it all happened a couple of years ago and I don't have access to any files. The major appears and I give my statement, explaining that I wasn't involved personally in the deal since our funds had no relationship with IFTG, the company at its centre, but that I knew that it was profitable for Vostochny. I also lay out how our accuser, Sherzod Yusupov, had himself personally negotiated the transaction and approved it. I name two or three people and companies who I am sure have all of the relevant documentation and can prove that no crime was committed. We are allowed to check the statement for mistakes before it is printed and signed by all sides. By now, it is about 7 p.m.

In a rare gesture of humanity, I am allowed to make a single phone call using my advocate's mobile phone. I call my wife, Julia, who is back at home in the UK, where we have lived for the last ten years. She answers hesitatingly, no doubt nervous of a call from a phone number she doesn't recognise. I can tell immediately from her voice that she already knows what is going on. She must have been under incredible strain today, but she is an unbelievably strong woman – truly the foundation stone of my life. We both almost lose it during the call but when I start to cry, she quickly regains her composure. She tells me exactly what I need to hear: that our family depends on me staying strong. It is tough love at its best, sobering and true. We discuss how to explain what is happening to our three kids and agree to wait to see what tomorrow brings – it is still unclear whether we are being subjected to a savage negotiating tactic or whether they actually intend to charge and convict us. I tell her, of course, that she shouldn't come to Moscow, even though she wants to support me.

I feel much stronger knowing that she and the kids are safe and out of reach of our enemies.

I have another couple of hours to wait before I am sent to an overnight detention centre. While I wait, a new investigator approaches me: a young man in his mid-30s dressed in a fashionable three-piece suit. Unlike the other officials I have met so far, he speaks very good English. Catching me in the corridor by the elevators, he asks how I am doing in these difficult circumstances. The question strikes me as odd and I suspect this is no chance encounter; he seems to be fishing for information. We have a brief and light conversation about some of the differences between America and Russia. He asks me, 'How much salary do American police investigators earn?' This is typical of the sort of question I often get in Russia, but I still find it ironic to hear in the corridors of Russia's Investigative Committee. I know what he is angling at, trying to show that his salary is a pittance compared to Americans in the same job. I tell him I don't know the figures, since I have never been directly in contact with America's criminal justice system, but I lowball a guess at $3,000 per month. He looks at me suspiciously, saying, 'Well, if that's all they get as salary, they probably get a lot of other benefits for free, like housing.' I realise there is no point trying to debate the subject as he clearly only wants his own prejudices confirmed. So, instead I simply change the subject.

Before long, I am put into handcuffs on the orders of the major, loaded into a cage in the back of a convoy truck and driven around Moscow for what seems like several hours, stopping occasionally to drop off or pick up other detainees. The cage, which I have to myself, is dark and it is impossible to see anyone else, though I can hear noises of at least three or four other prisoners locked in their own spaces. A wave of exhaustion from the stress of the day's events sweeps over me, so I try to close my eyes and rest, but it's impossible to find a comfortable position as the truck lurches and stops and starts abruptly, again and again. It is overheated too, as is often the case in Russian vehicles, so I swelter in my winter down jacket that I can't remove because of my handcuffs. Whenever someone is dropped off or picked up, the door opens for a few minutes, ushering in a swoosh of freezing Moscow air, initially refreshing but quickly leaving me shivering.

Veering between sweltering and freezing for hours on end feels like another intentional punishment.

Finally, the truck stops and it is my turn to be led outside. We have arrived at a temporary detention centre for those awaiting trial. There are apparently several such facilities in Moscow, each about three or four storeys high and with space for between fifty and seventy-five cells. I have no watch and my sense of time is off, but I gather it is well after midnight. I am ordered to take off my clothes and I'm searched from head to toe. They confiscate anything that might be either useful to me (like a pen and paper) or dangerous (my shoelaces and belt). When I have redressed, they lead me to a small cell, no more than 3m by 4m and containing three beds. Apart from that, there is one small shelf, an ancient metal teapot for boiling water, a sink, and a toilet area in the corner – in fact, just a filthy hole in the floor with a metre-high cardboard screen on two sides.

There are already two prisoners in the cell. I am initially apprehensive about how they'll receive me but I don't have to worry for long. One of them, Sasha, a barrel-chested Russian bear about 40 years old, immediately introduces himself. The other, Ildar, is a short, wiry Chechen in his early 20s. He is more reticent, not moving from his bed and only nodding vaguely to acknowledge me. When I tell them my name, Sasha asks where I am from. 'No way!' he says when I tell him. 'A real American? That's amazing!' They ask how I have ended up here. I decide to give them the short version. Then Sasha asks, '*Kakaya u tebya beda?*', which literally means 'What is the source of your trouble?' (The closest expression in America would be 'What are you in for?') It is the first of many times I am asked this question in the prison system. I check the paperwork given to me by the investigator, then tell Sasha I'm here on a charge of 159.4, 'fraud of large scale'. 'That's really cool!' he replies. He wants to know how much money is involved. I decide to downplay the figures so as not to appear too wealthy or grand. I tell him it's a dispute over a loan of 2.5 *million* roubles ($33,000), a factor of 1,000 times less than the real number. Sasha nevertheless strokes his chin and nods his head gravely, as if to acknowledge what a huge sum this is.

Sasha goes on to tell me his life story. He is a gregarious companion and takes pride in being able to show a foreigner the ropes of life inside. I learn that he's been married three times, in prison five times previously, and has been arrested this time for stealing someone's mobile phone. In between spells in prison, he works in the building trade installing windows. But, he tells me, it is hard to make a living this way, what with bills to pay and wives and everything else – you just can't get ahead. In comparison with life on the outside, he reassures me, prison isn't so bad. You don't have any bills to pay and you get to watch TV most of the day. But of course, he says, it all depends on which prison you are sent to. According to his own insider ratings of Russia's most famous prisons, he considers the nineteenth-century Moscow jail Lefortovo as the best he has experienced so far. He ought to post this stuff on a Prison TripAdvisor, I think to myself.

Ildar is much more reserved than Sasha. I never learn what he's been arrested for. Occasionally he yells out the window in Chechen, responding to shouts from some other Chechen prisoners in different cells. He spends most of his time exercising, forever doing press-ups. I tell him about a recent bestselling book in America called *Convict Conditioning*. That immediately gets his interest. We spend an hour comparing ideas on fitness training regimes, and Sasha joins in enthusiastically, too. He shows off his biceps that look like cannonballs. It's just the way he was born, he insists, and the same with his giant beer belly.

Eventually, I lie on my bed and try to sleep but with little success. The cell is stuffy and hot, an oppressive stench hanging in the air as if from accumulated decades of human sweat mixed with the indescribable horrors emanating from the toilet hole area. The lights are left on, presumably so the guards can look in on us periodically. The squeaky iron gates in the corridor clang open and shut all night long. Adrenaline continues to flow around my body as I try to process what is happening and what to expect next. I wonder if my case has gone public yet or if it's being kept quiet. And what about my colleagues from Baring Vostok? How are they coping in their cells wherever they might be? I'm still struggling to believe that this is a genuine attempt to arrest me. I just can't imagine that anyone can seriously try to construct a criminal allegation around a transaction from which we have derived no personal benefit and which had proven genuinely profitable and valuable to the bank. I figure that once a few senior people in the Russian government learn what's happening, there'll be a backlash against my accusers – perhaps even prompting an investigation into their historic investments, some of which really are suspicious.

I think about the reaction of the wider investment community to my arrest. I am well known for promoting Russia and defending the country's image as an attractive place to work and invest. But if word is out about my arrest, anti-Russian commentators in America are probably on TV right now, saying that my detention is yet more proof that no one is safe investing in Russia. I reckon this situation will cause damage to the Russian investment climate by a factor many hundreds of times larger than the amount at dispute with the shareholders. Surely there will be an appetite among the nation's intelligent and powerful to avoid such harm. As I lapse into brief and fitful sleep, I convince myself that I am merely being sent a message, and that tomorrow I'll be released back home.

★ ★ ★

It's about seven o'clock and I am sitting in my cell, struggling through my first prison breakfast: black tea with a cube of sugar, a slice of dark bread, and a strange glutenous substance that alleges to be oatmeal. It reminds me of the gruel eaten by Morpheus' crew in *The Matrix*, thin and tasteless but just about enough to keep you alive. When I'm done, I roll up my bedding and mattress and place it on top of my small bed, just as it had been left for me. Then I get dressed and await whatever fate has in store for me today. When the guards arrive to collect me, Sasha gives me some of his stash of *pryaniki*, a sort of Russian molasses cookie. It's his parting gift, along with a bear hug and a hearty 'God be with you!' A reminder of the decency and generosity of ordinary Russians that I have experienced so often in my twenty-five years here.

I am handcuffed and loaded into another convoy truck, this time heading for the Basmanny District Court. I will discover that this is the preferred court for Russia's Investigative Committee, as it approves almost 100 per cent of their recommendations. In fact, my advocates can't recall a single occasion when it has opposed the Committee's wishes. Over the years, it has been the setting for some of Russia's most controversial trials, like that of Mikhail Khodorkovsky. While I wait for my hearing, I am kept in a holding cell under the court. There are about ten of these cells, each around 3 sq m in size, with no windows. On the walls are scribbled messages, most referencing God or Allah. Each one is signed with the criminal statute number of the accused. One reads: 'God be with you! Mitya, 201.1'. Another takes a more defiant tone: 'Fuck them all! Ivan 160.2'. Last night's lack of sleep is catching up with me. I take my 'Dolomiti' black down jacket, roll it into a pillow and curl up on the rough wooden bench at the back of the cell. Before long, my eyes close.

When I rouse, I have lost all sense of time again. Have I been in this dungeon for an hour? Three? Five? Not knowing the time is, I realise, a special kind of torture for those of us used to modern, constantly connected lifestyles. Occasionally I hear someone being escorted into or out of the adjacent cells. Someone is brought into the cell next to me and knocks on the wall three times. I am not sure whether this is some kind of secret messaging system but I can see no downside to sending a return message. I knock back three times on my own wall. This is repeated a few times with the inhabitants of other cells and I find it oddly reassuring, providing confirmation that I am not alone.

Eventually, two guards open my door, put my handcuffs back on, and lead me out of the holding area. One of them gives me a heads-up, telling me that there are a lot of journalists upstairs, so I can cover my face if I want to avoid the cameras. I have always thought that is about the dumbest thing any person can do. A quick way to make yourself look guilty. I have nothing to hide or to be embarrassed about; I have done nothing wrong and I know who the real guilty parties of this piece are, so I determine to hold my head high as I walk into the court. I am not going to give those bastards the satisfaction of seeing me look afraid.

Even so, I am unprepared for the level of attention. Unless you have ever been the subject of intense media or paparazzi scrutiny, you can't really imagine what it is like to be exposed to the bright glare of a dozen video cameras and the snapping of throngs of photographers, each of them shouting at you in unison. There must be more than 200 people crowded outside the courtroom, but it is such a blur amid the flash of cameras that I cannot make out individual faces. It is a disconcerting assault on my senses. However, I do hear the unmistakable voice of my old driver and friend, Valera, shouting 'We are with you, Mike!'

The hearing is not about the merits of the case against me, but solely to determine what method of detention I will face during the planned investigation. The best result would be to be released on bail, but I might be detained under house arrest, or assigned to a 'prison isolation centre' (SIZO). The judge is Artur Karpov, whom I would later learn has adjudicated in several other notorious Russian criminal cases, including the infamous and tragic Magnitsky case during which Sergei Magnitsky, a lawyer who exposed corruption by state officials, died while in custody. In the courtroom I am put in a cage with glass walls, familiar to anyone who watches Russian TV. There are about twenty people allowed in court at any one time, and most of them seem to be journalists, although I am relieved to spot a few friends and colleagues, too. My advocates deliver a series of character reference letters from a host of my Russian friends (including the cosmonaut Alexei Leonov, entrepreneur Oleg Tinkov, the businessman and politician Ruben Vardanyan, and the internet pioneer Leonid Boguslavsky), as well as bail guarantees from influential Russian business figures, including Kirill Dmitriev and Peter Aven. There is even a letter in my support from the legendary Russian Olympic wrestler Alexander Karelin – a man I have never met! At least, I think to myself, I have not been abandoned.

Then the investigator reads the charges – the first time I am able to hear the details of the accusations against me. According to Yusupov, my colleagues and I have defrauded Vostochny by settling a 2.5 billion-rouble ($33 million) loan to PKB with shares in a technology company, IFTG, that they say are worth only $3,500. My advocates respond on a number of technical and procedural grounds as to why I should not be detained. Then, finally, it is my turn to speak. 'Almost everything you just heard from the investigator and from my accuser is false,' I begin. Then I briefly explain the real reason for our arrests, driven by the shareholder conflict in Vostochny. These commercial disputes are in the process of being addressed in the London Court of International Arbitration, I explain, where our accusers face potential liabilities of 17.5 billion roubles ($231 million). My belief that I have done nothing wrong is validated by the conclusions of the Russian Central Bank in a detailed audit report. I tell the court that I believe the accusations I face today are intended to help our accusers gain control of Vostochny and so avoid liabilities for their own actions. I also note several points in the accusation that are simply false.

My arguments seem to be making an impression on Judge Karpov, who visibly winces upon hearing my forthright description of the facts. His weary expression indicates that he understands he is now embroiled in a mess, rather than the clear-cut case that was probably presented to him. The support I have from figures influential in Russian society is doubtless food for thought as he ponders how best to proceed with this charade. He asks for a recess to run until tomorrow. I feel this is a hopeful sign.

I am kept in my cage while the press and other observers file out of the courtroom. I spot my assistant, Sasha, among them, and reach out to make a fist bump against the cage's glass wall as she walks by. She smiles and raises her fist to bump mine from the other side of the glass, before she is hustled away and scolded by the court security guards. Then I too am led out and loaded back into a convoy truck with several other prisoners. I am the last to be dropped off, and by the time we have made it round several different detention centres, it has been a couple of hours. Arriving at my new temporary detention facility, I am put in a cell with only one other prisoner. Mitya is a tall, wiry man with a shaven head in the classic Russian prison style. He has been arrested for theft. As he chain smokes, he tells me with pride about his early days in the 'business' in the 1990s, when he once 'persuaded' some railway officials to 'lose' a train car full of copper, which he managed to sell on very profitably. After he has regaled me with tales of his adventures, we are joined by a third prisoner, Alexander. I guess he is in his late thirties and his clothes suggest he is a prosperous man.

I find out that he owns a business in the aviation equipment sector, and that he is accused of selling important technology and secrets to foreigners. With his broken English, he tells me he knows who I am because he saw me on yesterday's news. Like me, he is clearly new to this whole system of Russian prison life and is visibly shaken up, breathing hard, moaning, and looking altogether miserable. Mitya, on the other hand, wants to ask me about Trump. 'What's he really like?' he says, assuming that I know him, since we are both Americans. I tell him that I have no personal knowledge of the man and then give my usual balanced assessment of the president, including his pluses and minuses. I can tell it's not the simple answer Mitya is after. He pauses briefly and says: 'Well ... anyway ... tell him hello from us! ... And to get rid of the sanctions!'

Time is pressing on and I try to get some sleep but a telephone in the corridor rings through the night at intervals of fifteen or twenty minutes. Just enough that I can't fall asleep. I close my eyes and try to rest at least, knowing that tomorrow will be another hard day. I breathe deeply, drifting eventually into a sleepless, trance-like state, visualising myself in a suit of armour that I wear to tomorrow's court hearing, and beyond.

Before I know it, I am eating breakfast again. It feels like *Groundhog Day* as I consume the same uninspiring food, put on my same jacket and hat, get handcuffed and loaded on to a convoy truck just like yesterday's. Back at the Basmanny court, I am stuffed once more into one of the same dreary holding cells. At least the wait is shorter today. After extensive press interest in my comments yesterday, this time journalists with video cameras are forbidden in the courtroom, at the request of my accusers. They obviously want to prevent anyone from publicising the real facts of the case. My advocates supply another wedge of character references from even more impressive Russian business figures, some of whom I don't know personally, but whom I know and admire by reputation. I am moved and encouraged by their courageous support.

Any expectations I have are tempered by my advocates, however, who tell me that my arrested colleagues have already been ordered to be detained for at least the next two months in special prison isolation centres. The chances that I will receive a different decision are remote. I imagine the many phone calls and meetings held by my supporters since yesterday, advocating on our behalf, but no doubt countered with lies being spread by my opponents. I recall Winston Churchill's description of Soviet politics as a fight between two bulldogs under a carpet; an outsider hears just the growling, and it's only clear who has won when the bones fly out from beneath the carpet.

I am canny enough to know that one can have many influential friends in Russia, but when factions are competing, it is the FSB who generally have the decisive voice. Clearly they are siding with my opponents, unmoved by the threat of reputational damage to Russia and its system resulting from the unjust arrests of myself and my colleagues. Judge Karpov, who seems fractious today, announces his decision that I should be detained in 'SIZO' for a further two months.

One of the witnesses at today's hearing has been the head of security at Vostochny Bank, and a henchman of Yusupov and Avetisyan, depicting himself as a 'victim'. He waits until after my sentencing and for all the journalists to leave and then starts filming me in my cage on his phone. I have the sense that he is getting a kick out of seeing me suffer. From his sadistic giggle, I gather he is livestreaming. I suspect Yusupov and Avetisyan are watching, perhaps popping the champagne corks. I try to remain expressionless and refrain from doing what I really want to, which is to shout at them all to fuck off and go to hell. It is one thing to fiercely defend your business interests, but what kind of person gets enjoyment out of seeing another human being suffer? If there really is karma in this universe, this security guy deserves to be reborn in the next life as a worm.

Eventually, I am taken back to the convoy truck. As I am shoved back inside the iron cage and the engine begins to turn, my mind races with images of the kind of misery that awaits me. I expect they will put me under increasing pressure to try to break me and make me confess to non-existent crimes. I imagine sharing a cell with a band of veteran 'thieves in law' notorious in the Russian prison system — the sort of organised criminals who have the status of 'made men' in jail. How will I cope? I have devoted almost my entire adult life to championing investment in Russia, and convincing other foreigners to share my optimism for the country. I have been notably successful in this, in large part because I genuinely believed it. Now I feel deeply betrayed, bewildered that I could be rewarded with such a fate.

I lean wearily against the wall of the cage, scrunched up in a ball with my handcuffs over my knees, trying to buck up my spirits and stay warm as two days of accumulated sweat begins to freeze on my skin. At last, the convoy truck grinds slowly to a stop. The guard, stretching stiffly after the long ride, opens the creaky metal door to go outside. It is a bone-chillingly cold Russian winter day, about -20° Celsius. After a few moments, I hear the footsteps of the guard, striding back towards the truck. He steps purposefully inside, unlocks my cage and leads me out. The truck is parked in what initially looks like the inner courtyard of a normal Moscow apartment building, except without the usual parked cars, or the customary aluminium 'rakushki' storage sheds, and other signs of residential life. But now I notice that this courtyard has no visible exit, and the windows of the surrounding buildings are all barred.

This, I discover, is Investigative Isolation Unit #1 at the notorious Matrosskaya Tishina prison – my new home for the foreseeable future.

2

Welcome to Alcatraz

I spot another guard standing outside the truck and wearing a different uniform, his arms folded across his chest. He says something in
awkward English. With his thick accent and odd intonation, it takes
me a few seconds to process and understand him: 'Welcome … to
Alcatraz.' From the grim smile on his face, he is clearly delighting in
the arrival of his new American prisoner. He doesn't intend for his
greeting to be reassuring and it isn't.

Still handcuffed, I am led through a heavy steel door and up some
stairs. I am not yet familiar with the prison rules so 'Hands behind
your back!' is barked at me at intervals. Every 30ft or so is an iron
gate, each requiring keys about 6in long which must be given two
or three rusty turns to unlock. As we enter the stairwell, one of the
guards presses a button, triggering a wailing siren louder and scarier
than anything I have ever heard before. It brings to mind the infamous
shower scene from Hitchcock's *Psycho*, but slowed down to make it
even creepier. Truly spine chilling. I wonder if this is all part of some
psychological game, but I realise there is a practical purpose. It alerts
other guards to the presence of a prisoner in the stairwell so that the
isolation for which this place is designed can be preserved.

When we reach the second floor, there are three more guards waiting for me – a sort of 'induction committee', who search me from
head to toe. They are all young guys, in their 30s, wearing camouflage
uniforms. Since my shoelaces and belt have already been confiscated,

there's nothing else for them to take. They ask a few questions for their forms and welcome me to Matrosskaya Tishina. I know it by reputation as an institution that has housed several famous and infamous prisoners; a place synonymous with misery and despair. In my mind, I see the image of a candle being snuffed out.

I am sent to a small room where a doctor makes a quick check of my temperature and blood pressure. I am surprised to see that my levels are normal, given the stress I am feeling. He also takes blood and urine samples and tells me I will be quarantined for three days while they are tested. I am taken to a cell and it is only now I realise that I haven't seen any other prisoners in this huge building full of cells. Prisoners mixing, I quickly learn, is considered to pose a risk of information sharing or witness tampering that might thwart investigations.

Compared with my cells from the last two nights, at least this one is clean and comfortable. There is a larger side table to sit at and write or eat, a proper toilet with full walls almost to the ceiling for privacy, and even an old TV. On the wall is a security camera, which recalls to me the Eye of Sauron in *The Lord of the Rings*. There is a small hole in the door (a *shnift*) for observation from the corridor, and a speaker through which commands are given. A list of the prison's rules, along with the rights and daily regime of prisoners, are also displayed. Although my spoken Russian is good, my reading is less so, so it takes a few days to get to grips with what it all says. But I do learn that if I have any complaints, I can contact the Ombudsman, Boris Titov. This is good news as I know Boris from business circles in Moscow. He has a reputation for honesty as well as forging good relationships within 'the system'. Useful to know.

A guard brings me to the shower room, and I take a hot shower by myself. After two and a half days of intermittently sweating and freezing, I need it badly. I am given just one bar of soap, which is for both washing and shampooing. The floor tiles have that slippery-filmy feel of a locker room shower just after it's been used by an entire football team. My allotted towel is the size and thickness of a small kitchen rag. But I stand under the hot water for twenty minutes, luxuriating and swearing that I will never again take for granted such a glorious indulgence.

The lights, it is quickly apparent, are kept on in the cells twenty-four hours a day. From around 10.30 p.m. until 6.30 a.m., they are slightly dimmed but never low enough to prevent the Sauron eye from watching and monitoring you even in your sleep. Feeling like a laboratory mouse under constant observation, I lie awake thinking of my colleagues who have also been arrested – all honest men and top professionals who have always acted with total integrity, and who have done nothing wrong. Now they too are in prison, all of them with young families, even younger than mine. It must be especially frightening for Philippe Delpal, a Frenchman who doesn't speak Russian. I feel responsible for them all.

In the morning I am given an iron bowl, a spoon, and a large iron teacup. The breakfast round is heralded by three metallic raps on the cell's steel door and the opening of a small square opening, about 12in across. I stick my bowl through, as I have been instructed. I can vaguely hear but not fully see the kitchen ladies who ladle oatmeal into my bowl, along with a big lump of sugar and a slice of black bread. The portions here are larger than in the temporary detention centres, and with the addition of the sugar the oatmeal is even edible. I find out that my bar of soap also has to do for washing up my bowl and cup after meals. This is all far from my accustomed lifestyle, but I realise that I can survive this. As I contemplate my bowl, I am reminded of a promise Mao Zedong made to his followers: having the Communist Party, he said, is like having an 'iron bowl', a symbol that you will be fed amply and reliably. Of course, millions of Chinese later starved to death during the Great Leap Forward. I am at least confident I won't die here because of lack of calories.

It is 8.30 a.m. and the guard comes to my cell as per his regular daily routine. This is the only time a prisoner is allowed to request anything. I ask if he can bring me any English books or newspapers. He explains that every request needs to be submitted in writing on an official request form (a *zayavlenie*) but, since this is my first day, he'll make an exception and check. When he comes back, he helps me fill out a *zayavlenie* for a Russian–English phrase book from the prison library. It is an ancient and well-worn copy, and the guard advises me to use it to decipher the rules on the wall.

I ask if it's possible to send a letter to my family. He says that normally it is but just now the prison censor is away on holiday. The censor has to check all post in and out of the prison to make sure no hidden, prohibited messages are getting through. 'When will he back?' I ask. The guard tells me it will be March or April. I suspect he's telling me a lie, messing with me. But, no, it turns out to be true. There is only one censor and he gets an eight-week holiday each year. The guard tells me that it is not possible for me to have any newspapers either. I am desperate to know what is being said about my case. He says I can subscribe to certain Russian daily newspapers but only once I have been assigned a permanent cell and have set up a 'personal money account' with the prison. This, he informs me, normally takes a couple of weeks to process and can only be done with a *zayavlenie*.

Late morning, I am taken by the guards up the *Psycho*-siren stairs to the top floor of the prison for my daily *progulka*, a one-hour period when all prisoners have the right to walk in the open air. Since this is a SIZO and not a normal prison, this occurs in small open-roof cells where no prisoner comes into contact with any other. These *progulka* cells have walls about 5m high, then an opening of about 1.5m (covered by barbed wire, but open to the air), topped with a corrugated metal roof. They are only about 20 sq m, with a small wooden bench fixed in the middle of the stone floor. Being mid-February in Moscow, it is bitterly cold. I'm guessing -20 degrees. I ask how I am supposed to avoid freezing. The guard circles his hand in the air and helpfully tells me to walk around until I heat up. Then he locks the heavy metal door behind me and I am left to my own devices. I jog briskly in tiny circles around the wooden bench, and, sure enough, after about ten minutes, I am feeling warm enough to unzip my coat. Music from the Retro FM radio station warbles from loudspeakers, a surreal soundtrack to the pair of machine-gun-toting guards who walk on a gangplank up above charged with surveilling the ten or so open cells up here.

When my hour is up, I feel refreshed and renewed as I return to my cell for the rest of the day. I fiddle with the cell window, which is lined with an opaque film to prevent you from being able to see anything out. At least it provides a little light and I discover it can be opened about 6in to let in some fresh air and offer a fleeting glimpse of what lies beyond. I stick my face into the gap and inhale deeply. Moscow's winter air and the sounds of normal life in the distance transport me in my imagination to a time when I am walking the streets again as a free man.

Dinner that evening is a bowl of soup and half a fish – overboiled, tasteless and full of bones. But I need the protein and eat the whole thing. I think how amazed my wife would be to see her husband, an Oklahoma boy raised in cattle country, devour it. But with a lot of free time and few distractions, I figure it's worth the effort to take that fish apart bit by bit with my bare hands. I treat it like a project. I guess I probably look like Tom Hanks in *Cast Away*, stranded alone on a remote island, slowly sucking on the legs of a crab while staring silently at the horizon. When I am finished, I switch on the TV in my cell, which shows all the main Russian channels. I watch a dubbed Hollywood movie, *Law Abiding Citizen*, starring Jamie Foxx and Gerard Butler. It's about a corrupt American prosecutor who lets a vicious killer free, and then the victim's husband comes back years later to gain revenge on them all. Mentally, I drift off into my own ridiculous revenge fantasies before coming back to reality.

When I try to get some sleep, I am relieved to find that Matrosskaya Tishina is quieter than the temporary detention centres. The *Psycho*-siren stairs are, thankfully, used only infrequently throughout the night. But there is something other-worldly about the place. I hear an assortment of strange sounds wailing periodically from outside in the courtyards. They make me think of phasers in *Star Trek*, zapping for about ten seconds, falling silent for minutes at a time, then zapping again. My sleep is further disturbed by my having to get up several times with a bad stomach. Must have been that fish. My volatile American stomach has not taken long to succumb to the combination of *balanda* (prison food) and my own questionable washing-up skills.

Around midday the next day I am sent to visit the prison psychologist, as per standard procedure. A psychological evaluation of each prisoner is made to decide to which cell – and with which group of other prisoners – you are to be assigned. I am initially suspicious that this is all a ruse aimed at extracting information from me for the criminal investigation, so I answer the psychologist's questions cautiously. But eventually I accept that the evaluation is genuine. He asks if I drink alcohol, take drugs, or ever feel suicidal. Yes, no, no, I reply. He asks me if I am a fighter or a negotiator. I tell him that I defend myself when I am cheated or threatened, but overall, I'm flexible and always willing to negotiate compromises. Hmm, he says, writing that down. Then he shows me eight pieces of cardboard, each of a different colour, and asks me to rank them in order of my preference. I go brown, blue, yellow, green, purple, red, grey, black. He asks me why I chose that order, and I play along, giving an apparently thoughtful but actually completely nonsensical and made-up explanation. When he is gathering up his things to leave, he stops suddenly and asks me, Colombo-style: 'Oh, by the way. Are you an introvert or an extrovert?' I guess this is to determine whether they will put me in a three-man or eight-man cell for the rest of my time here. I don't trust him and wonder whether I'll be assigned the opposite of whatever preference I indicate, so I hedge and say: 'Both.' He smiles and jots down my response before leaving.

It strikes me that I am still wearing the same clothes that I threw on during the raid on my flat days ago. If I had known that I was headed for a lengthy incarceration, I would probably have chosen something different to wear. But with gun-wielding FSB operatives yelling at me, such considerations were not at the top of my list of concerns. Now, though, I feel slightly ridiculous to be in prison wearing jeans and a Loro Piana Oxford shirt and sweater, along with black New Balance sneakers with the laces now removed. For one thing, it is completely impractical to wash clothes like these here, and almost a week down it's becoming a problem. At least my alpine ski hat has been great for pulling down over my eyes to block out the light when I need to sleep.

Later in the day, I meet one of my other advocates, Dmitry Savochkin. He may be more of a commercial lawyer than a criminal one, but he is always a welcome sight. Advocates must wait in a reception room, often for hours, while the guards review the schedule and bring prisoners into assigned meetings rooms on a rotation, ensuring that no inmate ever sees another. Advocates must leave their phones and other communications devices outside and are searched before being admitted to a meeting room in case they are carrying any contraband documents – in other words, anything that might actually be useful. Each meeting room contains a small scruffy table surrounded on three sides by stools bolted to a warped linoleum floor. There are bars on the window and the rooms are monitored with both video and audio devices, making it impossible to speak confidentially. When it comes to Russian criminal investigations, there's no such thing as attorney–client privilege.

Dmitry explains that he and my other advocates have only learned today where I have been held. He asks after my health and tells me that I'll be assigned a permanent cell tomorrow. Then we run through some details about the case and our planned appeals. After a while, we get up from the table and turn our backs to the door. He leans in and whispers in my ear some additional information about our defence, and I respond likewise. It must seem ridiculous but it is the only way to maintain any privacy from our opponents. He tells me my case is generating huge publicity in the Russian and international press, and that the entire business community supports us. He also says that my office will probably be able to organise deliveries of food and other provisions once I am assigned my permanent cell. The basic message is 'We are working on it, so stay strong'. I ask him to pass word to my family that I am OK, that the guards are so far following all the rules, and that they are not to worry about me.

Dmitry also manages to inform me that Matrosskaya Tishina is colloquially called 'Kremlin Central' because so many inmates are involved in high-profile cases being investigated with the highest level of scrutiny. In such cases, an informal approval for arrest and detention is typically sought from the Kremlin itself. The upside is that most prisoners here are being investigated for economic crimes, rather than violent ones, and that living conditions are better than the average prison. The bad news is that virtually no one gets released without a conviction.

After Dmitry has gone, I watch some Russian TV news and it is striking how much of it is about people being arrested, being paraded in handcuffs, standing in glass bubble cages in courtrooms. Viewers are given the impression that virtually everyone in the country, or at least all its business people, are criminals. At least I get some unexpected succour from the advertisements. A few promote state-owned giants like Sberbank and Gazprom, but most are for private companies, including many in which Baring Vostok funds have invested and played a role in moulding: Yandex, Tinkoff, and Avito, to name just a few.

I lie down on my bed just before the TV switches off at 10 p.m. I think of the strange dichotomy in Russia. On the one hand, entrepreneurs with big dreams, creating products that hopefully improve real people's lives. On the other, a state-controlled media system that usually depicts businesspeople as corrupt schemers. How ironic, I think, that I am lying here right now, having done as much as any foreigner to promote and develop projects for the optimists of Russia. I drift off unhappily to sleep, once more feeling betrayed and alone.

I am unsure how long I sleep for. My bunk comprises a solid metal lattice with zero flexibility, and the prison mattress is hardly made for comfort – about 3in thick, soft, and shiny from years of use, it appears to have been designed not to promote good rest but primarily to be easy for prisoners to roll up and carry under their arms when they are moved about the jail. I suffered a slipped disc a few years ago in my lower back, and my new sleeping arrangement is causing it to become inflamed. I tell the guard when he comes for his 8.30 a.m. meeting, and he helps me to write a *hodataistvo* (an application) for an additional mattress. He expresses his sympathy but warns me not to get my hopes up, pointing towards the ceiling and shrugging. This is the typical way for Russians to show that something depends on the approval of their superiors, which they deem unlikely.

Perhaps as a consolation, he brings me a copy of yesterday's *RBK*, a leading daily business newspaper. It carries an extensive, two-page article about my case. This feels like a breakthrough moment: the first time I have any idea about how my plight is being reported. The coverage seems balanced and allows comment from both sides. Certainly enough to convince any unbiased reader that the charges against me and my fellow defendants are obviously fake. The piece also includes quotes from several prominent Russian business figures, testifying to their belief in my character and integrity. You can tell a lot about the real views of any newspaper by the photos they select, and they have chosen one of me looking brave and determined at my hearing. Although that's not exactly how I felt in those stressful courtroom moments, it is a good indication that the media believes our story and is being allowed to print the truth, or at least enough of the truth. I re-read the article several times, calculating its implications and formulating what our next steps should be.

In the afternoon, a guard comes to take me to the prison doctor. This is in a different building within the same complex, but instead of walking the 100m there, I am sent by myself in a convoy truck to ensure my isolation from other prisoners. When I get out of the truck, a new guard says to me in English 'Don't shoot!', pointing his fingers at me as if holding imaginary pistols, ha ha. Like most Russians, his ideas about America seem based on films and TV shows, especially the police-detective shows beloved by the prison guards. As an American prisoner, I understand I have rarity value and I'm obviously a source of amusement. Because of the news coverage, they all seem to know about me, and I can feel eyes watching me with extra interest. Is this a good thing or a bad thing? I don't know. Some of the guards are decent human beings, but others seem like truly cruel bastards.

The doctor turns out to be a middle-aged woman with kind eyes but absolutely no smile. She is all business. I explain my back problem and she writes some things down in a booklet, then tells me I need an X-ray before any decision can be made. Do you have a machine, I ask. 'No, it's broken,' she tells me. But new equipment is scheduled to be delivered to the prison. When? 'Soon.' I do not hold my breath.

With this appointment out of the way, I have another – with one of my other advocates – at 5.40 p.m. With the meeting area closing at 6, this is the last slot of the day and we have to discuss everything very quickly. He tells me he has been kept waiting in reception since 10 this morning. An *operativnik* – an FSB guy, rather than a standard prison guard – knocks on the door and joins us, allegedly just to take my fingerprints for official records, but also to pass on warnings about restrictions around my communications with the outside world. He reminds us both that it is a criminal act to either send or receive any information prohibited due to the investigation. To emphasise this, he makes us stand against the wall with our hands above our heads while he searches all my papers and those of my advocate. Then he pats us down to make sure we don't have anything hidden in our pockets. By the time he is finished, it is past 6 p.m. and a regular guard arrives to take me back to my cell.

I work my way through dinner (cabbage and potato stew) and prepare myself for another night of broken sleep. As I continue to struggle to make sense of my new reality, I start to retrace the steps that have led me here. My mind turns back to 1991 and my arrival in Moscow as a naïve young man seeking to make his way in the world.

3

Genesis

If anyone had met me in 1989 when I was 21 and graduating from university, I would have seemed the unlikeliest person in America to ever even visit Russia, much less to build a career and family there. Yet just a couple of years later, I was part of a wave of young Americans and Europeans rolling into Moscow seeking fortune or adventure, and preferably both. Most of those other early expatriates had either some ethnic roots in what was then still the Soviet Union or had studied Russian at university. But neither applied to me.

My childhood in America was playful and down to earth, growing up as a middle child in a middle-class family in the middle of the country. I was born in 1967 in Milwaukee, Wisconsin, to parents of mostly Irish Catholic roots. We moved to Oklahoma when I was an infant as my father, an engineer, took a job in the burgeoning oilfield equipment sector. Like many of Irish origin, he was the kind of man who delighted in regaling the same twenty or thirty humorous stories and anecdotes, laughing uproariously with each retelling, while my mom rolled her eyes in the background. My mom was a straight-A student in science at university and could have pursued almost any career, but had four kids by the age of 26 and chose to stay at home to raise us. She was, I now realise, a saint.

We lived on a quiet and leafy street near the edge of a city expanding rapidly due to the oil boom. A vision of American middle suburbia, except the fact that there was wild undeveloped land just at the end of our street, about 100 acres of forest and fields with a red-muddy creek running through it. This was our Middle Earth, where we built tree forts and staged imaginary battles with our wooden swords and bamboo spears. There was me and Kevin, my older brother by a year, and we used to fight a lot, at least when we weren't terrorising our little sisters, Cathy and Beth, who somehow always trusted us despite the constant betrayals. Then on Saturday mornings we'd eat dough-nuts and sit on our brown shaggy carpet in front of the TV to watch cartoons, mostly *Bugs Bunny* and *Scooby-Doo* and *Superfriends*.

I was always a dreamer. The first book I remember reading was a children's illustrated anthology of Greek and Norse mythology. Odysseus was a favourite, with his epic tale of woe and adventure, struggling to return to his homeland after the Trojan War. I just never imagined I'd play out my own version across the continents a few decades later. From kindergarten through year 12, I always attended Catholic schools. Among the boys in our family, Kevin had the repu-tation as the smart academic one, and I was the athlete. At high school, Bishop McGuinness in Oklahoma City, I was obsessed with basketball and played two or three hours every day. I was never good at drib-bling, a vital part of the game, but I was tall, could shoot straight and apparently had sharp elbows, which are advantages in basketball, as in life. I worked hard enough, finally, to be co-captain of the school team and to receive some minor regional awards.

Away from the court, I wasn't great at anything else in high school, but I was decent at most things without doing much work. I got along well with all the different cliques in our school, and perhaps as a result was elected class president in my senior year and also 'Best All-Around' of our graduating class. I was also pretty good at talk-ing and arguing. That was especially useful in the philosophy and ethics class taught by Mr Thomas, one of those great teachers whose influence spans the years. His classroom discussions, which used the Socratic method to encourage critical thinking, gave many of us our first stirrings of intellectual curiosity. He taught not what to think, but how to think – more importantly, how to think for ourselves.

In hindsight, it was also at McGuinness that perhaps the first seeds of my interest in the Soviet Union were sown. Ms Hathcoat taught economics and, as part of her course, we read and discussed a book called *The Russians* by Hedrick Smith. The *New York Times* correspondent in Moscow in the 1970s, Smith was a natural storyteller. He related his first-hand experiences of life in Soviet Russia, the various ethnic groups, domestic life, and cultural habits. Through his evocative prose, you could almost smell the Soviet cigarettes and samovars and communal apartments. The book had little to do with practical economics, but Ms Hathcoat sensed that giving us some insight into daily life in what was then America's major adversary would help us better understand the reality behind events reported in the mainstream news. She was right. It was an inspired choice.

Oklahoma experienced an oil boom in the 1970s and early 1980s, mostly as a result of distant events in the Middle East that caused the price of oil to skyrocket. The ripple effects of those events could be felt in the prosperity of my friends' families. While our family holidays typically involved driving to my grandmother's house in Milwaukee or to the beach on the Texas Gulf coast, some of my friends' families started travelling to exotic places like Europe. It wasn't unusual for my friends' older siblings to get a small sports car as a present on their 16th birthday, when they became old enough to drive. Even my thrifty father started to take my mom on an annual holiday somewhere special, like San Francisco or Acapulco.

To earn my own spending money, I had a variety of part-time jobs starting from when I was about 13. Mowing the lawns of my neighbours, flipping burgers and working the drive-thru at McDonald's, hauling sheet rock on construction sites, driving a fork-lift at a factory, shovelling asphalt in front of the steamroller of a road-paving crew. Even today, whenever I smell fresh-cut grass, newly sawn lumber, or French fries coming out of the oil, I can close my eyes and be transported immediately back to those times. I especially remember the road-paving crew, which was like working in a blast furnace: pungent fumes from the tar boiler invading our nostrils, inescapable; the road behind us shimmering like a mirage in the sweltering Oklahoma heat; footprints from our boots sinking slowly into the sticky, melting asphalt beneath us. Men of my age are inclined to exaggerate the hardships of their youth and have an

almost ridiculous nostalgia for them. Yet these jobs were undoubtedly character building.

However, while we were on holiday at my grandmother's house
in Milwaukee in July 1982, my family's fortunes took a hit. My dad
worked for a company that sold casing, tubing, and other downhole
equipment to oil companies – not the big household-name ones but
smaller, independent businesses. His customers were mostly big-
talking oil men who perfected the art of skating on thin ice while
using other people's money. Sales contracts were agreed on the golf
course or over three-martini lunches. His customers rarely paid
promptly even when times were good; they always gambled all their
liquidity into the next promising exploration acreage or drilling
partnership. Banks competed to lend money even to risky start-up
ventures and investors from the East Coast were also piling in, believing that oil prices would go to $100 and it was a one-way bet.

But during that holiday, my father took a call in my grandmother's
kitchen as the rest of us sat at the table. He picked up the old rotary
phone, listened silently for a minute, and then quietly said, 'Oh, shit.'
I remember that moment as clearly as if it were yesterday, since it
was almost the only time I heard my father curse. A local bank in
Oklahoma City, Penn Square Bank, had gone bankrupt. As the biggest
lender to high-risk oil exploration ventures, this bank issued letters of
credit for their customers to pay suppliers, including my dad's company. Now those letters of credit were worthless. This day changed
everything for our family and for many other families in Oklahoma.

For the next few years, new sales essentially disappeared and his
company, along with other disgruntled creditors, tried desperately to
collect even cents on the dollar from their old bankrupt customers.
Unemployment in Oklahoma City reached between 10 and 20 per
cent and those fancy sports cars of my friends' older siblings were
repossessed. While my family were not in the direst financial straits,
we still had to cut new expenses to the bone. My dad informed all
of us kids that university costs were no longer something he could
afford unconditionally. He promised to give us enough money to
pay tuition at the local state university, and everything on top of that
would be our own responsibility. I remember the moment he told us

the grim news, and my mom stayed silent with a small tear forming in her eye. This tumultuous time left me with two deeply imprinted psychological traits: I have an inherent reluctance to borrow money or go into debt; and I can smell empty bullshitters from a mile away.

When the time came for me to go to the University of Oklahoma (OU), it was not only the practical economic choice but the most logical one too given my ambition at the time, which was – strange as it now seems – to become the Governor of Oklahoma. Like a lot of young Americans in the 1980s, I was impressed by the charisma and sunny optimism of Ronald Reagan, and found his conservative narrative compelling. Going into politics as a career seemed to make sense, and OU seemed the right place to go for anyone who wanted to pursue a career locally. (If there is such a thing as divine intervention, surely my avoidance of a career in politics is evidence of it! For this, among many other things, I should be eternally grateful.) As it turned out, I loved my years there. It was rowdy and hysterical at times, and I made some devoted friends. But it was also where I finally really stepped up my game academically.

I credit that to attending Officer Candidate School (OCS) in the Marine Corps in Quantico, Virginia, the summer after my freshman year. It was brutal, both mentally and physically. We woke every morning at 3.30 a.m., running or drilling most of the day through forced marches, obstacle courses, and intense physical training. My drill instructor, Sergeant Wallace, was a Vietnam veteran whose torso and head had been wounded by flames in the war, leaving scars and a perpetual grimace that made him terrifying even before he spoke. But it was truly scary when he screamed in your face, his gravelly, slashing voice attacking you like a buzzsaw. I developed a brain hack that helped me get through it. Not long before starting OCS, I had finished a film studies class at OU, where my final thesis paper was a study of Kubrick's classic film, *2001: A Space Odyssey*. The spectacular trumpet and drum score from the film's final scene was still ringing in my ears, and a vision of the mysterious Black Monolith was power- fully lodged in my memory. Somehow these helped shield me from the abusive words of Sergeant Wallace, who would have fitted much better in another Kubrick movie, *Full Metal Jacket*. I stared fixedly over his head – I was much taller than him – at an imaginary black monolith, with the majestic chords of *2001* playing in my head, thinking that even the ferocious Wallace was a puny and insignificant force in comparison. He noticed my indifference and tried a few times to break me, repeatedly poking the brim of his drill sergeant's hat into my face, but even that didn't faze me. After a while, he moved on to other cadets more vulnerable to his hazing. About one-third of our class broke down and quit before graduation. The course was only six weeks but it isn't a cliché to say that I went there as a boy and I left as a man. Back at OU, I now got only straight As and graduated near the top of my class.

It must have also improved my self-confidence or just the way people looked at me, because I now seemed to get job offers after every interview I attended as graduation beckoned. I had offers from the major oil companies like Exxon, Amoco, and Chevron, as well as big IT consulting companies like Anderson Consulting (now Accenture) and IBM, mostly for positions in Texas or California. But I also had an offer to join Salomon Brothers' investment banking unit in New York. In 1989, it was one of the most profitable firms on Wall Street, part of the 'bulge bracket' along with Merrill Lynch, Goldman Sachs, Morgan Stanley, and First Boston. It also had a reputation for the toughest, most unforgiving, sink-or-swim environment. Every year, they hired globally about 100 financial analysts straight from university, about two-thirds of whom worked in the New York office. After a two-month training programme, they were assigned to industry teams and expected to work seventy-hour weeks doing company valuations, preparing pitch books, and mostly low-level support work on transactions. Those who didn't sink were promised a fire hose of experience and the prospect of large bonuses. I knew immediately it was what I wanted to do.

After graduating, I blew my entire Salomon relocation bonus on a backpacking trip to Europe with one of my best friends. To save money for bars and nightclubs, we avoided even modestly priced youth hostels and mostly slept on trains or beaches for a month. I recall waking up early one morning in a park in Geneva, having slept in the rain under a bush that provided only meagre shelter, to find a poodle licking my face. As my bleary eyes followed the leash of the well-groomed dog up to its owner, I saw a look of genuine horror on the face of an aged, aristocratic-looking Swiss woman, mortified that her beloved pet was licking a hairy and scary homeless man.

That year, 1989, proved an extraordinary one in which to be in Europe, with the Berlin Wall falling and communist regimes toppling all across Eastern Europe. Although I didn't make it to Berlin that summer, we read about the fast-moving events every day in the *International Herald Tribune*, and frequently encountered breathless young backpackers returning from the east, recounting dramatic tales of adventure. I'm not a revolutionary by nature, but it did seem like a historic turning point that would open up this vast region to the rest of the world. Arriving back in New York in early August with two suitcases and not much else, I had to sleep on a friend's couch for a few days until my first Salomon pay cheque arrived. I made sure to read up on all the latest news about Eastern Europe too, although without any expectation of actually visiting. I remember standing outside Salomon Brothers' office before my first day of work, looking up at the shining skyscraper amidst the hustle and bustle of Wall Street early on a Monday morning. I had a stabbing feeling of trepidation in the pit of my stomach, and yet the hairs on the back of my neck tingled with excitement. I had no idea how clueless I still was about everything that mattered.

Among my Salomon analyst class, I was one of just a handful who'd attended a state university, with most coming from the Ivy League. This intimidated me at first, but I quickly realised we were all more alike than not. Some of my classmates became lifelong friends. It was a great environment for any young, single individual with a surplus of energy, working gruelling hours during the week but enjoying New York's raucous nightlife on the weekends. Shortly after I started work, there was a bestselling book, *Liar's Poker* by Michael Lewis, depicting the life of a Salomon associate a few years ahead of me. Lewis hilariously described the swaggering, foul-mouthed, aggressive trading culture that permeated the entire firm, and the necessity of developing a thick skin to survive it. Although Salomon's management was horrified by the publicity the book generated, the rest of us relished the notoriety we suddenly gained among our Wall Street peers.

I was assigned to work on Salomon's Energy team in corporate finance, covering oil and petrochemical companies, probably because they thought I would work well with the firm's clients in Texas, Louisiana, and Oklahoma. Unlike peers at Goldman or Morgan Stanley, the corporate finance team at Salomon Brothers were truly second-class citizens within the firm. The real nerve centre of Salomon was its legendary trading floor, feared throughout Wall Street. They might as well have been pirates, with cutlasses in their teeth, swinging on ropes to storm enemy ships every day, yo-ho-ho and a bottle of rum! But we in the corporate finance department felt more like servile workhorses, pulling heavy wagons uphill with blinders on our eyes, only seeing the road directly in front of us. We were contracted for two years, with the expectation that most of us would then leave for MBA programmes. I set my sights on only one place: Harvard Business School. With what was some recklessness in hindsight, I applied only there but somehow persuaded them to give me an offer. It was like a dream come true, but on reflection, the path I had chosen up until then was traditional and narrow, treading a straight line taken by so many others before me. For one thing, except for a month of backpacking, I had never been outside of North America.

On the off-chance, I reached out to Ron Freeman, then the co-head of Investment Banking in Salomon's London office, with whom I had earlier worked on the valuation of some North Sea oil properties. He was looking to expand the London office's energy coverage and liked the work I did. He offered me a job in London as a third-year analyst, if I could get a deferral of admission by Harvard, who quickly granted the request. I thought it was perfect: I would get a year of international experience in London, return to Harvard, and then pursue the rest of my life and career plans in the USA.

It was the summer of 1991. I was only weeks away from moving to London and had already shipped a few boxes of my modest belongings. Then one of my Salomon colleagues told me to check out that day's edition of the *Financial Times*. There was an article about Ron Freeman, who had resigned from Salomon and accepted a post as First Vice President of the European Bank for Reconstruction and Development (EBRD) in London. The EBRD had recently been created as a multilateral development bank with a focus on investing in the Soviet Union and Eastern Europe. Reading the article, my jaw dropped and my heart skipped a beat. As Ron was the only person I knew in Salomon's London office, it seemed like my perfect plan was crumbling to nothing. I called him on the phone, congratulated him on the new post, and then raised my situation. 'Damn,' he said, 'I forgot about you.' We brainstormed over the line but, with no one at Salomon London to sponsor my work assignments, it seemed like I would have a dull year even if the company honoured the job offer. Then Ron had an idea. What with the Soviet Union's reportedly vast reserves of oil and gas, he figured the EBRD would need some young financial experts to cover the sector. Why didn't I join him at the EBRD's London office instead of Salomon's for the year? With little to lose, and the prospect of travel to an exotic new region, I agreed immediately.

In the two weeks between leaving Salomon and starting work at EBRD that August, I took a short holiday to go mountain climbing with a friend in Switzerland. We were preparing to climb the Matterhorn and had gone to a shop in the village of Zermatt when I spied a startling headline in the *Herald Tribune*. A coup had taken place in the Soviet Union. Hardliners had taken over and the Soviet leader, Mikhail Gorbachev, was under house arrest. Besides the stunning historical implications, the prospects for foreign investment in the Soviet Union – of just the type I was expecting to do at EBRD – seemed to be evaporating before my eyes. Oh well, I thought. My cards were played already and there was no turning back; I might still find something useful to do for the next year working on projects in Poland or Romania, perhaps.

I set off with my companions to climb the Matterhorn. When we staggered back down to Zermatt three days later, I picked up a fresh copy of the *Herald Tribune*. On the front page was a huge photo of Boris Yeltsin standing on a tank. The headline read 'Coup collapsing'. It seemed that whatever would happen, my work in Moscow wouldn't be boring or uneventful.

4

Cell 604

I am snapped out of my contemplations of those heady days by the sudden intrusion of a voice over the speaker system in my cell. 'Calvey! Collect your things. You will be moved to a new cell.'

'OK,' I obediently respond. 'When?'

'Now.'

Just like that, my time in solitary is about to come to an end. I gather my meagre belongings: the iron bowl, cup, and spoon; one partially used bar of soap, which I wrap in a few layers of toilet paper; a toothbrush and toothpaste; a hand towel; and my mattress and bed sheet. I feel like a homeless man taking stock of his most sacred possessions. Placing these items in a neat pile on my mattress, I sit quietly at my table and wait. It is difficult to gauge how much time passes but it must be two or three hours before someone finally comes to collect me. Plenty of time for my mind to imagine what my new cell will be like and what sort of cellmates I will be living with. I figure it will go one of three ways. My optimistic hope is that things will be OK, but I fear it will be either bad or really bad. I keep picturing a cell filled with hardened criminals from the Russian Caucasus. If the 'hurry me up and then make me wait' approach has been designed to maximise my stress levels, it is working.

It is around 10 p.m. when four guards finally come for me. With my possessions spread out on my mattress, I roll it up into a bundle so that I can carry everything under one arm. The guards maintain

a silent and solemn air as I do this, offering no instructions and definitely no assurances. Judging from their stony silence and cold body
language, it is clear something very serious is about to happen. Any
hope I had that things may not be that bad quickly dissipates.

The guards lead me from my cell and to the stairwell where the
Psycho-siren operates. The shrieking alarm pierces the silence like a
sudden stab, tearing at my already frayed nerves. But as we trudge up
to the sixth floor, I know I have to get on top of my emotions. To
find at least some of the stoic composure that my wife has urged. 'If
it doesn't kill you,' I keep reminding myself in a bid to buck up my
courage, 'it makes you stronger.' Eventually, my guards bring us to
a halt outside cell 604. One of them knocks and looks through the
shnift into the interior. Then he unlocks and opens the huge steel door,
pushing me into what is to serve as my new home. I stand tall, trying
to put on a brave face, but my heart is beating wildly.

As I step over the threshold, I see not the one or two fellow inmates
that I am expecting, but seven of them, standing and looking straight
at me. Holy shit, two of them are monumentally huge. I stand nervously before them as the thick, heavy door clangs shut behind me.

Then I notice something unexpected. On each of their seven faces
is a warm, genuine smile. It is as if they all already know who I am.
There is just one empty bunk so I walk over to it and put down my
bedroll. Then each of the prisoners greets me in turn and introduces
himself. The first of the two giants, I now discover, is Sanych. He has
a big, burly beard and looks to be in his mid-40s. With a full head of
hair, he is also the only one of the seven not to have the classic prison
buzz cut. The other giant is 'Big Sasha', a few years younger than
Sanych and a good 2m tall with the broadest of shoulders. There is
another Sasha, too – Sasha Rostov – this one younger still, around
mid-30s with a steely glint in his eye but a big, energetic smile and a
deep, earthy laugh. Zhenya is the baby of the group at just 31 years
old, while the others – Andrey, Misha, and Grisha – range from mid-
30s to mid-50s. I will get to learn more of their individual stories in
the days and weeks to come.

It quickly emerges that my case is already famous among the prisoners here in Matrosskaya Tishina. They have been reading about me in

the newspapers for the last few days, and are in truth better informed about the case than I am. Whatever they have read, it has evidently not turned them against me. When they see that I have almost nothing with me, they all proceed to donate to me items of their own: clean T-shirts, shorts, sweatpants, sandals, a proper towel, plastic plates and cups. It is an embarrassment of riches compared to what I have got used to over the last few days. I am stunned by their generosity, thanking them as I tell them that it isn't necessary, but they insist.

By now, it's late and almost time for lights out, but they invite me to sit at the table in the middle of the cell and have some tea. I'm still learning their names and someone – I'm not sure who – pours for everybody. Then one of them makes a toast. '*Novoselye*,' he says simply as he raises his mug. 'Welcome.' Each of my new cellmates looks me straight in the eye as they join in with the salutation. Then one of them tells me in reassuring tones: 'Don't worry. Everything's going to be OK.' I am struck by the emotion of the moment. I am deeply moved by their display of basic decency – a reminder that humanity can thrive even in the most unlikely places.

I notice how they all address me from the outset with the Russian familiar '*Ti*', instead of the more formal '*Vi*'. It is not long, though, before the lights are switched half-off and everyone gets up from the table. As we make for our bunks, one of the guys pulls me aside and tells me that we have a mutual friend. This is an unexpected bit of luck and helps cement the bond between us. Then another cellmate seeks me out to give me a friendly warning. 'Even though here we are all decent guys,' he says, 'you should still trust no one. Never tell anyone anything about your case.' I appreciate his candour and note his advice.

By 10.30 p.m., as required by the prison rules, everyone is in bed but the stream of jokes and banter flows for a while longer. I join in too, adding a couple of salty anecdotes that I have learned on Russian hunting trips. These are received with collective laughter (I guess they sound even funnier coming from an American) and a comforting declaration: 'Ha ha, you are one of us!' With these words in my ears, it takes me a long time to fall asleep. The adrenaline is still coursing through me as my mind struggles to make sense of this unexpected, and apparently fortunate, turn of events.

When I wake the next morning, the cell is bathed in daylight that has forced its way through our two opaque and barred windows. It gives me the chance to properly take in my new home for the first time. The first thing I notice is how well stocked with provisions it is. There are bottles of water, instant coffee, apples, oranges, nuts, cheese, chocolate, cookies. Two small refrigerators are packed full with yoghurt, soups, kefir, milk, and prepared meals. When the guards come by with the usual delivery of prison breakfast, the other guys take one look at it and then send it away, saying they have their own stuff. Don't worry, they explain to me, whatever there is in the cell gets shared equally. I can have some of their food now, and when I get some of my own in, I will share it with them. Trust us, they tell me, what we provide for ourselves is much better than the *balanda* – a reference to the tasteless food inmates were given in the old Soviet gulags – served up by the prison kitchen. So, I help myself to oats mixed with kefir and honey, two hard-boiled eggs, and some coffee. The sort of feast I dared not dream of getting in prison. Life is looking up.

As the recipient of my cellmates' largesse, I am reminded of the urgency of getting a 'personal money account' set up. A friend or family member, or an advocate, is required to deposit some cash with the prison accounting department, following which the prisoner receives a statement confirming the amount in their 'account'. From this, they can pay for food from the prison's official supplier and get other household products (soap, detergent, etc.) from the prison's own dedicated shop. Officially, the system is designed so that prisoners do not retain any physical cash, so reducing the chances of inmates being subjected to threats or robbery by other prisoners. But I assume it also allows for the dedicated suppliers to make a tidy profit, operating in a literally captive market without competition. But none of the prisoners complain about it – the prices are reasonable and the consumers just glad to have a decent alternative to the prison-issue *balanda*.

The cell, which measures about 4m by 5m, feels cramped with eight of us in it. About half of the space is filled by the four double-bunk beds known as *shkanar*. As in every cell, we are surveilled on video by the Sauron Eye and from the corridor through the *shnift* in the door. In the middle of the room stands the *dubok*, a picnic-style table with fixed benches on two sides capable of seating three people on each. There is a teapot and a second curious contraption made from half a teapot, which I later learn is used to produce steam for heating up food. In addition, there is a single toilet(but a proper one fully enclosed by walls for privacy), a sink with a mirror above it, and a TV. There is also a small space for hanging coats and storing shoes, but my cellmates each keep the rest of their belongings under or beside their bunks. In one corner sits a collection of traditional Orthodox Russian religious icons. Most of my companions, I discover, are religious and pray at the icons first thing each morning. Religious adherence, it turns out, is more prevalent than smoking in 604, with only two of them partaking – an extraordinarily low proportion for a cell in a Russian prison.

I discover there is a rotation system forever in play among the pre-trial detainees at Matrosskaya Tishina. Some are eventually convicted and sent to penal colonies, with new prisoners arriving constantly to fill the empty spaces. Long-term detainees are moved to new cells every six months or so, to prevent a 'block' from forming in any specific cell that might prove disruptive. The average period of pre-trial detention is somewhere between one and three years. Several of the guys in cell 604 have already been here for more than a year, so this is their third or even fourth cell. They know plenty of the other detainees held in the prison, having shared a cell with many of them at one time or another.

Around mid-morning, the guards bring us together for our daily *progulka* in the fresh air. It gives me the opportunity to get a clearer picture of the cell hierarchy. There are essentially two groups: on one hand, the 'young Turks' (Andrey, Sasha Rostov, Misha, and Zhendos) and, on the other, the older veterans (Grisha, Sanych, and Big Sasha). Most of us immediately start walking in a circle around the bench in the middle of the open cell, but Zhendos takes himself off to a corner of his own, where he practises a sort of dance for a few minutes, seemingly to get himself into his desired frame of mind. Meanwhile, Sasha Rostov, forever an individualist, trudges determinedly in a straight line back and forth, studiously removing himself from the circuit the rest of us have assumed.

As the hour progresses, the activities vary. After about ten minutes, Grisha strides to one corner and lights up a cigarette. He is joined by one of the others and they strike up a conversation. Sasha Rostov and Andrey, both apparently former boxers, move to the sides and begin shadow boxing. The rest of us take it in turns to use the bench for press-ups or dips, continuing our circuits around it in between. Every ten minutes or so, someone gives an almost imperceptible hand signal to indicate the walkers should switch direction. Walking on a gangplank above us are two guards armed with machine guns, looking down at our cell and apparently several other similar cells where prisoners are also having their *progulka*. All the while, Retro FM blares from the radio with its mix of hits from the '70s, '80s, and '90s.

After we get back to our cell, the guards tell us to get ready for *banya*. Are they being serious? A *banya* is a traditional Russian sauna – not what you typically expect to find in prison. Of course, it turns out this is the guards' idea of a little joke. Here, the *banya* is just the normal shower rooms. As a prisoner, I am entitled to one shower per week, but if I have enough cash on account I can buy a second one. At a cost of about 200 roubles ($3), it is money well spent. As always, painstaking effort is made to ensure that prisoners are unable to communicate with anyone from outside their own cell, so the guards organise shower times on strict rotation.

Later in the afternoon, I catch coverage of a speech by President Putin live on the TV. One of his main themes today is the criminal justice system. I gather he has been motivated to address the subject in part by the fevered reaction in the Russian press and among the business community to my arrest. Everyone in our cell watches with intense interest. Realising that my own fate might hang in the balance, I am nervous and unsettled. I feel like a seasick sailor adrift on a stormy sea, trying to avoid being cast overboard. The President doesn't comment on my case specifically, but astonishingly he does say that Russia's investigators have got out of control. It is unacceptable, he declares, to arrest businesspeople before there has been a detailed investigation and clear evidence of guilt uncovered. It's almost unheard of for Putin to criticise his security agencies, and he never admits that they have made mistakes. My cellmates nod to themselves gravely, looking at me and saying, 'This is because of your case.' None of us know if his comments are a sign of genuine changes to come, or just a tactical comment to deflect pressure from the business community. But this can only be positive for my case, my cellmates think. I won't have to wait long to find out, anyway. My appeal hearing is scheduled for tomorrow.

As evening approaches, I try to wind down ahead of the coming tests. After dinner, the entire population of cell 604 sits down to watch a film on TV. It's called *Once Upon a Time in Love*, an Italian movie dubbed into Russian. It begins with the scene of the heroine, a beautiful young woman, at the beach in her swimsuit. It is enough to bring all conversation to an abrupt halt, our rapt attention remaining unbroken for the rest of the film. It's actually a very funny comedy, in which the impoverished hero tricks this beautiful rich girl into falling in love with him, and we frequently break out into raucous laughter. From the dread I had felt about moving into this cell just twenty-four hours ago, I find myself feeling ... what? An unexpected lightness as the film plays. But more than that, a sense of camaraderie. We may not yet be firm friends, but these are not the terrifying spectres out to harm me that had filled my imagination yesterday evening. Sometimes bad things happen to good people. Sometimes good things happen to bad people. But sometimes, when you least expect it, good things can happen to good people. This is just such a moment. Cell 604 is not the gateway to an underworld I feared, but an oasis in a bleak wilderness. My seven comrades, I am to discover, are among the bravest and most decent guys I have ever met.

5

Brothers in Arms

I'm a fervent believer in free markets in the tradition of Hayek or Friedman. But the rules in cell 604 about sharing property and food, as well as those around assigning work, are as close to a system of communism as I have ever experienced. And I soon come to believe that prison is probably an environment where communism actually works better than the alternatives. With eight of us packed into our cell, we are a tight knot of humanity amid the otherwise isolating conditions of Matrosskaya Tishina. Dividing out our supplies, tasks and duties on the basis that we are all equal stands us in good stead.

Take food and provisions. Everyone gets an equal share of what there is, even though some people's families contribute more to the overall supply. Whenever someone receives a special item – like the time Big Sasha gets a smoked fish from his wife to mark his birthday – there is an unspoken understanding that the chief recipient gets the first and largest portion, but that the rest is still to be shared among the remainder of us. If anyone were to try to keep something for themselves, I imagine it would breed resentment and lead to serious problems in cell harmony. Anyway, sharing your special treats with the others gives you a sense of pride and even boosts your self-esteem.

As the days pass, I get to know each of my inmates a little better. Grisha, the oldest of us, is an ethnic Armenian Muscovite who has previously served as Russia's Deputy Minister of Culture – a man who has truly inhabited the upper echelons of society. He is both intelligent and *intelligentni*, or 'cultured'. He has an air of experience about him, and an ironic look in his eye that suggests that nothing ever surprises him. It is obvious that the other inmates of the cell respect him, not least because he seems to know more about Russian law than most advocates. Football is a big deal in 604, and Grisha is an avid supporter of Spartak Moscow, historically one of the country's most successful clubs. He is also a fierce dominoes player.

Coming down in age, next is Sanych, also known as Sanya, the giant with a mighty beard. His name is a derivation of Alexander, sometimes used instead of Sasha. I discover he is a general in the Russian Army, with a background in military engineering and construction. He was responsible for building many large civil and military infrastructure projects throughout Russia and the Commonwealth of Independent States, and he's brought his practical skills with him into prison. I think of him like a human Swiss Army knife, able to fix almost anything, from the refrigerator or the sink to someone's bad back or sprained ankle. He even serves up a wonderful dinner salad. It is soon obvious that, like Grisha, he is also a big football fan, although his loyalties unsurprisingly lie with CSKA Moscow, once the official team of the Soviet Army and still a force in domestic and European football. Sanych is capable of impressive spontaneous bursts of profanity, as only a true Russian military man can produce.

Misha, also known as CoCo (for reasons I have never established), is an Armenian from the south of Russia. He is full of zest for life and a big joker, forever telling anecdotes to keep us entertained. When he speaks about his work, he says he is engaged in the trading business – a description he delivers with a sly smile. I later learn he is being investigated for narcotics dealing.

Big Sasha is another Muscovite, but half Armenian, half Azeri – a rare combination. His background is in the construction business. He is truly a gentle giant, with an insatiable appetite and appreciation for good food. He is a natural storyteller, with a particular taste for the nostalgic, and has a habit of humming tunes to himself as he goes about his daily tasks, usually some old romantic song or another. He also loves dominoes and is typically Grisha's partner in the cell's dominoes tournaments.

The smaller of the three Sashas, meanwhile, hails from Rostov. Everyone simply called him Sasha, but to avoid confusion in my own mind, I thought of him as Sasha Rostov. He is at once fiercely individualist but also true and loyal to his friends, even as he seems hard and unforgiving to his enemies. I am of particular interest to him as he is currently working hard to learn English. So too is Zhenya – or Zhendos, Zhos or even Zhack, as he is also known. A computer hacker from St Petersburg, around 30, he is often teased by the others as the baby of the group but he takes it well. He is clearly smart but he never reads books. Instead, he seems to be the main handler of the TV remote control. His football loyalties lie with Zenit St Petersburg, which adds some additional spice to the inter-cell soccer rivalries.

Practising English is a big deal in 604. The last of the inmates, Andrey from the Russian Far East, speaks the language almost fluently but is always striving to improve himself. Even in prison, he keeps up subscriptions to both *The Economist* and the *New Yorker*. Like Big Sasha, he too has a background in the construction business. A former boxer, it is clear he remains strong of body as well as mind. But he is kind too, with a true and easy smile counter-pointed by melancholy eyes. A natural leader who commands the respect of his comrades.

And we are comrades. Working together to make life as bearable as it can be. Everyone, of course, washes their own dishes and makes up their own beds, but we take it in turns on rotation to clean the entire cell every day. The floor and table are washed, the toilet and sink cleaned, and so on. I am pleasantly surprised by the standards of cleanliness we communally expect of ourselves. Unlike my time in the temporary cell, here we have proper cleaning products and detergents purchased from the prison's authorised supplier. No one cut corners when it's their turn to clean, nor would they be able to get away with it if they tried. With eight men in such a compact space, life inside these four walls would quickly become unbearable without such a system.

Our laundry regime involves everyone washing their own clothes by hand in round plastic buckets, then rinsing them under the tap at the sink as best we can before hanging them to dry – either on one of the radiators or across a clothes line improvised out of stretched trash bags. Ropes and wires are unsurprisingly banned from cells, along with shoelaces and anything else that might feasibly be used for self-harm. Nor are we allowed any metal utensils besides a single spoon each. The knives and forks we use are plastic. Given these restrictions, prison life demands invention, and Russian ingenuity never ceases to amaze me.

The guys in 604 have designed several things to improve daily life. We have air fresheners made from dried orange or mandarin peels, which are set alight with matches and allowed to burn slowly. Yes, it really does work! Newspapers are folded neatly to form small boxes for extra storage, while ropes are made out of trash bags along the same method as the washing line. We can then hang T-shirts or towels over them to create a small curtain between bunks and give ourselves at least a little privacy. Cardboard toilet paper rolls come in handy too, connected into a long stick that we use to jam the windows open at night. But the most important invention is the steaming device, made out of an open teapot (no lid) on to which a large plastic bowl is placed. As the plastic bowl has holes punched in the bottom, it channels steam efficiently from the teapot, so if you then perch your iron bowl on top of the plastic bowl, you can astonishingly use it to cook almost anything: soup, stew, noodles, etc. America is a land of invention, but I don't think American prisoners ever designed anything so simple but so ingenious.

At around four o'clock each afternoon, the guards open the hatch ('*karmyak*') in the cell's big metal door and deposit whatever deliveries have arrived from the outside. When I get a big consignment from my colleagues in Baring Vostok a couple of days after my arrival, the guys stare at the array of items before bursting into laughter. There is an enormous amount of food and drink, plus bags of clothes, shampoo, soap and more. I am pleased to see I have some new clothing – two sets of sweatpants and sweatshirts, a few T-shirts, and warm socks. This is much more practical for Matrosskaya Tishina, since they can easily be washed and dried compared to the jeans and button-down shirt in which I arrived. I am a bit embarrassed by it all, but at the same time I feel reassured, like the cavalry has arrived. I can almost hear the bugle playing as my delivery is unloaded. The rest of the guys are smiling to each other, knowing that they are going to share in this abundance, in accordance with the cell's sharing system.

Together with supplies the others have received from their families, we have more than thirty different items of food and drink, including soups, pasta, salads, bread, crackers, fruit, cakes and coffee. Our two small refrigerators are packed full, after Andrey has patiently unloaded and reloaded each item with a skill and precision that utilises every square centimetre, like in Tetris. Bottles of water are stacked against the wall in a giant 2m-high tower, and plastic shelves groan under the weight of apples and oranges. Cell 604 is transformed into a mini-supermarket.

Dinner reminds me of a scene from *The Godfather*. The one where Don Corleone's lieutenant, Clemenza, teaches the boss's son Michael how to make spaghetti meatballs 'because you never know when you're gonna need to cook for twenty guys'. Luckily for us, Sanych is trusted by the guards with an hour's loan of a metal knife. It is a harmlessly dull kitchen knife but Sanych wields it with the precision of a celebrity chef on TV as he chops and slices cucumbers, tomatoes, garlic, dill, and radishes to make a salad. We steam up a big bowl of pasta and Andrey tosses in some meats and sausages, channelling his own inner Clemenza. The only thing missing is wine or vodka but, sadly, alcohol is strictly prohibited. Still, it is a memorable meal and we linger at the *dubok*, our kitchen table, for a long time, making sure to enjoy it fully.

When I am lying in bed a little later with a full belly, the necessity of ear plugs and eye patches hits me. Sleep is proving elusive against the backdrop of snoring and with the lights left constantly on. Of course, the guys end up sharing some of their spare ear plugs and eye patches with me, and for the first time since I have been taken into custody, I almost manage to sleep through the night. But the next morning is cold and windy. At the morning *progulka*, snowflakes swirl ferociously around the barbed wire above us, before floating slowly down to the floor. To stay warm, we all jog briskly in a circle for the full hour, leaving a circle of trodden dirty snow around the bench. Towards the end, I asked Big Sasha a naïve question of some kind, like how many of the prisoners here does he reckon are innocent of what they've been put inside for. He looks at me and smiles. 'Ahh Michael … you still have the smell of the free life [*volye*] about you,' he says, as if no seasoned veteran of prison would ever even think to ask such a silly question. I may be finding my feet in 604, but there is still much for me to learn.

After *progulka*, I am taken to Matrosskaya Tishina's new hospital section, where word has it they have an X-ray machine. A chance to get my back properly looked at. To get there, I am driven a short distance in a convoy truck to a different building within the same prison complex, from where I am guided on foot through the old Matrosskaya Tishina hospital. It is a shocking experience. The state of the facilities puts me in mind of that old classic film with Steve McQueen and Dustin Hoffman, *Papillon*, about a thief convicted of murder and ordered to serve his life sentence in French Guiana. The scene that greets me is of old crumbling brick walls, barren empty cells for sick prisoners, and an eerily sad atmosphere of decay, as if the whole place is crying out with the misery of decades. I see only two prisoner-patients when I am there, both bald, pale and thin as rails. They peer at me like I am an alien from outer space. From my recently delivered consignment of clothes, I am wearing my old Bosco 'Sochi Olympics' tracksuit, which is more practical than what I had before, but too flashy for normal prison attire. I feel utterly out of place in this medieval hospital-dungeon, but I really don't have anything else to wear just now. I try, no doubt unconvincingly, to keep a rugged look on my face as I trudge onward with the guards.

Finally, we turn a corner and enter the new part of the prison hospital. It is like being teleported forward several centuries. Everywhere is whitewashed, with banks of modern computers and shiny new equipment, most of it still wrapped up as if it has just been delivered today. A few doctors and nurses mill about in the very latest professional hospital attire. For a moment, I seriously wonder whether this might not all be for my benefit. A modern variation on the 'Potemkin Villages' built long ago to convince Catherine the Great that the far reaches of her realm were more developed than was really the case. Is this a performance to persuade this American of Russia's advanced facilities? I am seen by a calm, serious-looking doctor who quizzes me on my condition and carries out an X-ray of my spine. There follows a consultation between various medical staff but the guards haul me back to my cell before I am told of their conclusions.

Back in 604, all the talk is about whether the President's recent speech on the state of the nation's criminal justice system will impact any of the investigations or trials we face. At this point, I have neither asked nor been told what each of the guys is accused of. But I am dismayed to discover that some of them have already been in Matrosskaya Tishina for over three years, under investigation but yet to be tried, much less convicted of anything. Whether or not any of them are guilty, the overall atmosphere is of quietly seething rage against what they all recognise as an arbitrary and immovable system. The consensus is that our only realistic chance of a path through the legal quagmire is some kind of Putin-inspired amnesty or reform. That's why his speech has triggered such intense discussion. Someone argues passionately why he thinks this might be a real turning point, but the others wearily accuse him of naïveté. 'Hope dies last,' someone says – one of my favourite Russian expressions, and perfectly apt just now.

My fourth day in cell 604, 23 February, is a Russian public holiday known as 'Defender of the Fatherland Day'. It was originally intended to honour military veterans, but these days encompasses a broader recognition of the men of Russia. It comes just a couple of weeks before the larger and usually more extravagant celebration of International Women's Day on 8 March. Sanych, of course – as a real Red Army general – is offered congratulations repeatedly. It is an opportunity for me to talk of my own interest in Russian military history, like the stories of the soldiers at Stalingrad, Kursk, and other epic Second World War battlefields.

Somehow – and oddly given that this is a day to celebrate Russia – the conversation turns to the English language. It is by no means the first time this has happened. Sasha Rostov and Zhenya, in particular, are always coming to me to check how to correctly use some English idiom or another. Slang proves particularly bewildering. What does 'gonna' mean and is it the same as 'I got to'? What does WTF mean? And LOL? What is the difference between a 'sucker' and something that 'sucked'? What does it mean to 'work it out'? Or when a person is a 'show off'? Such questions frequently veer into conversations about what life is like in the UK. How much does a beer cost? How much does it cost to take your wife to dinner at a restaurant? Do English people really wear tweed jackets and hats like Sherlock Holmes?

Sometimes Andrey circles obscure words from *The Economist* or *New Yorker* – the kinds of words you won't find in a standard dictionary – which I then translate and explain to him in Russian. Zhendos, being true to himself, mainly asks questions about how to get girls to sleep with him: 'How do I say ... take your clothes off!' Sasha Rostov, on the other hand, is interested in America, asking which places he should visit when (or rather, if) he ever gets out of here. I first describe the urban wonders of New York, then the breathtaking natural beauty of the American West. But I can see none of this is really piquing his interest. Northern California, San Francisco – still no tremendous enthusiasm. But when I describe San Diego – standing on a warm, sandy beach in your shorts, fish taco in one hand and cold beer in the other, with beautiful, tanned girls in bikinis all around – he immediately shouts 'YES!' Bullseye.

Yesterday, the 22nd, happened to be George Washington's birthday, a fact oddly enough reported on the Russian TV news. The guys all thought this was very funny, given they are now sharing a cell with an American. They made a toast at dinner for old George – no vodka, but cranberry juice (*mors*) in our plastic cups. I suppose the dollar bill is so ubiquitous that George Washington's face remains one of the most recognised on the planet. The moment reminds me of a joke from the 1990s, when dollars, or 'bucks', were almost as commonly used in the streets of Moscow as the rouble. A Russian businessman travels to the USA and, when he returns, his friends all ask him what it was like. 'It was great,' he tells them. 'But the funny thing is, their American dollars are exactly the same as our bucks!'

Today, Defender of the Fatherland Day, sees some friendly US–Russian rivalry. One of the guys tells me: 'Well, America may be a great country, and English is probably the dominant global language, but your language pales in comparison to Russian when it comes to swearing and curse words.' He then demonstrates some of the fantastic verbal combinations that can be strung together in 'mat', the swearing quasi-dialect of the Russian language. 'Bet you can't say that in English,' he says with a grin.

But I take up the gauntlet. 'Well ... actually, you can say those things in English,' I inform him. And then I set about demonstrating the versatility of just a single word – the F-word. I whip through 'fuck off', 'fuck you', 'what the fuck', and 'what a fuck up', explaining the entirely different meanings of each. I spot Sasha Rostov and Zhendos immediately grabbing their notebooks and writing it all down, asking me to repeat each several times and practising the various phrases themselves. We proceed to more complex combinations, such as the nuanced difference between 'a fucking idiot' and 'a fucking shithead'. I explain how 'motherfucker' is not meant literally, but is an excellent expression that serves to cover a multitude of different kinds of unpleasant people. Immediately, the guys come up with the names of individual investigators and other officials to whom the term can be well applied. Finally, I explain how the F-word can be used as a noun, a verb, and an adjective all in the same sentence: 'That fucking motherfucker is totally fucking fucked.' By this time, all of cell 604 have their notebooks out and are furiously scribbling notes.

Eventually, as they fend off writer's cramp, the guys grudgingly admit that the English language is much cooler than they had previously thought. Maybe still not quite as cool as the Russian language, but definitely a close second. I'll take that. And so, on 23 February of all days, I have acknowledged the great richness of Russian civilisation while also defending the honour of my own motherland. It is symbolically like the meeting at the Elbe in April 1945. As they say in Russian, '*pobedil druzhbu*' – friendship won in the end. And from this moment on, 'fucking awesome' becomes the unofficial slogan of cell 604.

Later in the evening, we settle in front of the TV to watch the recent Russian film about the 1972 Soviet Olympic basketball team, which defeated the Americans for the first time to win the gold medal. It is a fascinating true story, even though a painful and controversial topic for me and most Americans because of the infamous events at the game's end when officiating errors caused the final three seconds to be replayed three times. Of course, since it is a Russian film, the Americans in the film are portrayed as bullies and whiners, which really isn't true, while the Soviet players are all portrayed as heroes (which they probably were). But I can't complain, since it is no different to the bias in American films like *Miracle on Ice*, the story of the US men's ice hockey team's epic, against-the-odds victory over the Soviets at the 1980 winter Olympics.

This film and the discussions in cell 604 today remind me just how similar Russians and Americans are in many ways. We both inhabit big countries, with lots of wide-open natural space and a disparate range of racial and ethnic groups. Both populations are naturally patriotic so that, while often critical of our own countries, we instinctively rush to defend our countries from criticism by anyone else, whether justified or not. And we both have our own unique national sense of humour. There are obvious cultural differences, of course, including very different views of society and hierarchical relationships, but we have a lot more in common at the human level than that which separates us. (Yes, Sting, of course the Russians love their children, too.)

The television proves an important tool in unifying us inmates of 604. Each weekday evening, we watch the Russian comedy shows *Year of Culture* (*Goad Kulturi*) and *Police on Rublyovki*. I don't normally tend to like popular TV comedies, but these two are clever and genuinely funny – a huge hit in the cell. They poke fun at the 'system' just enough to be credible, but not enough, of course, to be dangerous. The night after Defender of the Fatherland Day, we gather around the screen again, this time to watch the World Cup basketball qualifier between Russia and Finland. Russia are down by 11 points with ten minutes to go, but come roaring back to win by 15. There are lots of shouts of '*Ura!*' – the traditional battle cry of the Russian armed forces since medieval times. I often root for Russia's national team except when they are playing America or Great Britain, so I join in the cheers and a good time is had by all. I am beginning to lose that feeling of being the sore thumb sticking out.

6

Trailblazer

I visited Russia for the first time in early 1992. I was on an EBRD work trip from London and it was just a few weeks after Mikhail Gorbachev had made a Christmas Eve broadcast from the Kremlin to announce the immediate dissolution of the Soviet Union. The Soviet state anthem was played for the last time, the hammer and sickle solemnly lowered down the flagpole, and the Russian tricolour hoisted in its place as the country took its first teetering steps into an unknown future. No one quite knew what to expect. As I heard Robert Strauss, the US ambassador to Russia, note sagely: 'If I was a young man and had just $10,000, I would move there right now and bet it all on Russia. But if I was an old man with $10 million, I would still only bet $10,000 on Russia.'

Arriving with a knowledge of the local language restricted to *Da* ('yes') and *Nyet* ('no'), my first impressions of Moscow were grim. It was a strangely colourless place – everything seemed to be either grey or brown. The people I met on the street struck me as unwelcoming, especially older people, who scowled back at me if I ever accidentally made eye contact. And everywhere there was a pervasive, strangely unpleasant aroma, probably resulting from a combination of cheap Soviet tobacco and the peculiar cleaning liquid only ever used in the Soviet Union. An intangible heaviness permeated everything.

For most people, there was no sense of the excitement of a new nation getting on to the front foot, full of opportunity and promise.

Indeed, these were the darkest days for most Russians since the Second World War. Older citizens, in particular, felt vulnerable, unprepared and unable to adjust to whatever new opportunities might be emerging. Instead, they worried as inflation wiped out their savings and they found themselves priced out of the rapidly expanding black market that was coming to dictate who could buy what consumer goods. Not long after my arrival, I visited the celebrated GUM department store, a magnificent nineteenth-century building in an absolutely prime location right on Red Square. Not so long ago, it had been as close to a palace of consumerism as the USSR got, with long queues snaking around the square. Now, its ground floor still had shops selling Levi's jeans, ice cream and other desirables, but the second and third floors were virtually empty, save for a battalion of grandmothers (*babushki*) selling their old porcelain plates, silver cutlery, religious icons, and whatever else they could lay hands on to make a little cash. I felt genuine sadness seeing their desperate circumstances, depressingly aware that there was nothing I could really do to help thanks to the scale of the problem.

A woman I met a few years later told me a story of her first encounter with a Western brand from around this time, when she was a university student still living with her parents. Her father was a construction engineer on a modest salary, part of which he had used to purchase a product recently introduced to the capital: a Snickers bar. When he arrived back at the family apartment, he reverently showed the delicacy to the girl and her mother. In awe, they set it on the kitchen table, where it remained for three days – a suitable delay in which to build up anticipation before they consumed it. When the moment finally arrived that weekend, the girl's father carefully opened the wrapper and took out the chocolate bar, sliced it into small sections and gave one to each family member. The little that was left was shared with the grateful neighbours.

The economy soon found a momentum of its own, based on the ingenuity of young Russian entrepreneurs and a growing throng of Western firms only too eager to satisfy the pent-up demand for consumer goods. While the shelves or kitchens of traditional Soviet shops or restaurants lay mostly bare, cheap private kiosks appeared organically and spread quickly all across Moscow, like wild mush-rooms after an autumn rain. Stuffed full of Marlborough cigarettes, Wrigley's chewing gum, Tuborg beer and other inexpensive Western brands, these informal kiosks raked in vast sums of roubles for their shady owners and their protectors in the bureaucracy. For wealthy 'New Russians' and adventurous expatriates, a few private cooperative restaurants, like Krapotkinskaya 36, offered a fancy but dimly lit and slightly seedy dining option – only for dollars, and only if you didn't mind the gangsters or their bodyguards who might be sitting at the next table. All around, if you knew where to look, the commercial landscape was changing.

It was a fascinating time to find myself in Russia, but of course, I was there for my job … and what a job it turned out to be. The EBRD was, and still is, an extraordinary institution. When I arrived for my first day at the London office in late August 1991, I was among the first 100 or so employees. Nowadays it employs thousands. When I joined, the entire banking department consisted of only about twenty people, so that we could all meet in a single conference room in the bank's office on Leadenhall Street. However, that would not last long. It was soon expanding like wildfire, growing from 100 to more than 1,000 employees in only eighteen months. We sometimes felt like we were a modern Noah's Ark, except instead of animals, we'd welcome on board a procession of two bankers of every nationality. The polyglot atmosphere, along with an initially slightly chaotic organisation that hadn't yet given way to bureaucracy, made it a ridiculously fun place for a young person to work. Some EBRD colleagues from that early adventurous cohort, like Charlie Ryan, became my lifelong friends.

I was still only 24 years old but serendipity gave me some advan-tages that enabled me to grab responsibilities beyond those that I felt I deserved. Not least, in those early days I was the only EBRD banker who had any experience working on projects in the oil and gas sector. It gave me valuable knowledge that couldn't easily be learned by gen-eralist professionals, so other bankers were initially content to cede that huge territory entirely to me. Perhaps fortunately, I looked older than I really was too, so although I never lied about it, many clients assumed I was perhaps 30. In addition, I was almost the only person at

EBRD who had previously worked with Ron Freeman, who, as First Vice President, was effectively the bank's chief investment officer. Ron was instinctively comfortable with me as a former Salomon guy, so I got invited to tag along with him to a lot of high-level meetings, especially anything involving an energy angle.

Whether deserved or not, I was getting unique exposure for some-one of my age. Among the VIPs I met were the Prime Minister of Kazakhstan, the Russian Minister of Fuel & Energy, and the Turkish Minister of Finance. I had lunches and dinners with CEOs of major oil companies, including a few times with John Deuss, a notorious oil trader who was then trying to position himself as chairman of the historic Caspian Oil Pipeline – a character who could easily have played the villain in a Bond film, with his dapper attire, odd accent, and suspiciously high-level connections (but no cat). On another occa-sion, I flew to Baku (the capital of Azerbaijan) with a senior team from British Petroleum in the BP chairman's private aeroplane, and joined the first meetings for what eventually became the Azeri International Oil Consortium. Whenever an oil company approached EBRD for financing, the project ended up on my desk, and I was soon busy analysing a dozen potential opportunities with no one yet besides Ron to report to.

Although I visited Moscow several times for the EBRD, in fact I was usually passing through, connecting onward to distant locations where oil and gas fields existed. My travels gave me an extraordinary opportunity to experience the Russia beyond the capital, and other far-flung reaches of the old Soviet Union. I became familiar with lesser-known regions like Tyumen Oblast in Western Siberia, the Yamal peninsula, and Komi Republic. I remember disembarking the aeroplane on my first visit to Siberia in mid-winter. Immediately, the blast of cold air almost knocked me off my feet. It was -40°C, so cold that even the contact lenses on my eyes started to freeze. I had to stagger around with my eyelids nearly closed to keep the lenses just above freezing temperature, opening my eyes only as necessary to maintain my bearings and not fall down. It felt like I was stumbling drunk through a nightclub through a barrage of strobe lights, except it was outside in the broad daylight and I was stone-cold sober.

Sadly, my youthfulness eventually caught up with me. At some point, Ron was reminded of exactly just how old I was, concluding that it really was inappropriate for someone so young to be managing so many projects by himself. He told me to engage a recruiter and start the hiring process for someone older to become the head of EBRD's oil team. It is not every day that you are tasked with hiring your own boss, but that being the situation, I decided to tackle the assignment with relish. In hindsight, some of the interviews I conducted seem ludicrous. How odd it must have appeared as I asked candidates – some of them twenty years my senior – the typical, banal recruitment questions like 'Where do you see yourself in five years?' Ron, of course, retained the final say on who got the job, and we ended up hiring the ex-treasurer of Amoco, a major US oil company. He was a very capable and experienced individual, but he was used to delegating to junior subordinates. Once he arrived at the EBRD, he didn't get involved in the details of analysis or the structuring of transactions. So, I essentially carried on with my work just as before. Recognising that energy projects were likely to be one of the biggest sectors for EBRD lending and investment, we also brought on board a couple of very smart Russians seconded to us. Former professionals from Vnesheconombank (formerly the Soviet Union's Bank for Foreign Economic Affairs) like Sergei Popov and Dmitry Maslov joined the team, as we together took the main responsibility for EBRD financing of Russian oil projects.

As I got to know Sergei and Dmitry and some other Russian colleagues better, I was invited to their homes and met their families. I realised that my initial impressions of Russia were superficial and that I had definitely not grasped the essence of the country. I came to understand the remarkable resilience of its people, and was soon convinced that they would survive and rebound from their current condition. I learned too that they are among the most generous, hospitable, dependable, and true friends that you can find anywhere in the world. I didn't speak the language yet, but I immediately appreciated the unique Russian sense of humour. Something else helped me to fit in, too. Perhaps because of my Irish roots, I could drink a lot of vodka without totally losing control of my senses. That meant I could meet my new Russian friends head on in their drinking sessions, refusing to shy away as most foreigners did. It helped persuade them to embrace me as a kindred spirit. 'Mike, you are one of us!' I heard on many occasions. My love affair (and sometime love-hate affair) with Russia, which has now flourished for well over a quarter of a century, did not take long to catch light.

It was lucky I got along well with Sergei and Dmitry, because we had some dense, challenging work to wade through. I was mainly focused on arranging project financing for joint ventures between Russian state-owned oil companies and foreign oil firms. Unlike at Salomon, the financial analysis part of these projects was easy, as there were always ample reserves of easy-to-produce conventional oil to exploit. Far more complicated was how to legally structure the transactions so that the projects would be successful, and the Bank could be confident of getting its money repaid. With the collapse of the Soviet Union, Russia scrambled to create new laws governing commerce and investments, and eventually developed a sound and sensible legal code that generally resembles those in most other major international economies. But it took time to be done comprehensively, and the initial framework we were dealing with in 1992 and 1993 was confusing and often contradictory. I always remember the first legal opinion I received for one of my EBRD projects, which started with the ominous words: 'In 1917 ...' It went on to explain the nuances of Soviet law and how the new Russian legal system related to it. After reading just a single page, I knew the opinion was totally useless, and threw it straight in the waste basket. It was clear that we would have to use our common sense and be creative ourselves in defining new legal concepts to make sure our loans were actually enforceable. We spent hundreds of hours with lawyers and oil company executives, structuring transactions, negotiating terms and crafting legal documentation. The EBRD ended up financing most of the first foreign oil joint ventures in Russia, and the documentation for those transactions, along with EBRD projects in other sectors, served as precedents for many other projects that followed. Miraculously, considering the volatile path of Russia in the 1990s, every single one of these oil projects was implemented successfully, and the EBRD eventually repaid in full.

After the first several months at EBRD, I realised that I was in on the ground floor of something special. As much as studying for a Harvard MBA had been one of my dreams and ambitions, I felt that the EBRD had set me on a learning curve so steep, in a country with so much potential, that I couldn't afford to step away for two years. With a heavy heart, I informed Harvard that I would pass on their offer of admission, and decided to stay at the EBRD (still working out of London) beyond that first year. I then set about researching what opportunities that were to study a part-time Masters from my new base in England. I applied to and was accepted by the London School of Economics' MSc programme in International Finance.

With a heavy workload in my day job allied to a hectic travel schedule, I missed a lot of my lectures at the LSE. But I made up for it by taking most of my annual EBRD holiday allowance just before the exams, cramming intensely for a few weeks, and doing just enough in the tests to pass all my courses. Although I felt most of the classes were overly theoretical and of little value to practitioners, I nonetheless picked up invaluable knowledge in two subjects in particular – International Economics and Emerging Markets Equity Investment. For these alone, the entire programme was a worthwhile one. All the while, I was getting a different sort of education from the EBRD. Not least, on how tumultuous life and events in Russia were.

It was my 26th birthday, 3 October 1993, and I was flying from Nizhnevartovsk in Western Siberia to Moscow on an aeroplane chartered by an oil company seeking project financing from the bank. After we had been in the air for a couple of hours, there was an unexpected and unwelcome announcement. All of Moscow's airports had been closed until further notice. There was, apparently, a major civil disturbance happening in the city. A stand-off had developed between the then Russian President, Boris Yeltsin, and the parliament that he had just recently ordered to be dissolved in favour of rule by presidential decree – a move he argued would hasten reform but that was not authorised by the constitution. Parliament retaliated by impeaching Yeltsin and barricading itself inside the Russian White House, its Moscow home. As tensions escalated and street fighting swept the city, the authorities determined to close the airport as a security precaution, presumably to prevent the arrival of reinforce-ments sympathetic to the parliamentary rebels. Our aircraft circled Moscow several times, waiting for any change in circumstances, but the radio remained silent. When we started to run short on fuel, some kind of agreement was at last reached between the cockpit and ground control, giving us permission to land at Moscow's Vnukovo airport.

Once we'd touched down, there were no ground handlers to direct the aeroplane to a slot. The craft sat motionless on the runway for several minutes until the pilots took matters into their own hands, taxiing us manually towards the gates of the main terminal. No one came to meet us or answered our radio calls, and we were parked up for several more minutes deciding what to do next. Finally, the pilots opened the door, lowered the stair ladder, and we all climbed down on to the tarmac. We walked hesitantly over to the terminal building, checking doors to see if any were open. After three or four tries, we found one that was unlocked and entered the terminal. Once again, there were no staff in sight. We wandered through the silent, empty terminal – luggage in hand – until we finally came to a crowded arrivals hall, buzzing with a mixture of energy and anxiety. There were dense swarms of people crowded around each of three TV sets suspended from the ceiling. On the screens was live coverage of the storming of the Russian White House by pro-Yeltsin special forces troops. I approached one of the swarms and peered up at the screen just as the TV showed troops securing the building, which was smoking after a barrage of tank shelling and grenade bursts. We all watched spellbound as the two leaders of the insurrectionist parlia-ment, Alexander Rutskoi and Ruslan Khasbulatov, were led away from the White House by Russian troops. Moscow had promised never a dull moment; from the time I'd seen the news of the failed coup against Gorbachev when I had come down from the Matterhorn three years earlier, it never failed to deliver surprises.

By 1994, I was living virtually full-time in Moscow and had a new job (more on that later). The pace of change in the city was staggering, making it, on the one hand, frustratingly dysfunctional by any practi-cal measure, and on the other, constantly entertaining – especially for the young expatriate community that I was now part of. We worked hard – typically, six days a week on a seemingly never-ending flow of new projects. But what made those years unique were all the crazy episodes that occurred away from work. Life for an expat in 1990s Moscow was equal parts bizarre and marvellous.

There was a camaraderie among the investment community, even among competitors, since we felt a bond of common experience in what we all felt were historic times. Traffic jams had yet to become the bane of Moscow life and you could still drive from one end of the city to the other, right through the centre, in twenty minutes. On Friday evenings, virtually all of us went to a pub on Znamenka street, not far from the Kremlin, called Rosie O'Grady's – one of the city's first Western-style drinking holes. For the rest of the weekend, it was smoky evenings in nightclubs like 011 and Titanic, where there seemed endless legions of beautiful girls – Russia's greatest natural resource. This was a time when if you really wanted to impress a date, you might take her to Pizza Hut, which was considered a high-end restaurant and one of the cool places to go.

But the most iconic bar of Moscow in the 1990s was undoubtedly the Hungry Duck. Its lifespan was brief, but you could fill an entire book about the goings-on that occurred there. It was a real den of decadence, with a proven and clever business model: women only before 10 p.m., with unlimited and almost free shots of vodka or Jägermeister on offer, then after 10 p.m. men were allowed in for a hefty admission fee. Once inside, cheap drinks were no longer on offer. Instead, the prices were stiff. The owners of the bar made a fortune. For any young man with two arms and two legs seeking female companionship for a night, the Hungry Duck was about as close to a sure thing as ever existed. But its frenetic energy got tiring after a while. The same ten or fifteen songs sung raucously by a sweaty crowd in endless repetition, teetering around a littered floor sticky from spilled drinks. Watching the frenzied horde eventually left me feeling lonelier than when I arrived.

In any event, the Hungry Duck's massively profitable existence came to an abrupt and ironic end. One of the bartenders was a strikingly handsome African man who was accustomed to entertaining the women guests before the doors opened to men at 10. When he wasn't serving the excitable crowd shots of vodka, he would jump up on the bar, take off his shirt to reveal his chiselled frame, and dance while the Soviet national anthem was blasted out at full volume. The women absolutely loved it but, unfortunately for the owners of the Hungry Duck, someone filmed one such episode. The footage circulated rapidly until it ended up on the desk of a Russian bureaucrat. The sight of a half-naked African man dancing to the Soviet anthem, with a throng of screaming Russian women grabbing at his legs as he strode up and down the bar, apparently offended the puritan official's sense of propriety. The bar was closed on short notice by municipal order, bringing to an end the life of the legendary Hungry Duck as we had known it.

Personally, I always wanted a deeper connection with Russia than high times with expats could offer. I still didn't speak much Russian in the mid-'90s, which was a barrier to how deeply rooted I could become in the country. Nonetheless, I was already developing a genuine affinity with Russian culture. On weekends, I would often walk around Moscow's parks, neglected and run down in those years, but still wonderfully grounded expressions of real life. I would see families grilling *shashlik* (skewered cubes of meat) over small beds of coals, students earnestly doing their gymnastic-type physical exercises, and old men playing chess while wearing hats made from folded newspaper, each revealing their own distinct personality. I immersed myself too in the country's literature and music. I followed a few Russian rock groups, like the avant-garde Kvartal, and sometimes went to see their gigs in crowded little Moscow bars, surrounded by a young and entirely Russian young crowd very different from the expatriate scene. I also developed a love of Russian cuisine of the type that every babushka in every Russian village has made for generations: all kinds of hearty soups, like *schii, rassolnik, ukha, solyanka*; the best dairy products in the world, especially *kefir* (a yoghurt-like drink) and *smetana* (a sour cream); cabbage and meat pies; *pelmeni* (dumplings) and *golubtsi* (stuffed cabbage leaves); half-salted cucumbers; *mors* (a drink made from berries), *kvas* (a drink of fermented rye), and much more. In the small canteen where I worked, there was a cheerful, round and altogether extraordinary woman called Lyudmila, who cooked these dishes (and many more) with an unrivalled mastery. The tantalising aromas as she prepared lunch every day were enough to melt the heart of even the most reluctant foreigner.

Travel continued to inform my developing relationship with the country. I frequently took overnight trains to visit prospective companies. It could be stiflingly hot in the cabins, since the windows were fixed shut, but it was just about survivable if you boarded with a sense of humour and the standard ration for a Russian train journey – a kilogram of salami, a loaf of black bread, a jar of half-salted cucumbers, and a bottle of vodka. Air travel was preferable to going by train but still sketchy in those days, often featuring old Yak-40s that had already been out of production for a decade and a half, and which were so poorly maintained that a successful landing was routinely greeted by an eruption of cheering from relieved passengers. Hotels, too, were still mostly of Soviet vintage, characterised by bad design, under-investment, and often corrupt managers who had seized ownership since the collapse of the USSR through underhand means. I recall staying in a hotel in Petrozavodsk, Karelia, in the middle of winter when the heating was not working. At night, I lay fully clothed under the blankets, even wearing my overcoat and wool hat, and watching my frosty breath wisping in the air as I tried, in vain, to fall asleep. But it felt more like an adventure than great hardship, and I and my contemporaries rarely complained. We embraced the chaos, energised to be living in truly exciting times.

Of course, there was a dark side to the 1990s in Russia too. It was a time when official structures for imposing the rule of law were fractured, weak, and corrupt. Into this void, organised criminal groups stepped in and flourished. They were there in the usual, predictable areas. Running casinos and dealing narcotics, and selling protection services to small businesses, where they offered to shield them from unwanted bureaucratic interference. There was even a special term for this – to have a 'roof' (*krisha*) for your business. Of course, it was the mafia groups themselves often instigating the very bureaucratic raids that they then offered to help 'solve'. Sometimes, territorial battles between rival groups played out on the streets in Moscow and other cities, with gun fights and bombings not uncommon. Thankfully, I would never have to deal myself with any of these mafia groups. The path I was set on led me to working with companies that were more complicated than the mafia could easily understand or manipulate. Generally speaking, they targeted 'rent-collecting'-type businesses, ones where they didn't require a lot of brains to take advantage. For me and my colleagues, as long as we could recognise the mafia types in the nightclubs and had the good sense to stay away from their girls, we managed to avoid problems.

The 1990s was an uncomfortable time for many Russians as the nation transitioned to a free market economy. Swathes of the population felt a sense of disorientation now that the certainties of the Soviet times were no more. But for others – most of them young, energetic and enthusiastic – there was suddenly the chance to make previously unimaginable amounts of money – both honestly and dishonestly. I had my experience in the gas and oil business, and natural resources would prove a booming sector. But it was a dangerous playing field with many ruthless competitors. I started to see my opportunities elsewhere. I wanted to move away from the big beasts using their muscle to dominate the natural commodities markets to a sector where my natural entrepreneurial spirit and skills lent me an advantage. My time in Russia had already shown me that there was a vast, pent-up and un-met consumer demand for almost everything. I saw the potential to create huge value in the early formation of brands and platforms. My working life began to pivot towards smaller, entrepreneurial, consumer-focused ventures. Here was where I would truly make my mark in Russia. And, though I could not possibly have foreseen it, where the long pathway to my unjust arrest and imprisonment truly began.

SECTION 2
MARCH 2019

7

No End in Sight

As I acclimatise to life in cell 604, I still cling to the dream of getting out quickly. By now, there has been a torrent of articles in the Russian press about my case, and any reasonable person reading them would conclude that I am innocent. It's obvious that the case against me is motivated by the shareholder conflict within Vostochny Bank, rather than any genuine concern about the alleged fraudulent transactions being investigated. More importantly, dozens of influential Russians are speaking up in my defence, not just famous businessmen but even some government ministers and heads of state companies. If such statements are appearing not just in the usual opposition newspapers but in the mainstream Russian press, which is famously docile and under control of the Kremlin, it must mean that support for me extends even within the President's administration. This gives me a glimmer of hope.

But in Russia 'the security system' can never admit a mistake for fear it might set off a chain reaction that will jeopardise its entire legitimacy. I am regularly reminded that the investigation against me, and efforts to somehow prove my guilt, are grinding on. One day, I am taken to an interrogation room to meet with my advocate, Dmitry Kletochkin. Next to him, I see the same passive-aggressive major who conducted the original search of my flat.

He has brought with him a laptop and portable printer to print and sign an important preliminary procedural statement, which he needs to press forward with the investigation. Nonetheless, I can tell from the major's demeanour that he regards me and my situation differently now. He must still 'go through the motions' like a loyal soldier, of course, regardless of truth and facts. Russian investigators broadly believe that all businessmen are guilty of some crime or other, so I doubt he thinks that I am genuinely innocent of everything. But I sense that he no longer believes the specific accusations made against me.

When the statement has been printed and signed, the three of us stay in the room and chat for another fifteen minutes or so. The major sighs, leaning back in his chair, and starts to speak. It turns out he's a fan of the NBA. 'I guess now I'll never get to visit America and watch the Milwaukee Bucks play,' he says ruefully. I reassure him that there is still time for a happy ending for everyone, if the case is closed and we all move on with our lives. I will even buy him the Bucks tickets myself, I joked. But he and Kletochkin both shrug their shoulders, gesturing up to the ceiling, a classic Russian gesture to indicate that the destiny of my case depends on forces outside any of our control. I'm pragmatic enough to understand this, so I figure it's better to foster a reasonable, if not friendly, working relationship with them. I'll direct my rage and energy elsewhere, where it might actually make a difference.

We continue to chat, sharing childhood stories, which is amusing given the differences in our Soviet and American upbringings. It must come off a bit like the 'Four Yorkshiremen' sketch from *Monty Python*, each of us boasting about some difficult summer job we each had when we were 15 years old: 'Tell it to the kids these days, and they'll never believe it.' When we at last get up to leave, the investigator reaches in his pocket, takes out a piece of candy and hands it to me, as if to say: 'I'm really sorry for ruining your life, but I hope you understand it's nothing personal.' I shake his hand and leave, unable to forget how ruthless and hardened this man had been towards me just a week or so ago. It is a shockingly cynical system, even if the blame doesn't lie mainly with him or any other lower-level soldier within it.

Not many days later, I receive a visit from Boris Titov. I have known him, though not closely, for several years because a company he owns, Abrau-Dyurso Champagne, is a well known and success-ful in the Russian market. But he has come today in his official capacity as the Ombudsman appointed by the Russian President to help defend the interests of entrepreneurs. He has the right to visit prisons, inspect conditions, and meet with inmates. He tells me that he is trying to help me and the other Baring Vostok detainees. We have the support of the entire Russian business community, he says, and there is widespread understanding that our accusers are lying. As he mentions some specific people trying to help me, I am invigorated and feel that maybe we do have a chance. Of course, our meeting takes place in one of the usual advocate meeting rooms, where everything is recorded and monitored, so we are both careful in our remarks.

He asks about my health and the living conditions in prison. I tell him that the guys in 604 are surprisingly supportive and that we get along fine. When he presses me for any complaints, I mention the issue with my spine and the request for a second mattress, which was denied. Otherwise, the guards have so far been careful to follow the rules. My real grievance is fuelled by outrage about being in here at all, and I would much rather our supporters focus on getting us released, instead of working to achieve minor improvements in the conditions of our detention.

It turns out that Titov visited cell 604 just before our meeting, when I was elsewhere meeting one of my advocates. I learn that he interviewed my cellmates, asking whether I was able to communi-cate with them fully in Russian (which I am), and how I'm doing psychologically. He also made the time to ask each of them in turn what they are 'in' for. I gather they don't normally get so much direct attention from the Ombudsman, and they have seized the opportunity to complain about their own various health issues. My cellmates are impressed that he is paying such personal attention to my case – and by extension to them – and I can feel my credibility with (not to men-tion usefulness to) the 604 team rising.

Shortly after Titov's visit, two things happen. Firstly, that same evening, I am delivered a second mattress. Then Misha (CoCo) is moved to a different cell. This is how I learn that Misha is being indicted for selling narcotics – a different category of crime compared to the rest of us in 604, all accused of 'economic crimes'. I will not forget Misha's friendliness and generosity when I arrived, and his spirited sense of humour. But I guess someone determined that it might be bad PR for an American businessman like me to be housed with a drug dealer, so he is moved to a different cell.

I have one more meeting, the day after the one with Titov. A senior consular officer from the US Embassy arrives to meet me, turning up with a translator. I am not sure why a translator needs to be there, considering that the consular officer and myself are quite capable of conversing in English, but I gather this is required protocol. We meet in an area of Matrosskaya Tishina that I haven't been in before, a section of small, closed rooms on the ground floor, where prisoners can speak to outside visitors. The compact, windowless room is really just a cubicle, divided by a sound-proof glass panel and big enough for no more than two people to sit on either side. The only way to hear each other across the glass is via a telephone. Standing right behind the consular officer and translator throughout is a tall, veteran Matrosskaya Tishina guard, whom the 604 guys have already pointed out to me as an FSB man.

The consular officer is mostly interested in my health and well-being. I repeat the same message I gave to Titov: that I feel fine (except for my spine) and that the guards are so far following the rules. I take the opportunity to re-emphasise my innocence, and that my friends and colleagues are working actively on my defence strategy. He tells me that Ambassador Huntsman, whom I know well, fully supports me and is ready to give whatever help is needed. I reply that public comments of support from the ambassador are very much appreciated, as are other US government efforts to get me released, but I urge him to refrain from giving any ultimatums to his Russian counterparts. Given the current poor state of US–Russian relations, I am concerned that such a strategy will backfire. Russia is less susceptible to American government pressure than many smaller countries not yet under sanctions, so any ultimatum will likely only result in a hardening of the forces against me. I fear I will become a bargaining chip in a broader puzzle of diplomatic relations, in which case it might take years for any deal to be finalised.

There are two other major considerations that warrant a carefully calibrated diplomatic approach: Baring Vostok funds have many other Russian investments, and I also have several Russian colleagues now under arrest. My main priority is to get out of prison, of course, but if it happens solely as part of a political trade with the US, it has the potential to jeopardize Baring Vostok's entire Russian portfolio. Even more pressing is the worry that my arrested Russian colleagues will receive even harsher treatment than they've already experienced. We are all effectively hostages and need a comprehensive agreement that gets us all out of this hole together. That said, it is comforting to know that there are powerful potential 'sticks' that US and European governments have the capability of wielding should we eventually be convicted. The thought of my accusers partying in their Italian villas with money taken from our jointly owned Bank, while we sit in a penal colony in Siberia, is too much to bear. When I return to cell 604, the guys as usual ask how the meeting went? 'BZ,' I reply. In a Russian prison it's short for *byez izmenenie*, meaning 'no change'. A phrase you hear a lot whenever someone returns to the cell from a court hearing, or from a meeting with their advocates.

It is a Thursday morning nine days after I joined the cell when I am summoned to an appeal hearing about my two-month detention. As I gather my papers and prepare to go, the guys all give me fist bumps and 'God be with you!' Andrey, who faces being summoned at any moment for his own final day of hearings, asks me if I need any advice or help. I am struck by his selflessness and thoughtfulness, given the huge stress he must be under just now. The consequences of my minor appeal hearing are dwarfed by the potential magnitude of the sentencing decision he faces. I tell him I will be OK and wish him a successful outcome in his case.

I don't actually leave Matrosskaya Tishina for my appeal. Instead, I join the courtroom in Moscow's City Court (MosGorSud) by videolink. TV cameras are briefly allowed to film before the hearing starts, but are excluded from covering any of the actual proceedings. I recognise a few faces watching on, including Alexander Branis from Prosperity Capital, a well-known corporate governance activist and an astute investor. I raise my fist in the air when the TV cameras roll, to show that I am OK and ready to fight to prove my innocence.

I am happy with the way my advocates forcefully make their arguments, dealing mostly with technical issues of law. This hearing isn't about proving my innocence, but rather to determine whether or not there are proper grounds to detain me while the investigation is being carried out. That said, I give an address highlighting that I *am* innocent, explaining why our accusers are acting for their own mercenary reasons. I know my arguments will make little difference to the judge, even though any fair system of justice would immediately dismiss the case on account of my opponents' improper motivations. Really, I am speaking to win the attention of the journalists there, knowing that they will likely report what I say, and that this might just help eventually to nudge the case in our direction.

In the event, neither my arguments nor those of my advocates are even considered. The judge takes a recess of only five or ten minutes to decide she will confirm the previous decision of the Basmanny court. I am to be detained until at least 13 April. She delivers a ten-page ruling, seemingly oblivious to the fact that the length of the decision proves it was made in advance of today's hearing. She reads aloud in the crisp, staccato cadence that I come to recognise as the characteristic style of Russian judges. It reminds me of the brisk intonation of American and British auctioneers, delivered with the same gusto whether they are selling an Old Master at Sotheby's, or cows at the Oklahoma State Fairgrounds.

When I return dejectedly to cell 604, it is with 100 per cent certainty – and not just the 99 per cent I had when I left for the hearing – that it is to be my home for the foreseeable future. At first, I sit alone for a few hours, feeling heavy and powerless. I don't feel like engaging in conversation with the others. But eventually I decide that I need to make the best of a bad situation and use the time to maximum advantage. Otherwise it would be like letting those bastards defeat me. At a minimum, I think, I should be able to use my time in isolation to finish some great books that I have long wanted to read, and to improve my fitness to the level of the other 604 guys, matching their workouts at morning *progulka*.

But even as I pledge to keep looking forward, it is a struggle. My main sadness and frustration is because I am missing several important family events. The complete information blackout in here means that I don't know what my wife and kids are thinking or how much they understand about my situation. When I allow myself to contemplate this, it makes me absolutely miserable. I can only imagine how worried they must be about me, probably assuming that I am caught in some kind of living hell but unable to help me in any way.

My despondency intensifies on 1 March, the birthday of my wife, Julia. It is a particularly notable one this year, a special round-numbered one, and it makes me so sad to be separated from her. At least I am able to arrange, via one of my advocates, to send her flowers and a huge teddy bear. In Russian, a teddy bear is called 'Mishka', and it is the nickname my wife has for me (at least, when I'm not in trouble with her). So, it is a symbolic gift of sorts, a stand-in Mishka while the real one is away. Word eventually gets back to me that she loves it. But on the day, I feel only gloom, reinforced by my upset that I cannot help my kids, Sasha and Niko, with their respective entrance exams and university applications. I have very fond memories of a college tour I once took with my oldest son, Mishuta (Michael Jr, but *also* sometimes called Mishka), and we definitely bonded on that trip. But now I am denied that same chance with my other kids. I wonder if they will ever forgive me. I also worry that what is happening to me is affecting their chances of getting into university at all. I have more experience than my wife with the US and UK education systems and I fear the kids won't be able to navigate it successfully without my guidance. This is one of a parent's core priorities, and now I have let them all down.

I lie on my bunk most of the day, seething at the injustice of my situation. I am sure that my arrest must be seen as a huge irony among political analysts in the West. I have a reputation among them as an American who actively promotes investment in Russia, even after the geopolitical situation soured in 2014 with the annexation of Crimea. I am counted as one of few experienced foreigners in Russia who have remained optimistic about the country, regularly arguing that the situation on the ground in Russia is better than it is commonly portrayed in the international press. This being the case, I'm probably the last American they ever imagined would be arrested here. The only explanation is that my accusers have skilfully manipulated top decision-makers with false information about me. To be portrayed as the 'bad guy', and even a criminal, just doesn't make sense, and is so unfair.

But I have to remain strong. Things could be worse. I think about my BVCP colleagues, Ivan and Vagan and Philippe, as well as Maxim from PKB. They all have kids younger than mine, and families that probably need them even more than mine need me. And I know, too, that my situation is a dream compared to what Andrey and the others in 604 are going through. At least I still have some hope of getting released or acquitted. They have almost no chance. Their strength in the face of such odds makes me ashamed to feel sorry for myself.

8

The Labyrinth

To be cast into the Russian judicial system is to find yourself pawing through a seemingly endless labyrinth. When Dante finds himself descending towards hell at the beginning of the *Inferno*, he is urged: 'Abandon all hope, ye who enter here.' Matrosskaya Tishina, in particular, is a place where bad news arrives often. But I never stop being impressed by the fortitude of the guys in cell 604. Somehow they don't break down, almost always keeping a stoic face while contemplating their fate.

Although my cellmates all have a firm grasp of the allegations against me – how could they not, given the media coverage – I never really discuss the crimes *they* are accused of, or delve into the details. I expect the others to heed the same advice Sasha Rostov gave to me when I first arrived in cell 604, telling me not to share with anyone the details of my own case. Nonetheless, one of my cellmates, in a bitter tirade about the unfairness of the system, reveals that he is accused of bribery. He is alleged to have given an expensive watch as a gift to an official who had influence over approvals for a construction project his company was working on. He insists, of course, that the man was his friend and the watch had nothing to do with any project. In any event, this kind of behaviour should come as no surprise. While it is theoretically possible to get the go-ahead on construction projects in Russia without resorting to under-the-table incentives, insiders say such an approach would likely stretch out the planning approvals process by years, often destroying the economic basis for taking up the project in the first place. Of course, bribery is wrong and should be punished. But what about the other companies, contractors and officials in Russia who give and receive bribes without ever being arrested? Who decides whom to arrest and on what grounds? An overhaul is required so that everyone is on an even playing field if the intention is to really clean up the system. But all of us in the cell know that the playing field in Russia is inherently uneven; many are rewarded but others get punished, usually for reasons unrelated to any alleged offence.

One Monday morning, Sanych is called away for a hearing into his case. We send him off with fist bumps and encouraging exclamations of 'God be with you!' all round. He does not get back to the cell until around ten o'clock that evening. It has evidently been another long, disappointing and inconclusive day. But he smiles grimly as he tells us that at least he enjoyed having the opportunity to tell them all what a bunch of bastards they are. I have no doubt that he delivered his message with the colourful vocabulary that we have come to expect of him. It might be a small victory but it feels good to hit back at 'the system' any way we can.

One of our favourite TV shows in the cell is a comedy series called *Police on Rublyevskoye*, all about a corrupt (and often inept) police unit in a rich Russian residential district. It's hilarious, with some priceless jokes and scenarios. In one episode, for instance, the local police chief decides he has bad karma as a result of his corrupt misdeeds. He sets about trying to reverse his karma by working honestly and doing acts of benevolence. But as he does so, he predictably encounters mishaps and is confronted by an array of unintended consequences, until he eventually realises that it is simply impossible for him to make amends. We all love the show in cell 604 but I am surprised that it is allowed to be shown on a state-controlled Russian TV channel as it makes fun of endemic corruption, which the government would never admit.

As the investigation into the claims against me progresses, I meet regularly with my own advocate team. It is an incredibly frustrating process. The biggest challenge we face is trying to plan a legal defence without knowing what evidence my accusers are using to support their claims. Banking and securities deals often involve complex legal documents and the devil is in the details. I have only had indirect involvement in the financial transaction on which I'm being accused, although I was briefed on it by colleagues. I certainly know enough to be certain that we have acted in good faith in the interests of the bank throughout. We have received no benefit from it, it was done transparently, and the bank has suffered no loss or damage. In other words, I know we have done nothing wrong. But I also know the real motivations of our accusers: they are determined to take permanent control of the bank and to avoid responsibility for their own actions in relation to the bank's finances.

We are fighting blind. Without access to my old emails, phone messages, and files, we are left to hopelessly second guess what they might pluck from those records with a view to using them against me, doubtlessly out of context. All the members of the team at Baring Vostok who have any knowledge or involvement in the bank merger have been arrested, and all our physical files, phones, and computers were seized during searches of our Moscow offices and our various apartments. The remainder of the Baring Vostok team are no doubt trying their best to learn the facts indirectly, via advocates searching back through our servers and cloud-based data for whatever scraps they can retrieve, but this is like trying to find a needle in a haystack.

My hands are further tied because I am not allowed to speak to any of the other accused or to any potential witnesses, even under the supervision of investigators. Even communication with my own advocates is severely constricted, and they are prevented from bringing me the necessary documents to refute the charges against me. Nor is there any 'attorney–client privilege', since conversations conducted in the prison meeting rooms are all monitored. All the while, the state investigators will be calling witnesses and subjecting them to interrogation. They have at their disposal the unspoken threat of further arrests as a means of frightening people into confirming their own version of the 'truth', while at the same time scaring away those witnesses who can prove our innocence. I feel like I am having to defend myself while blindfolded and gagged.

At one of our meetings, however, my advocate manages to smuggle in some press coverage of my case. He has mixed it in with some of his other legal papers, so the guards – usually so hot on making sure I never get my hands on material that they don't want me to have – neither confiscate it nor try to prevent him from showing it to me. It feels like contraband even though it shouldn't, since there is nothing illegal about having access to public news.

Normally, at the end of every meeting I have with my representatives in SIZO, the advocate must press a button on the wall to summon one of the guards. My pockets are then searched again to make sure I haven't been given anything, before I am escorted out of the meeting room and taken to my cell, walking with my hands held behind my back. Along the way, we pause at several gated 'checkpoints' where the guard radios ahead to request permission to proceed. Checks are made to ensure that there are no other prisoners in the next section of corridor, enforcing the ban on no communication between inmates. But on this occasion, I at least have the satisfaction of having seen the press reports and commentary, which gives me a better idea of what is going on in my case.

Sometimes their vigilance in denying me things strikes me as petty in the extreme. At one meeting, my advocate tells me he has tried to bring in a photo from my wife, but the guard downstairs had confiscated it. What potentially dangerous image did this photo convey? It is a snapshot of Julia with the bouquet of flowers and giant teddy bear I sent for her birthday. My advocate had pleaded with the guard that he at least be allowed to show it to me briefly, without actually handing it over. After all, he reminded him, we would be searched before leaving the meeting room. He appealed to the guard's better nature, explaining how much it would mean both to me and Julia if I could just see the photo for a moment. Besides, it clearly had absolutely no relevance to my investigation. But the guard – one of the real bastards in the prison – flatly refused.

That's why getting to see the press coverage counts as a triumph, even if only a minor one. The reporting itself is, I am relieved to see, balanced and mostly positive. Some of the Telegram channels, which operate outside the control of the Kremlin, are particularly damning about my opponents. But it is not altogether reassuring. There is one article, published by a second-tier Russian news outlet, which suggests I was arrested because I have been involved in funding the Russian political opposition. The suggestion is absurd, almost hilariously so. I have always studiously avoided any involvement in Russia's politics, as I believe all foreigners – and especially business-people – should do when they are guests in someone else's country. In any event, only a masochist would invest heavily in Russia and then support the political opposition. Disconcerting as it is to read, at least I am aware of the kind of fables being spread by my enemies in their crude attempt to influence the system against me. I trust that the forensic searches to which all my phones and computers are currently being subjected should conclusively put any such theories to rest. I am pleased, too, to see in the same article that several senior public officials, including Foreign Minister Sergey Lavrov, are openly contradicting such accusations and pointing out the damage my arrest is causing to Russia's international reputation.

On another occasion, I am visited by two representatives of the *Obshestvennaya Palata* (the Civic Chamber), a body with responsibility for helping citizens interact with government authorities. They monitor various activities by the government that impact citizens, including criminal justice. Although, of course, I am not a Russian citizen, their remit apparently includes oversight of cases like mine. One of the representatives is a part-time journalist with the *Nezavisimaya Gazeta* (which roughly translates as 'Independent News'). They ask a lot of questions, covering everything from which bunk I have and my views on the prison food, through to how I'm getting along with the other guys in my cell and whether the guards are following the rules. I keep my answers brief but try to convey that, overall, I am OK. A couple of days later, a complimentary and positive article about me appears in *Nezavisimaya Gazeta*.

In my first five weeks in Matrosskaya Tishina, I receive three visits overall from members of the *Obshestvennaya Palata*. It is clear that I am being treated as a special case. The other 604 guys tell me they expect to get such visits only once or twice a year, and then they are typically perfunctory affairs. The extra attention I receive is presumably because of the huge press interest in my case. On one visit, the pair of representatives are accompanied by the particularly tall guard/FSB man who had previously shadowed my meeting with the US consul. On this occasion, one of the *Obshestvennaya Palata* guys asks me a couple of questions posed to him by a Bloomberg journalist whom I know. Specifically, he wants to know what I think of President Putin's economic policy, and whether I still believe in investment in Russia. The way the questions are posed, within Matrosskaya Tishina and within earshot of an FSB guard, obviously makes this an awkward encounter. For one thing, there is no good answer I can give. I will get into trouble no matter what I answer.

I simply reply that I won't comment on any political questions, but I still believe I will be found to be innocent, and want to express my sympathies to my colleagues who are also wrongfully detained. The guard clearly sees the question as a provocation. Even before the *OP* guys can write down my answer, they are hustled out of the room. I later learn that one of the representatives gets into serious trouble and is formally reprimanded for asking these questions. Such a reprimand is overly harsh and unnecessary, but probably not surprising to the *OP* guys, given the nature of 'the system' in which we and they are operating.

One day I ask the guys in cell 604 their opinion as to what the biggest problems are with 'the system'. They all laugh as if my question is both ludicrous and naïve – the type of question, in fact, only a foreigner would ask. From their vantage point, stuck in Matrosskaya Tishina while under investigation, the problems with 'the system' are so extensive that it would take them volumes to fully describe. But when pressed to name just what they consider the single biggest problem, each of them cites the same thing: a lack of independent judges. My experience of Russian judges previously was confined to those in the commercial arbitration courts, to which we have sometimes been called to defend one of our fund's portfolio companies. Altogether, I have come away with a generally positive impression of them, and our funds were almost always successful in defending our rights there. But in criminal cases, judges are afraid to rule against the recommendations of investigators or prosecutors – and especially the FSB – for fear of themselves being accused of some misdemeanour and being put under investigation.

I spend a lot of time thinking about what seems to me most wrong with 'the system'. Among the major problems are endemic corruption, a topic that is commonly speculated about in the press. But even looking at 'the system' in the most forgiving light, it is backwards by design. Fundamentally, it treats the accused as guilty until they are proven innocent, instead of the other way around. In fact, it treats the accused as guilty, period. Once someone is accused and an investigation initiated, the investigators and prosecutors rarely let go of their prey and stubbornly refuse to admit that any mistake might have been made by them. To admit error is to seriously damage their career prospects and is a course of action to be resisted at almost any cost – even if it means aimlessly carrying on a futile investigation for years. Investigators even have a special term for it. Prisoners are 'marinated' in SIZO until they are ready to confess their guilt.

A major article in *Vedomosti*, a leading Russian newspaper, while I am in SIZO, bears this out. The piece reveals that of the criminal cases that go to trial in Russia, there is a 99.8 per cent conviction rate. For cases initiated by the Interior Ministry, a portion are closed before going to trial based on lack of evidence, and in a few rare cases a defendant is found by the judge to be not guilty. But for cases initiated by the Investigative Committee, it is extremely rare for any to be closed before going to trial. In the rare instances when one is, it typically results in a formal demotion in rank for those involved in investigating it. And when the FSB initiates the investigation, the accused is always found to be guilty. When I asked my advocates about it, they said there are no precedents – zero – of cases initiated by the FSB when a Russian judge found the defendant to be not guilty.

There is, moreover, a highly arbitrary aspect to Russian justice. One person will find themselves subject to a criminal investigation, while someone else with an almost identical legal fact pattern will go ignored by investigators. There is a well-known Russian expression, 'The toughness of our laws is compensated for by the lack of strict enforcement.' Like many jokes, it's funny because it's true. My own case is a great example of this arbitrary nature. At the root of the investigation, a transaction that was disclosed transparently to our opponents and which caused no damage to anyone, and from which we gained no benefit. Meanwhile, our accusers carried out more than twenty transactions that were not disclosed to us and which caused huge financial damage. And yet, my colleagues and I are marinating in prison while our accusers enjoy their lives without any apparent risk of investigation.

Over lunch one day, Big Sasha starts teasing Zhendos, saying he ought to stay longer in SIZO than the rest of us because he hasn't 'reformed'. The rest of us, Big Sasha jokes, are ready to be rehabilitated. Zhendos takes it all in his stride, treating it as the good-natured ribbing it is meant to be. He predicts that he will, in fact, be the first of us to get out, since the crime of which he is accused typically carries only a year-long sentence. It prompts another long discussion about the failures of the system, uniting us in a boisterous condemnation of Russian sentencing standards, which are wildly arbitrary.

Not long after, there is a news report on TV about the arrest of the deputy governor of Ryazan, in the south-west of the country. The journalist mentions Sasha Rostov in his report, which unleashes a new torrent of cursing and comment in 604 about 'the system'. Normally feisty and argumentative, Sasha Rostov withdraws from the conversation to brood over this latest news. I still don't know what he is being investigated for, and now does not feel like the right time to ask.

Despite our feelings towards 'the system' being largely in concert most of the time, every now and then deeply ingrained differences show themselves between Western perspectives and those of Russians. One such time comes after Andrey approaches me about a *New Yorker* article he has read, which has troubled and confused him. It is about 'Whistleblowers', which in Russian translates the same as *informer*, or *stukach*. In Russia, a *stukach* is someone to be despised, while the *New Yorker* article presents them as brave and honourable. Is he missing something, Andrey asks? I try to see it from his perspective and agree that for every 'good' whistleblower, there are probably an equal number of 'bad' ones motivated by selfish or cynical interests. Then I give him a few theoretical examples where a whistleblower can be regarded as honourable. He mulls it over carefully but I don't think he's convinced.

I soon learn of another weapon in the investigators' armoury that tips the balance further in their favour. It is called 'the Box' – a room containing two small, windowless closets (the 'boxes'). We have one just down the corridor from our cell. Prisoners are temporarily put in these boxes for all sorts of reasons. Sometimes prisoners are held in the miserable Box for several hours, presumably as a form of psychological pressure. More typically, it's to allow a full search of their cells in their absence, or more briefly to prevent contact among prisoners in the corridors. One day I am taken there for fifteen minutes after returning from a meeting with one of my advocates. When I get back to 604, I find only Sasha Rostov, himself only having just arrived back. He tells me that the others were taken out ten minutes ago for their weekly *banya*. I am uncertain why I have been sent to the Box and can't believe the guards have been so petty as to do it to deprive me of my right to a shower. Sasha Rostov and I figure it must be because they wanted to search the cell without being noticed. They often do this, apparently, when all the inmates are away at *progulka* or for *banya*, to rummage for hidden contraband and also (so it's said) to photograph any notes or papers kept by the prisoners.

I am already careful in this respect. Even though I have nothing to hide, I don't want any notes I write with instructions for my advocates or work-related *aide-memoires* to fall into the hands of the investigators, and perhaps even our opponents. I'm the kind of person who remembers things better if I write them down, even if I never refer to the note again. I know I can't afford to leave such scribblings in the papers by my bunk, or even thrown away in the trash. It might be a symptom of paranoia, but to keep information secret from the 'other side', I have taken to making up code words for key things, and use a scrambled word format to make my notes illegible to anyone but myself.

A few weeks into my incarceration, I hear news reports of the arrest of Mikhail Abyzov, a prominent businessman and ex-government minister. I don't know him, so cannot judge whether there is any truth to the charges levelled against him. But the parallels to my case – the extensive press coverage, testimonies given on his behalf by well-known Russian business leaders and officials, and rumours of high-level FSB men who are lined up against him – creates a sense of déjà vu. It seems like a long line of dominoes falling inexorably, one after the other.

Most of the time, in my logical mind, I remain convinced that there will be a way out of this labyrinth into which I've been cast. I determine not to be one of those who abandon all hope. I know that my enemies have tentacles that stretch into the far reaches of government. If they did not, then I wouldn't be here in the first place. But I have my own influential supporters, people I sense are communicating at the very most senior levels that the allegations against me are unfounded, and more importantly explaining how they are damaging Russia's economy and reputation. Most of the time, my head tells me that rational thinking will win the day. But there are darker moments. Those days of no movement, or backwards steps. And then, I wonder, is the game so skewed against me that I cannot win? And how long will the game go on for? How many weeks, months or years will I need to battle before I taste freedom again, and see my family?

Thankfully, I am always eventually able to snap myself out of these destructive patterns of thinking. But I am weighed down by worry for my colleagues who are also being held. I know our business has deep enough pockets to be able to strike a financial deal that, if necessary, will likely bring this ordeal to an end. I refuse to strike a bargain that involves me admitting to a crime that never happened. But what if the authorities are hell-bent on finding a scapegoat? Someone to whom imaginary crimes can be attached in order to save their face and prevent them having to admit that the entire investigation has been misguided? My cellmates warn me that this is the typical outcome of almost all Russian criminal cases. I need to find a way to engineer an outcome that allows the system to save face without anyone on our side being made the fall guy. A difficult task, indeed.

9

Opportunity and Turbulence

The year 1994 was a pivotal one on my path to this point. Big for Russia's economy and big for me. Personally, it was the year that I completed my Master's degree and began to realise that the early excitement I had felt working for the EBRD was wearing off. It was becoming clear that the real opportunities in Russia lay not with oil projects involving large corporations, but rather with smaller, entrepreneurial ventures focused on consumers. This was also the year that the government's programme of mass privatisation kicked in and the private sector at last began to emerge as a force. Anyone with a bit of financial acumen could sense that this was a once-in-a-lifetime opportunity.

I was already itching to move on from the EBRD when I was contacted by a group of people planning to launch one of the first investment funds for Russia. This would prove to be a moment of serendipity that would change my life forever. But before I explain, a little history. Back in the eighteenth and nineteenth centuries, the famous London-based Baring Brothers had a leading position in international finance and served as official bankers even to Russia's tsarist regime. Over its long history, the institution had been responsible for financing major infrastructure projects ranging from the Louisiana Purchase for the USA to the Trans-Siberian Railway for Russia. Now, in 1994, the firm's asset management arm, Baring Asset Management

(BAM), teamed up with an investment boutique, Sovlink, with a view to raising a pioneering investment fund for the former Soviet Union.

Sovlink was started in the early 1990s by Terry English, a former commodity trader from Phibro (formerly Philip Brothers), then affiliates of Salomon Brothers. These firms did substantial business in commodity trading and finance with the Soviet bloc via credit facilities mostly with Vnesheconombank (VEB), the Soviet foreign trade bank. When the Soviet Union ended and VEB curtailed its activities, there was a big gap in the market's financial lubrication that caused commodity trading volumes to fall sharply. Terry partnered with a Russian colleague to form Sovlink with ambitions to address this gap, convincing Salomon, along with the British insurer Sedgwick and VEB, to become initial shareholders in the company.

BAM, meanwhile, was already an experienced manager of listed equity funds in emerging markets, especially in Asia. In addition, it had recently raised a fund to focus on Central Europe and the former Warsaw Pact countries then in the process of joining the EU (such as Poland, Hungary, the Czech Republic and Slovakia). It was a logical next step for them to raise a similar fund to focus on Russia and other former Soviet countries.

Having joined forces, BAM and Sovlink approached the obvious potential anchor investors, the EBRD and the International Finance Corporation (IFC) – a member of the World Bank Group, with a mission to encourage private sector development in less-developed countries – to help sponsor their planned new fund. Both the EBRD and IFC at the time were enthusiastic about sponsoring funds for Russia, but they disliked listed equity investments – that's to say, investments in publicly listed companies. Instead, they preferred to back funds that invested directly into private companies (so-called private equity funds). They also insisted, naturally, on having dedicated investment teams within the fund management structure to focus on their specific fund. Thus, with an eye towards improving their chances of securing these anchor commitments, BAM and Sovlink hired me and another former EBRD man, Richard Sobel, to work full time on their new fund. Richard was well known and liked inside the EBRD, and was also a well-regarded presence in the nascent Moscow investment community. The EBRD and IFC consequently agreed to commit to around 25 per cent of the new fund's capital, on condition that the other 75 per cent came from private sector investors.

Raising capital for a private equity fund is normally a lengthy process in which potential investors conduct an exhaustive review of the fund management team, taking in their track record and strategy for moving forward. Although Richard and I had both made investments in Russia for the EBRD, there was not yet much in the way of track record. Besides, the types of investments we'd overseen were very different to what we planned for the new fund. There was probably no way we could convince normal private equity investors to back us for a first-time fund like this. Our plan, then, was to raise the funds using BAM's regular approach: structuring it as a listed company, and targeting mutual funds and wealthy individuals as investors.

The timing couldn't have been better. Under the Russian government's privatisation scheme, vouchers corresponding to a share of national wealth had been distributed on an equal basis to virtually all Russian adults and children. It is estimated it reached about 98 per cent of the population. These vouchers could then be exchanged for shares in state-owned enterprises that were about to be privatised. Over a two-year period, some 15,000 firms moved from state control to private hands. The programme was structured this way to reduce the likelihood that companies immediately fell under the control of the already well-connected or of organised crime. But, of course, most ordinary people had little idea how or where to invest. Most instead decided to cash in their vouchers, which fell largely into the hands of the existing management of the enterprises. The process typically involved burly men in black leather jackets standing outside the factory gates, with thick wads of cash in their pockets, handing over small sums to individual workers who queued up to exchange their share certificates. Although the valuations were often unfair and there should have been more protections in place, the managers behind most of these buy-back schemes at least understood the businesses and sometimes helped steer their companies into real profitability. Moreover, members of Yeltsin's economic team, like Anatoly Chubais, argued that the quick transfer of ownership into private hands ensured that the Communist Party would be unable to easily reverse the march towards a market economy if they ever regained power – a persuasive argument. That said, at this time, the very largest and potentially most valuable enterprises were not fully privatised, with the state retaining majority control on strategic grounds.

The scheme was certainly not without fault, but at least it did facilitate a rapid phase of privatisation and won the attention of large global investors. Nonetheless, there were as yet still few foreign-listed investment funds to provide easy access for international investors. This was a gap we sought to fill. We went on a roadshow to win over investors, trading heavily on BAM's hard-won credibility in emerging markets. By November 1994, we had succeeded in raising $160 million in capital for what was called the First NIS Regional Fund (NIS being short for New Independent States, to distinguish it from CIS, the acronym of the Commonwealth of Independent States formed after the collapse of the USSR and which excluded the Baltic States). Of this, 60 per cent was initially allocated for investment in private companies, and 40 per cent into 'liquid' shares of Russian companies. Richard and I essentially co-managed the fund, with him travelling between London and Russia and me moving to Moscow permanently to head up a small local team. We were off to the races, or so we thought.

Unsurprisingly, some of our first investments were disasters – a result of our greenness in the market allied to generalised economic turbulence. For example, our bet on the Garden Ring Supermarkets chain in Moscow, and another on a sawmill project based 750 miles north of the capital in Arkhangelsk, both ended as 100 per cent write-offs. There were assorted reasons for these early mishaps. Sometimes, it was a case of poor execution by the wrong people heading up the companies. Other enterprises held real promise but were entering the fray way too early. And some were simply bad ideas altogether. But for all the slip-ups, we also made some highly successful early invest-ments, including into Sovintel (later GTS, a fixed telecom operator) and Vimpelcom, a mobile operator. When we invested in the latter, it had only 2,000 mobile subscribers; today, it has more than 100 mil-lion. In 1996, it became the first Russian company to make an IPO on the New York Stock Exchange, earning our fund a strong early win. We also invested the 40 per cent listed equity allocation into some promising but as yet poorly known opportunities. We identified, for example, the best of the oil holding companies, rather than their better-known production subsidiaries, before the market generally recognised that this was where real value was likely to be generated.

We also arranged to buy, via brokers, a 2 per cent stake in Yukos, a company destined to become a giant in Russia's energy sector. The shares mostly came from employees who had received them during the company's privatisation. The powerful Menatep Group eventually bought 96 per cent of the company through notorious privatisation tenders, so it turned out that at one point our tiny fund owned half of the remaining 'free float' of shares. I recall going by myself to the first annual shareholders meeting of Yukos, held in a nineteenth-century palace on Moscow's boulevard ring. Security was tight as you entered the building. I had to pass through two metal detectors before a hulking security guard searched me from head to toe with a magnetic wand. I had arrived about half an hour before the meeting's scheduled start time, and was shown into a large, ornately decorated room, probably a former ballroom or grand hall. There was a large rectangular table at its centre that could seat about thirty people, and I saw a few faces I recognised already there.

Among them was Sergei Muravlenko, the general director of Yuganskneftegaz, the main oil-producing subsidiary of Yukos. I had met him years earlier when I worked at the EBRD. I remembered thinking back then that he was the epitome of the tough, command-ing Soviet oil man. Now he was the centre of attention around the table, and I assumed that he was the dominant figure in Yukos. Its CEO was a much younger man, Mikhail Khodorkovsky, and it didn't seem realistic to expect that a youthful Moscow banker would even try to control, much less dominate, such a powerful Siberian oil baron. But when Khodorkovsky entered the room, the atmosphere changed and it was clear who really held the power. Muravlenko seemed to deflate before our eyes, looking down at the floor. Khodorkovsky was completely in command of the room and, of course, completely ignored me. I sat in silence watching the show. Within a few years,

Khodorkovsky would briefly be Russia's richest man. It was already clear to me in that meeting room that he had no interest in minority shareholders like our little fund, so we sold our shares shortly afterwards. Although I briefly regretted selling, we were lucky to do so when we did, in light of what subsequently happened at Yukos, and were able to earn the fund a solid profit and an early win.

By 1997, the Russian market had grown in both size and sophistication. There were now several funds focusing either on listed companies or private equity opportunities. It was clear that to try to do both was both inefficient and unsustainable. Richard and I felt that direct investment was likely to offer the better long-term opportunity, but BAM remained focused on investments in listed companies made via stock exchanges. They fundamentally didn't understand the private equity model, and were not willing to stump up the money to enable us to hire a team necessary to do the job properly. Nor were they willing to share enough of the fund's performance fee to incentivise the team to commit long term. Richard was growing increasingly disappointed until he decided to resign to pursue raising his own fund.

The corporate world often requires a shock to bring top management to its senses, and so it proved. Shortly after Richard left, BAM agreed to cede greater control of the fund to Baring Private Equity Partners (BPEP) and to my management team. This was a good move. After a rogue securities trader in their Singapore office almost brought Barings to its knees in 1995, the bank had been bought out by the Dutch ING group. BPEP instinctively understood the private equity business, and with ING as their new parent company, they promised to provide seed capital to any new fund we raised. By the end of 1997, there was further restructuring, and around the same time we also bought out Sovlink's stake, giving our small team in Moscow still more ownership.

We held a contest in our Moscow office to come up with name for the new company, and 'Baring Vostok' won the day. *Vostok* is the Russian word for 'East' – an appropriate brand since our operations were obviously to the east of our parent company and most of our investors. *Vostok* was, furthermore, the name of the Soviet spacecraft piloted by Yuri Gagarin on the historic first manned flight into space back in 1961. It seemed a fitting reference to the scientific and technological prowess of the countries in which we were investing – what we saw as the key to the success of real entrepreneurial ventures, in contrast to the reliance upon copious natural resources that other investors were relying upon.

As well as BPEP, we had several highly respected independent board members for our first fund, giving our young team advice and credibility. I still count several of them among my friends, and they proved great mentors over the years. Men like Arthur Hartman, whose distinguished career in foreign service included a stint as the US ambassador to the Soviet Union, and Dudley Fishburn, a former British Member of Parliament and editor of *The Economist*.

As life was progressing professionally, so too was it personally. I had met a woman, Julia, at a birthday party of a mutual friend in 1996. She was stunningly beautiful and obviously smart, but most of all, she was disarmingly genuine. Talking to her at that party, it felt like only the two of us existed, and we made the kind of connection that leaves you entranced long afterwards. I knew immediately that she would be my wife. The only problem was that I wasn't yet ready to get married. I hesitated to even get back in contact, fearing that I would slide quickly into marriage and my treasured bachelor days would be gone forever. I held out for a couple of months but couldn't shift the memory of that first unforgettable conversation. I could resist no longer, so called and asked to meet her for lunch. About six months later, we were happily engaged to be married, and tied the knot in May 1997. Our first child, Mishuta (Michael Jr), was born a year later.

I was now a family man, with a job I loved. But the economic sands were shifting again. Russia was firmly in the grip of the oligarchs – a relatively small coterie of well-connected individuals who had exploited the tumult of the immediate post-Soviet years to acquire once state-owned businesses, often for a fraction of their real value. These were men who had rapidly made unimaginable fortunes and dominated not only the nation's economic life, but its political intrigues also. Their rise had been accelerated by the infamous 'Loans for Shares' scheme in 1996, which was motivated by Yeltsin's political expediency and ended as one of the most corrupt episodes in economic history. Vast riches were earned through rigged privatisation tenders, each run by a specific oligarch group who had secured those rights by providing loans to the government several months earlier. They used their control of the tenders to ensure no competition and dirt-cheap prices for themselves to buy control. As if this wasn't bad enough, the money they previously 'lent' to the government was actually indirectly financed by the government itself. Several of the oligarch banks, like Oneximbank and Menatep, served as treasury agents to the Russian Finance Ministry. They held large volumes of roubles deposited in government accounts, so that when the 'loans' were made, it was simply a matter of debiting one government account and crediting another within the same bank. The money never actually left the oligarch-owned banks. It is hard to imagine a more cynical operation to privatise some of the world's most important natural resources assets, and it was bound to create a backlash in the future.

In those days of rapid capital formation, if a project couldn't earn 50 per cent annually with little risk, oligarchs weren't interested. We had neither the capabilities nor the desire to compete for the types of opportunities the oligarchs pursued; it wasn't 'our type of sport', as Russians say. And they were not interested in the new entrepreneurial companies we chased, where the potential rewards came with risk and the prospect of years of hard work.

By 1997–98, it was clear that the Russian stock market bubble was unsustainable. After Yeltsin's 1996 election victory, the Russian Trading System (RTS) Index soared to all-time highs, but lacked the fundamentals to support it. The only metrics used by most foreign portfolio investors were asset-based, like the valuation of a company per barrel of oil reserves or per ton of production capacity. There were none of the traditional financial measures like earnings or cash flow multiples, since almost no companies produced independently audited financial statements. Following a couple of years of stellar returns, Russian investment conferences became the most popular among emerging markets, and new investors who hadn't a clue about Russian reality started piling into the market. I recall listening to a new European investor breathlessly extolling the attractions of 'Montenegro' as one of the great electrical utility assets in the world. After a couple of minutes of listening to his optimistic pitch, I realised that he was talking about Moscow's long-established power-generating company, Mosenergo. This type of ignorance was an obvious sign that the market was overheating and headed for a correction.

The government's fiscal position was unsustainable, too. There were more than twenty types of tax in the convoluted Russian tax code, but almost nobody paid them. Tax evasion seemed like the national sport. Barter schemes and *veksels* (bills of exchange) became commonly used by many enterprises as real cash liquidity dried up, contributing to the artificial nature of company financial accounts (where they existed at all). Teachers, nurses, police officers and other state workers didn't receive regular salaries because of the chronic government budget deficit. Meanwhile, oligarch-owned banks, probably in collusion with public officials, actively speculated in the government bond markets, so that annualised yields on local government bonds reached 50 per cent by 1998. In those circumstances, making loans to the real economy became unattractive in comparison, although, of course, no government can afford to pay such a cost on its bonds for long. Optimists put all their hopes on a bail-out from the IMF, but that could only ever be a temporary fix in lieu of real reform.

The collapse came in August 1998. Despite an IMF bailout, Russian markets went into a steep downward spiral, eventually forcing the government to default on its debt. The rouble devalued sharply, from 6 to the dollar to 24 in a single week. Battle-hardened Americans could look back on major USA market upheavals like 'Black Monday' in 1987, when the US stock market fell by 23 per cent. But such 'crises' were merely minor corrections compared with what was going on in the Russian market stock market, which fell by *98 per cent* over the course of 1998. That means that if you had $1 million invested in the Russian market on 1 January, by New Year's Eve that same year it was worth just $20,000. A virtual wipeout. One global investor told me in late 1998 that Russia was like the *Titanic*: it had sunk to the bottom of the ocean, and would never be brought back to the surface.

On the day of the default and devaluation, 17 August, I was on holiday with my wife in Portofino, Italy. When the news broke, Julia's first thought, practical as ever, was for the roughly $3,000 she had in savings on her Visa debit card with Inkombank, a Russian bank that was now surely destined to go bankrupt. We immediately raced to one of the shops in Portofino, saw that the card was still working, and spent the next two hours madly dashing to spend every last dollar on clothes and food. We completed the mission just moments before the bank declared bankruptcy and all of its cardholders' funds were blocked.

I remember those days in Portofino for another reason, too. Anyone who has visited there will know it as a postcard-perfect, quaint, stylish fishing village, usually with a collection of very expensive sailing yachts moored in its tiny harbour. That August, as Russia careered into financial collapse, a huge, modern ocean liner sat in the harbour, dwarfing all the beautiful sailing yachts around it. Its only passengers were a Russian oligarch, Vladimir Potanin, one of his male friends, and at least fifteen Russian and Ukrainian girls, partying wildly day and night. I admired the male–female ratio on his yacht, but it struck me as incredibly cynical that Potanin was so conspicuously flaunting his wealth on the very days that his bank (Oneximbank) had defaulted on its bonds and suspended depositor funds.

Julia and I cut short our holiday, and when we got back to Moscow, we found the shops were closed. They were prevented from reopening because it was impossible to know how to properly price their merchandise after such a sharp and sudden currency devaluation, and there were no functioning banks to manage their money anyway. Our son was just 4 months old at the time, and we faced the calamity of there being no Pampers available to buy anywhere in the city. We had only about ten days' supply left in the apartment. If we got down to two days, I had plans to take extreme measures: a run to the Finnish border. I kept my Land Rover Discovery oiled, full of petrol, and ready to go on short notice. Thankfully, I never had to put the plan into action. After three or four nervous days, the shops reopened and our Pampers supply was replenished.

One benefit of the government's economic shambles was that by the end of the year there were signs that it was finally ready to address its previous failures. When no one will lend money to a government and printing more money is not an option, there is no alternative but to run a government budget surplus. Work started on implementing real economic reforms – the first steps to creating a sustainable foundation for the government finances, and key to the economic boom that eventually followed.

It has become almost commonplace to quote the Chinese, for whom the word for 'crisis' is the same as for 'opportunity'. But it clearly has a fundamental truth. This was the time that Baring Vostok really took the shape that later became famously successful: a journey only possible after the events of 1998. Despite the stress of those turbulent days, I quickly realised that predictions of *Titanic*-type catastrophe didn't reflect accurately what was happening on the ground. As usual, average Russians responded to the crisis with resilience and adaptability. It is often said that the difference between successful people and the rest is how long they spend feeling sorry for themselves when things go wrong; I was impressed by how Russian entrepreneurs working in the real economy faced reality, quickly adjusting their costs and adapting their businesses to survive in the new environment. Moreover, the devaluation had – as often happens in emerging markets – overshot on the downside, leaving Russian exporters with a much sharper competitive edge (their goods were now much cheaper in relation to those of their foreign rivals) and greater scope for profitability. Within a few months of the devaluation, it was clear that the large export sector would be a locomotive to drive recovery.

Nor was the outlook for Baring Vostok's funds as bad as it appeared on the surface. I and Rory Landman from Baring Asset Management, who had taken over as the main manager of the First NIS Fund's listed equity portfolio, had decided to sell most of the fund's listed shares position in mid-1997, near the peak of the market before the collapse. With the proceeds of these sales and from Vimpelcom's IPO, the First NIS Fund had distributed a $100 million dividend in December 1997, giving shareholders back more than 60 per cent of their original investment, and leaving $30–40 million in the fund. Of the fund's fourteen remaining private companies, several suffered deeply from the fallout of August

1998, but others seemed poised to benefit if they could just secure an injection of capital. Buoyed by the December '97 payout, our shareholders felt more bullish than investors in most other funds and actively supported us to continue investing. That $30–40 million of cash – together with a vital fresh capital commitment of $15 million in early 1999 from the EBRD and IFC, and a further $25 million from ING – became a hugely valuable strategic reserve in a country where almost all other financial market players were reeling from their debts and unable to make any new investments.

The economic tempest that blew through Russia between 1994 and 1998 exposed many of the obvious failures of that era's Russian governments. The cynical excesses of oligarchs, the chaos in government policy and lack of responsibility among officials had brought the country to its knees. But the financial deprivation of ordinary Russian people in those years naturally led to a yearning among them, as well as among foreign investors, for more order and accountability. Longer-term consequences of such a new 'order' were not yet apparent. After the tempest, the priority for all was to rebuild. And for Baring Vostok, it was full steam ahead.

10

Levelling Up

Before 1998, Baring Vostok's team had comprised a mix of foreign and Russian professionals, including many talented individuals, but together we were still not really capable of seriously penetrating the local market. Since I hardly spoke Russian yet, we probably had a bias in our hiring prior to 1998 that resulted in employing the Russian candidates best able to articulate their ideas in English, rather than those with the greatest overall competence and potential. Our network at the time was also dependent on local brokers and other intermediaries. As a result, we were only addressing a small part of the real market for entrepreneurial opportunities. We needed to radically overhaul our team, giving it much deeper local roots and capabilities.

Step one in any textbook management restructuring is to get the wrong people off the bus, and then bring the right ones on. Rather than simply hiring new people, Jean-Michel Broun (one of the other partners) and I initially thought it might be faster and more impactful to merge with a leading local investment team. We reached out first to Alfa Capital, a private equity subsidiary of Alfa Group, then a rapidly growing banking-financial group. Alfa Capital had a strong track record and we had already partnered with them on a successful co-investment, so we knew their investment team well. We felt that the combination would be a great fit, as each of us had capabilities the other couldn't replicate on their own. The parent company, Alfa Group, had barely survived the 1998 Russian financial crisis and needed to focus their scarce liquidity and capital into their core banking and natural resource assets, so they quickly responded favourably to our approach. Alfa Group was interested in alternatives that reduced their financial burden of growing Alfa Capital further. But as negotiations developed, I could feel that a formal merger of our two companies would impose a lot of headaches associated with having two 'corporate' shareholders, ING and Alfa Group. And I sensed that Alfa Group's owners would be extremely hands-on and probably interfere in the way I wanted to run the team and business. Instead, we were able to persuade Alfa Group's owners that it would be better and simpler if Baring Vostok just hired most of the senior team from Alfa Capital without Alfa Group becoming a shareholder in the firm, avoiding all the complications of a three-party merger.

Thus it happened that Baring Vostok was dramatically reinforced by the arrival in late 1998 of Alexey Kalinin from Alfa Capital, a talented negotiator and natural relationship builder, who initially became co-managing partner alongside me. He had a PhD in Electrical Engineering, but his huge size made him resemble a giant Russian bear more than the scientist that he was originally by profession. Several other key Alfa Capital people from their investment, legal, and security departments also joined us. We kept a friendly, but arms-length relationship with Alfa Group and our funds ended up making two highly profitable investments together with them – in CTC Media and Golden Telecom. Although Alfa Group later developed a hostile reputation, we never had any disagreements with them and our collaboration together was very successful.

The merger also gave us access to resources to solve the myriad annoyances that could otherwise plague daily life in Moscow. Sometimes in unorthodox ways. Jean-Michel Broun was too thrifty to buy his own car and grew accustomed to simply hailing and negotiating with random drivers on the streets, as was common practice in Moscow at the time. One afternoon, he hailed such a car after buying a case of wine in a store, and told the driver he needed to make one additional stop at a supermarket before going home. Foolishly, Jean-Michel left the wine in the back seat when he went into the supermarket, although at least he was wise enough to take note of the car's vehicle registration number. Sure enough, the car and the wine were gone when he returned ten minutes later, bags of groceries in hand.

Jean-Michel reached for his mobile phone and called our colleague Anatoly, one of those who had joined from Alfa Capital and now in charge of Baring Vostok's security. He had been a colonel in the FSO, a powerful entity responsible for Russian presidential security, before he retired to work in the private sector. From his office, he looked up the vehicle registration using his access to official databases, figuring out who the driver was and where he lived. He then drove to the man's apartment, arriving less than forty-five minutes after the incident happened. Hearing a knock on his apartment door, the driver opened it with a big smile and a half-empty bottle of wine in his hand, apparently expecting guests to join him in drinking their unexpected bounty. He must have almost had a heart attack when he saw Anatoly standing there, holding out his old FSO badge. Apologising profusely for what he claimed was a 'misunderstanding', the driver quickly returned the case of wine, now with one vacant compartment. After a few nervous seconds when Anatoly said nothing, the unlucky chap rushed back to the kitchen and came back with a bottle of cognac, which he slid into the empty space. Anatoly shook his hand and left, bringing the case back to Jean-Michel, which they then proceeded to drink together. It was poetic justice.

It was around the time of the merger that we decided to hire a couple of famous figures to enhance our profile. The first was Alexei Arkhipovich Leonov, a celebrated cosmonaut and the first human ever to walk in space outside a spacecraft. His illustrious career saw him twice honoured Hero of the Soviet Union, the highest accolade available in the USSR. Kalinin already knew him well as Leonov had been president of Alfa Capital. I was introduced to him at an intimate dinner along with Kalinin in early 1999. The idea of him joining Baring Vostok immediately interested me, even though I didn't yet understand what role he would play; Leonov was open-minded but understandably cautious, as a small foreign-owned company run by a bunch of guys in their early 30s must have struck him as a bit unpredictable.

We met at Serena Restaurant, the first of the lauded 'Novikov' restaurants in Moscow, famous for its fresh fish and huge vodka selection. My Russian was still weak then, but it was slightly better than their English, so we spoke in their native language. Leonov, I think, was charmed by my Oklahoma accent. He said it reminded him of his dear friend, Tom Stafford, a fellow Oklahoman and a legendary American pilot and astronaut. (Stafford was commander of the Apollo portion of the famous 1975 Soyuz–Apollo mission, the first link-up in space of American and Soviet spacecraft. When the capsules linked together, millions watched on live TV as the hatches opened and Leonov reached his hand across, dragging Stafford to the Soviet side. I was eventually introduced to Stafford via Leonov, and he became a dear friend.)

That day in Serena, I was in awe at meeting this legend of Russian space exploration, listening to him recount story after story from his breathtaking career. The dinner quickly became a vodka-fest with many heartfelt toasts. Before the main course was finished, he spontaneously suggested we all drive out to his house in Star City, to continue with an after-party. Otherwise known as Zvezdnyi Gorodok, Star City was the centre of the Russian space training programme about 30 miles from Moscow, where foreigners were historically allowed only with special permission. We got to his house around midnight, and stayed up until about 4 a.m. eating raw frozen moose meat brought back from a recent hunting trip, served with just salt and pepper and raw onions, and washed down with copious amounts of whiskey and Armenian cognac. All the while, we shared the rudest Russian and American jokes we could think of, laughing uproariously. At the end of this night of cultural exchange, Leonov wrapped me in a big hug, and said 'Mike, you are one of us!' – that phrase I will hear again often over the years, including in cell 604. Leonov and I became fast friends from that moment on.

Being around him brought me some extraordinary adventures. Once, we were invited on a hunting trip by the Mayor of Vladivostok and the general in charge of Russia's armed forces in the country's Far East. Staying aboard a small military vessel on Ozera Honka, a lake half in Russia and half in China, we enjoyed a vodka-fuelled weekend mostly involving great revelry and storytelling, punctuated by the occasional hunts at dawn and dusk for wild duck and geese. We were all in a barracks-like group cabin after an epic dinner one night, with Leonov and the general already fast asleep and locked in a snoring competition. Half-tipsy from vodka as well as jet-lagged, I lay awake on my bunk bed, jolted frequently by the thunder of their unpredictable snoring patterns. From a porthole next to my bed, I gazed for hours at a full moon shining down on a Chinese fishing village on the distant horizon. I couldn't stop thinking to myself, 'How did a boy from Oklahoma end up here?'

I would discover that Leonov was not just the charismatic hero of the Russian people, but also one of the wisest, most generous, and most human of human beings I have ever met. I was struck, many times, by his uncanny ability to relate to, and connect with, people of any level or background, from top government officials or CEOs to bus drivers, farmers, and factory workers. The many hunting trips we took together over more than twenty years, and the birthday parties and family dinners at his home together with his wife, Svetlana Pavlovna, are among my most cherished memories. And when he occasionally travelled with the Baring Vostok team on business, it was always a sensation when he arrived. Simply having Leonov as part of our team helped to ensure constructive community relations, and every regional governor in the country couldn't wait to welcome this famous cosmonaut and hero.

It was through Leonov that we met and hired another useful advisor, Vadim Victorovich Bakatin. Originally a construction engineer, under Gorbachev he was spotted as a talented, reform-minded manager. He was appointed variously as head of the Kemerovo and Kirov Oblast administrations, head of the Soviet Interior Ministry, and, for four months in 1991 after the failed coup, boss of the KGB. But by the time he was working for us, he was long an outsider to the government and its security structures. In the last months of the Soviet Union, he had given American officials, on behalf of the government, detailed plans of where the bugs were hidden in the American Embassy in Moscow. According to Bakatin's memoirs, it was intended as a gesture of openness – a symbolic one, as the bugs had long since been discovered anyway – but to traditionalists in the KGB it was anathema, helping bring an abrupt end to his career in officialdom. For us, he provided advice about some industrial sectors in which he had contacts and experience, like building materials. But he was especially brilliant at explaining Russia's history and its future prospects to potential investors, often over dinners in renowned Moscow restaurants. Investors sat rapt as they listened to his stories about the Gorbachev years, told with his own characteristic modesty and sense of humour, and his wise observations about Russia's path forward. Like the Leonovs, he and his wife, Lyudmila Antonovna, became my dear friends.

Alongside building the right team, we were also looking to consolidate our position in the Russian private equity market by taking over management of some failed funds. One of these was Sector Capital Fund, and the takeover proved a lot of headache for little financial reward. But it did bring one gigantic benefit: of just two of the Sector Capital staff we retained, one was Elena Ivashentseva, a woman destined to be counted among the most successful investors ever in Russia, and eventually across global emerging markets.

With our strong new line-up, we set about reviewing the First NIS Fund's portfolio in light of the financial crisis. There was some triage, as always after a deep crisis, and we had to write off a few investments. To others we injected vital follow-on capital that not only ensured they survived but paved their way to eventual great success. One of these, Burren Energy, was the first blockbuster success for our funds, going public on the London Stock Exchange and then being acquired by the Italian oil company ENI for $3 billion, giving us a huge return on our initial outlay. We had another big win when GTS, the fixed telecom operator that had expanded from Russia into Western Europe, went public on NASDAQ during the telecom boom of 1999–2000. The success of these two investments – almost entirely based on their activities outside of Russia – proved a Godsend for our fund's investors.

These successes took place against the backdrop of still more upheaval in the Russian political scene. The end of the century saw a chaotic climax to the topsy-turvy years since the collapse of the USSR. President Yeltsin's remaining political capital was evaporating quickly both at home and abroad. Tensions with the West rose sharply when a coalition of countries led by the US intervened militarily in war-torn Yugoslavia, despite sharp Russian objections. A bloody war with separatist rebels in the republic of Chechnya had also taken its toll, especially when apartment bombs blamed on the separatists ripped through four Russian cities, including Moscow, in September 1999, at the cost of several hundred lives. Yeltsin was gone as President by the end of the year, his approval ratings at a nadir. His chosen successor was a previously little-known official who had climbed slowly up through ranks of the KGB to hold important civic positions in both St Petersburg and Moscow. Most recently, he had been Yeltsin's prime minister, gaining popularity and finding his voice through an aggressive response to the latest Chechen war. To many, he also seemed to be a serious and competent administrator. The sort of man the West hoped it might be able to do business with. As Tony Blair, British Prime Minister at the time, commented: 'Vladimir Putin is a leader who is ready to embrace a new relationship with the European Union and United States. He wants a strong and modern Russia and a strong relationship with the West.'

Even amid the fallout of the 1998 financial crisis and the changing of the political guard, most of our fund's companies performed well, often exceeding the upper range of our revenue projections. But success came at a price. Perhaps predictably, we were the subject of hostile takeover attempts by Russian oligarchs that threatened to destroy any chance our fund had of making a profit. The main route of attack was through the portion of the First NIS Fund's portfolio invested in privatised former state-owned companies. Even though we hadn't directly invested in any privatisations, but rather purchased shares afterwards, there was always a lingering risk with any privatised company of title challenges that unscrupulous raiders might attempt to exploit.

The broad tactic was for the predator to arrange for some 'unaffiliated' individual to buy a very small number of shares of a target company in the secondary market, then file lawsuits against the company claiming that the original privatisation was somehow flawed. By their argument, all subsequent share transactions, including the ones to which our funds subscribed, were invalid and so, they demanded, ought to be reversed. This would effectively wipe out our fund's shareholding. In parallel, and obviously not coincidentally, we would be approached by intermediaries enquiring whether we were interested in selling the fund's stake, while noting that the 'uncertainties about title' meant that the shares were no longer worth very much.

We faced just this type of hostile situation with our investment in the Syktyvkar Paper Company. Oleg Deripaska was an oligarch whose fortune derived principally from the dominant position he carved out in Russia's privatised – and very opaque – aluminium industry. He now had his eye set on muscling in on the forestry and paper sector as his next area for expansion, with Syktyvkar identified as a suitable crown jewel. When this was going on, Yevgeny Primakov, recently retired as Prime Minister, could see that such attacks risked damaging the investment climate, and potentially Russia's international relations. To allow reputable foreign investors to be expropriated through such an attack would cause damage far in excess of the value of the enterprise at stake. I was told that he personally called Deripaska, and, although I don't know the content of their conversation, the lawsuits against Syktyvkar were withdrawn the very next day. Our programme of modernisation for the company proceeded as planned, and it was later acquired by the Neusiedler Group of Austria, becoming a key part of a global forestry group.

An assault on our holding in SladCo, a confectionery business achieving success in Russia's Urals and Upper Volga regions, proved trickier to fend off. SladCo was the subject of hostile interest from a Russian competitor, GUTA Bank, which at the time owned Red October, a leading Moscow-based confectionery brand. SladCo, like Syktyvkar, had invested heavily, overcome massive operational challenges and become a leading player in its sector. Of course, it was this very fact that attracted attention from rivals keen to inherit the foundations of success without putting in the years of risk and hard work required to build them.

The mini-oligarch pulling the strings of the SladCo raid refused to admit publicly that he was behind it. As such, he was immune to any potential PR scandal associated with his actions. Eventually, I was able to fix a meeting with his son, one I arranged to secretly record, in the hope of capturing an admission on tape as to who was behind the scheme. It was the first time I had ever resorted to such clandestine behaviour, and in my twenty-five years in Russia I would repeat it only once more.

Initially, the son stuck to his script. 'It's a shame that such hostile raids happen these days in Russia,' he told me. 'I'm not behind it, of course, but I am ready to help solve your problem by buying the company.' Although, of course, he pointed out it would not be for very much money, given the risk involved with all the ongoing lawsuits. I called his bluff, telling him that we could dispense with the lies and discuss what was really going on. At this, his tone changed and he admitted that he was indeed sponsoring the attack, and felt confident that he would triumph if matters went to the courts. Then, he ominously said, we would see how we viewed the price of our company after the courts validated his victory.

When the meeting ended, I felt like 'We had him!' He had admitted to his role in the hostile takeover. But when I replayed the tape with our security team, the conversation was completely inaudible. The clever guy, anticipating our strategy, had brought a jammer that blocked the recording entirely. We were left to challenge his claims through multiple rounds in Russian arbitration courts over more than a year, before finally securing a decision in our favour. We had preserved our fund's title and eventually sold SladCo to Orkla, a Norwegian food group. It was some struggle, but we finally made a solid profit. And the hard experience gave us a belief, valid or not, that we could protect what was rightfully ours through the Russian courts.

By 2000, the robust performance of our First NIS Fund made it possible to raise a new fund, the Baring Vostok Private Equity Fund, with $200 million in fresh capital. By then, Russia's private sector was growing rapidly and finally achieving serious scale. Revenue growth rates of 30–40 per cent annually were common in consumer goods, telecoms, and media sectors, among others. But it was the internet that offered the biggest opportunity of all – with Elena Ivashentseva taking the lead in that sector for us. As a company we had adopted a slogan: 'Building businesses for the future.' It epitomised our philosophy and differentiated us from our local competitors, as well as from typical private equity peers in other countries. We saw our role as backing entrepreneurs to do the things that make growth sustainable – building strong teams, innovating to improve the customer experience and stay ahead of competitors, and prioritising the long term over the short. As such, we spent most of our time not on new transactions, but on helping existing portfolio companies. We valued partnership, too. We shared the benefits of success, and also the costs when things went wrong, both with the enterprises we backed and within Baring Vostok itself.

In hindsight, the timing of this second fund couldn't have been better. Russia was at the beginning of an extended consumer boom, coupled with soaring oil prices that boosted government finances. Putin's administration – influenced by key figures such as German Gref and Aleksey Kudrin – initially set about major reforms that radically transformed the economy: a complete overhaul of the tax code and budgeting system, a new land code, and new civil code. Furthermore, unlike most oil-rich countries that squander their oil revenues, the government of the 2000s, still carrying the scars of the fiscal failures of the 1990s, saved a portion of its oil revenues in a strategic reserve. But in the moment, the timing of our fund felt far from perfect. Because of the instability in Russia, international investors didn't even want to talk to us about investing money in the country. I travelled all over the world to meet investors, leaping whenever one finally agreed to hear me out. Altogether, I met more than 120 investors in one-on-one meetings, of whom only eight eventually invested. Even then, it took two painful years to actually secure all the commitments. It required a thick skin to get rejected so many times and keep on going without losing hope or confidence in our strategy. I felt at the time like a salmon, swimming almost alone against the current.

And then the world changed again. On 11 September 2001, I was sitting at my desk in Moscow. It was around five in the evening when a colleague told me to get to a TV and switch on CNN. Watching in Kalinin's office, and standing next to Alexei Leonov, we were at first incredulous, and then filled with fear and anger as it became clear that an orchestrated terrorist attack of unprecedented scale was under way. At 6 p.m. Moscow time (10 a.m. New York time), we saw the first tower of the World Trade Center collapse in flames, the instant deaths of thousands of people caught on live TV. It was horrific. Half an hour later, the second tower also collapsed in a maelstrom of fuel and flames and smoke. Back in New York, I had worked at Salomon's office at 7 World Trade Center, directly across the street from those two mighty towers. Among the throngs I had watched in 1990 scurrying to their offices in those buildings every day, many had now just perished, right in front of my eyes. With no words to express the unfolding tragedy, we silently embraced each other, then left for our homes to comfort our families and watch the ongoing news.

We set up a team meeting for eight o'clock the next morning. One I will never forget. The entire Baring Vostok team, about thirty people, assembled in our office's main conference room, and we started the meeting by standing together for a full minute of silence. You could have heard a pin drop. The emotion was palpable, but also the feeling of solidarity. It was a rare moment when good and evil seemed clearly defined, with no shades of grey in between. All decent human beings felt the same at that moment. Russians, having been the target of terrorist attacks themselves, were among the first and strongest supporters of America on that day and in the weeks ahead, and I was proud to stand among Russian colleagues and friends who so clearly sympathised with my motherland.

After the minute of silence, we sat down to face the fallout for our business. Someone gave a quick review of the status of our funds' liquidity, capital position, and counter-party risks, then we turned to our portfolio companies with the same analysis. Although delivered in voices strained with emotion, the reports were brisk, sharp, and with just the necessary details to provide clarity. We concluded that there were a couple of companies likely to require an urgent injection of capital, but most were in a solid position. Having assessed our vulnerabilities, we then turned to ideas for how we could invest proactively at this time. Watching my colleagues soberly and professionally carry out this balanced analysis and come to firm decisions, even as markets were panicking all around, was one of my proudest moments in Baring Vostok. I knew we had built an organisation ready to prosper in any conditions.

11

The Good Times

The events of 9/11 came on the heels of the dot-com crash, when the stock market bubble that had ballooned around internet start-ups exploded spectacularly. This had far-reaching consequences for Baring Vostok, not least because ING, our Dutch parent company, suffered steep losses and, under pressure from the Dutch banking regulator, decided to abandon further investments in private equity funds. For some parts of the Baring Private Equity Partners group, this was a fatal development, but for us it was a tremendous opportunity. We were able to negotiate a buyout of the ING/BPEP stake in our management company, just when our funds were becoming financially independent of any external sponsors. ING had been great supporters and gave us a wealth of institutional wisdom over the years of their sponsorship, but the timing was perfect for us to break free and become fully independent.

It was about then, as we were preparing for an upcoming annual investor meeting in Moscow, that Vadim Bakatin asked me whether it would be useful if Mikhail Gorbachev came to our main dinner. 'Are you serious? Of course!' I said. Although unpopular in Russia since he tried to pursue a middle road that failed to satisfy either the hardliners or the liberals, Gorbachev is justly viewed globally as one of the great figures of the twentieth century. I knew our investors would love the opportunity to meet, and speak with, such an important, historic individual. Bakatin had worked closely with

Gorbachev during the *perestroika* years as Interior Minister and had remained in contact afterwards. Gorbachev accepted Bakatin's invitation and agreed to attend.

When I asked Bakatin two weeks before the event if everything was still on, he reconfirmed. Same thing two days beforehand. I was still nervous, of course, that Gorbachev would cancel at the last minute, so we didn't announce anything to investors. We rented the main dining room of Moscow's National Hotel for the event, its giant windows looking directly across Manezh Square at the Kremlin.

However, when the cocktail reception began, we waited in vain for Gorbachev to join. An hour passed, then two hours, and still he didn't arrive. Bakatin paced the corridors anxiously, and then angrily, as Gorbachev didn't answer his phone. By 9 p.m., we couldn't wait any longer, and had to seat everyone for dinner. I told Bakatin not to stress about it: these things happen, and the investors didn't know he was supposed to join us anyway. After everyone was seated, Bakatin uncharacteristically stood to make the first toast. 'Friendship,' he proclaimed, followed by a lengthy pause. Then: 'That word used to mean something. But not anymore, apparently.' His face was pale and etched with emotion. As someone translated into English, the investors looked awkwardly at one another, confused. I started to think about damage control and how to intervene to change the subject. But right at that moment, Gorbachev walked into the room, saying, 'Vadim, don't be so emotional.'

Jaws dropped as the former leader casually walked across the room and took a seat at the head of the main table, in between me, Leonov and Arthur Hartman, who had been President Reagan's ambassador to the Soviet Union in the 1980s when Gorbachev ruled in the Kremlin. Apologising for his lateness, Gorbachev pointed at the Kremlin walls across the square, explaining that he had unexpectedly been called to a meeting with President Putin just an hour ago. He took a glass of wine handed to him by a waiter, and proceeded to talk for an hour, unscripted and uninterrupted, about the past and Russia's still unclear future. He shared witty and poignant anecdotes about the major figures – Thatcher, Kohl, Mitterrand, Reagan – of an era that truly changed the world. When he finished talking, our investors gave him a lengthy standing ovation, still too stunned to fully process what they had just witnessed.

Fast forward to the mid-2000s, and I could see that the structure of the Russian market was changing, creating still more space for us to grow. The old oligarchs who had dominated the Yeltsin era were gradually being subdued, either submitting to the new political reality in the country or exiting the scene altogether. Few of us who were veterans of Russia's financial markets in the 1990s shed a tear, for instance, at the arrest on fraud charges of the founders of the Menatep Group, whom I had encountered initially when our fund was briefly a shareholder in Yukos. They had been among the most cynical of the oligarchs in that era, and our fund had been a direct victim of their aggressive tactics, through our mutual shareholdings in Volgatanker, an oil transportation business. During our settlement negotiations over Volgatanker, Platon Lebedev (a close ally of Mikhail Khodorkovsky) personally threatened me. 'Do you know what administrative resources are? Do you know what I could do to you just like that?' he had asked me, snapping his fingers in my face. I did, of course. He was referring to his ability to leverage his political connections to his own ends, a practice so widespread that the term 'administrative resource' became a common one in Russia. It is true that Khodorkovsky changed his behaviour in the early 2000s and began to manage Yukos transparently and very successfully, and after suffering through a long prison term he is now a champion of Russia's civil society. But at the time I couldn't forget how Menatep acquired their assets and fortune in the first place.

In any event, it seemed the changing landscape played into our hands and Baring Vostok's Fund II enjoyed several blockbuster successes. Out of nineteen investments, thirteen earned a profit more than twice the fund's initial investment, including six that earned more than 500 per cent returns. The two most outstanding, in CTC and Yandex, were both initiated by Elena Ivashentseva and counted among the most profitable ever made by private equity funds in any markets.

CTC was an independent TV channel launched in the early 1990s with a view to becoming a leading player nationally. It raised more than $200 million from mostly American institutional investors, hired experienced global TV executives, and invested heavily in network infrastructure and programming. But by the mid-'90s, the Russian advertising market was still tiny, and competition for ad revenue from the sudden proliferation of new independent channels fierce. The 1998 financial crisis seemed like the nail in the coffin, erasing any expectations of market growth and causing the company's foreign investors to seek to abandon the company altogether. Elena was aware of CTC's position since Sector Capital Fund had been among the company's earlier investors, and our friends at Alfa Bank had become a 25 per cent shareholder in the company's Russian subsidiary. But we could see CTC's long-term promise, especially if we could overhaul the management. Our Fund II bought out some of the American institutional investors, and Modern Times Group (MTG) of Sweden also moved in and bought out some of the others. Elena and I joined the board representing Baring Vostok funds, and with our investor-partners and the new management, led by the uniquely talented Alexander Rodnyansky, oversaw a radical repositioning of the company. The network's audience share rose from around 3 per cent pre-1998 to roughly 8 per cent by 2004, while company revenues soared by more than ten times. The company completed an IPO on NASDAQ in 2006, and our fund sold its stake a couple of years afterwards. Our $10 million investment returned $400 million.

Yandex was a much slower and longer road, but the success even bigger. Elena had met Arkady Volozh, Ilya Segolovich and other founders of Yandex in 2000, shortly after it launched as a new search engine for the Russian market. The platform's algorithms and software worked much better for Russian-language searches than Yahoo, Google, or any of the other big global players. But there were still big questions about whether such a platform could attract paying customers or advertisers: in the entire year in which we invested in the company, Yandex's total revenues were just $12,000. There were other investors already circling the company, but we managed to persuade Arkady and other Yandex shareholders that we were best placed to help the company grow and succeed. We led a consortium that put in $5 million, the only funding Yandex ever raised until its IPO. It took much longer for the company's revenues to grow and achieve scale than we expected after the dot-com bubble burst, and many observers predicted that Yandex would never be commercially viable. Even though its costs were low, it burned through our $5 million at a rate of $1 million per year.

Around this time, Google tried to buy the company for $100 million but was rejected. Several months later, it returned with a second bid of $250 million. For most Yandex shareholders, this would have resulted in a profit of more than fifteen times over their cost, which seemed like a miracle amid the crash in US and global tech companies. Several smaller Yandex shareholders were keen to accept the bid, even though Arkady and the Yandex team wanted to remain independent and continue to develop the business. Elena and other board members exercised a veto of the bid, which outraged some shareholders, but we were convinced that Yandex's potential value was in the billions, not the millions.

This faith was well placed. Yandex became the only company in the world to defeat Google in the battle for market share without any kind of regulatory protection or barrier. In China, the only other major market besides Russia that Google doesn't dominate, such barriers were essential for Baidu's success. Yandex succeeded solely on superior technology and innovation. When Yandex completed an IPO on the NASDAQ in 2011, it was valued at $8 billion. Arkady became a well-deserved billionaire, and around a hundred Yandex employees earned more than a million each. For our funds, our $2 million net initial investment in Yandex (our fund's share of the $5 million our consortium put into Yandex's parent company) eventually sold for more than $900 million – a staggering 450-fold return.

Among those who don't understand entrepreneurship – including many of Russia's investigators and prosecutors – there is a belief that one person's gain is always someone else's loss. They think business is always a zero-sum game. But real entrepreneurial endeavours are a win for everyone, with ripple effects far beyond those directly involved. The success of a company like Yandex inspires hundreds of new entrepreneurs to launch their own businesses. It is an example of entrepreneurship at its best.

Buoyed by the success of the First NIS Fund and then Fund II, we were able to quickly raise Fund III in 2005 and Fund IV in 2007, with total capital of approximately $1.5 billion. We now had an enviable list of investors, including some of the world's most prestigious pension funds, sovereign wealth funds, university endowments, and funds of funds. The process of raising capital for Fund IV was so easy in comparison with previous funds that it made me nervous. Instead of the gruelling, two-year marathon required to raise Fund II, we handled most of the primary meetings with US investors for Fund IV in just a week. We camped in the comfortable London, New York, and San Francisco offices of UBS, our placement agent, and most of the prospective investors travelled to meet us! For the first and last time in my life, they pitched to convince us to take their money, and not the other way around. In fact, we had to scale back investor appetite in order to close the fund at a reasonable size. We held a party in Moscow to celebrate becoming the first ever Russian private equity fund to raise more than $1 billion in capital. It was a mighty validation of our success, but I recall telling my partners: 'Remember this moment, because it may never happen again for the rest of our lives.' It simply felt too easy, and I couldn't recall any previous success that wasn't accompanied by struggle along the way.

These were heady days but we didn't have to wait very long for a very nasty surprise. The global financial crisis of 2008 sent shock waves that almost capsized every fund in Russia. But unlike the crisis of a decade earlier, this one wasn't triggered by problems in Russia itself. Instead, the globalisation in financial markets meant that the collapse of major US institutions like Lehman Brothers reverberated across the planet. Falling oil demand in 2008 caused the oil price to crash from $150 down to around $40 per barrel, which in turn led to a sharp devaluation of the rouble, from 23 to the dollar to around 36. As in 1998, this caused a panic in the Russian financial markets and a spike in inflation, mainly the result of the rising cost of imports and the inability to quickly substitute imports with local goods. Interest rates rose sharply as banks needed to pay a huge premium to keep their depositor and investor funds in roubles, rather than dollars. With funding costs so high, new investment ground to a halt and companies focused on building or preserving liquidity: 'cash is king' ruled once more.

Moreover, in Russia there was a geopolitical dimension to the 2008 crisis. Tensions between Russia and Georgia had been simmering ever since the election of Mikheil Saakashvili as Georgia's President in 2004. He was an impressive anti-corruption reformer who strongly favoured European integration, and his reforms certainly made Georgia much more transparent and democratic – a level of progress unmatched in either Russia or Ukraine, where corruption remained deeply entrenched. But at the time, I feared that his approach was needlessly provocative towards Russia, even if motivated by good intentions to give his citizens the European future they desired. When NATO ministers in April 2008 took a formal decision that Georgia and Ukraine 'will become members of NATO', I thought: 'My god. This is going to end badly for everyone.' In August that year, Russian forces invaded Georgia amid escalating tensions around Russian support for the separatist enclave of South Ossetia, whose campaign for independence had spilled into open conflict. I was on holiday with my family in the USA at the time, and I was stunned as I watched news footage of Russian tanks rolling across the Georgian border.

A ceasefire was announced after a few weeks, but not before Russia recognised declarations of independence by South Ossetia and another Georgian province, Abkhazia. For investors in the USA and Europe, the sight of Russian tanks crossing into a neighbouring country seemed to shatter whatever remained of the idea that the country was on a long-term track towards convergence with European institutions. From this point on, Russian asset prices always contained a discount factor reflecting geopolitical risks and tensions. Even after the subsequent 'Obama Reset' of relations with Moscow (a reset whose eventual failure was symbolised by a typo in the banner at the signing ceremony prepared by US officials, which used the Russian word for 'Overload' (*peregruzka*) instead of reset (*perezagruzka*)), this discount factor couldn't easily be erased from investor's minds. In hindsight, the invasion of Georgia should have been seen as a watershed moment, causing us to suspend further investments in Russia by our funds. But at the time, I felt the situation wasn't entirely Russia's fault, and that there were still powerful long-term factors that would eventually repair geopolitical relations, and which made new investments compelling.

In terms of the economy, the devaluation of the rouble quickly proved a powerful medicine again, boosting the profitability of exports, stimulating local production to substitute imports, and keeping the federal budget with only modest deficits. By 2009, growth resumed. Throughout, we were lucky not to face a liquidity crisis like most hedge funds or oligarchs or banks did at the time. We had fresh capital reserves and no debt, so we were able to continue investing. Of course, the devaluation had an immediate negative impact on the US dollar valuations of our companies, but most survived the crisis and many continued to grow rapidly, in many cases eventually far outpacing the impact of the devaluation.

As the decade drew to a close, on a personal level I saw how, one by one, many of my expatriate friends were leaving Russia to return to their motherlands: America, France, Britain, Israel, Italy, Australia, and elsewhere. There were just a few dozen of us left from the original early '90s cohort. By now many of my closest friends were Russians, and I no longer viewed myself as an expatriate in Moscow with a planned departure date. In 2009, I decided to buy a house in the UK and become resident there. My kids moved to UK schools, but I was still spending more time in Moscow than London. I figured that if my kids wanted to be teachers or journalists or doctors, they would probably be better off making their careers in the UK or USA, but if they wanted to become entrepreneurs or go into business, Russia might be their best bet. This half-move to the UK seemed likely to best equip them to make their own choices for their futures, while allowing me to focus on growing our business in Russia.

Moscow in the 2010s was completely transformed from the city I knew in the '90s. It now had some of the best and most stylish restaurants in the world – and not only the expensive ones in the centre, like those of the legendary Novikov group, but thousands of modest but charming new places away from the centre, and accessible to most Muscovites. There were shiny apartment buildings that had been fancily renovated, but also huge new developments aimed at the rising middle class. Locals grumbled that they were too expensive for those on average incomes, and this was true, but gradually they became affordable to an increasing number of Muscovites, especially after mortgage financing became available for the first time. The Bolshoi Theatre and other opera and classical music venues were restored to their magnificent best, and the city teemed with street jazz cafes and hundreds of new or renovated small theatres offering comedy, kids' shows, and music to suit any taste. Apartment building courtyards that had been strewn with broken bottles and garbage in the '90s were now mostly well maintained, and often boasted newly built play-grounds. But surely the biggest turnaround was in the parks. Until recently they had been ruled by drunks and filled with tired attrac-tions left over from the 1950s, but now they had landscaped gardens and bright new activities for families. The good life was opening up in Moscow (and St Petersburg too) not just to the wealthy, but to those on regular incomes, too.

I was travelling in Russia's regions more than most Russians in this period, and got to observe many of the regional capital cities, too. Life for their typically million-plus populations was unmistak-ably improving overall as well. There were new pedestrianised areas, fresh shopping facilities, decent cafes, and new housing projects. The improvement was from a much lower base than Moscow, of course, and I still witnessed many instances of poverty, but the progress was undeniable compared to what I had seen twenty years earlier. However, conditions away from the main metropoles were much worse. In the villages, life often remained impoverished and even hopeless, especially for the few remaining young people who tried to build their lives there.

It was common at the time for Western observers to dismiss Russia's economy as solely driven by natural resources. John McCain once quipped that Russia was 'a gas station masquerading as a country'. The view fitted a convenient narrative, but my experience was different. Natural resources were indisputably important for Russia, especially in terms of tax revenues, but I saw hundreds of entrepreneurial enter-prises growing rapidly in a competitive market. How could Baring Vostok companies grow by 30 per cent every year unless the economy was becoming more diverse and innovative? Seeing Russia through the eyes of ambitious entrepreneurs with whom I worked made me optimistic for the country's future. Looking back, maybe their excitement for what lay ahead, coupled with the firm's success, insulated me from 'Russian reality'. I was not naïve to the country's deep-rooted structural problems, including corruption, but I believed that the country was overall getting better, even if there were worrying political signs. My optimism often outstripped that of my Russian colleagues, but I attributed this to Russian cultural pessimism, not to my own biases or Russians' inherently better appreciation for the country's risks. Many times in meetings with investors, I said – and I believed it at the time – that only a dishonest person, or someone who had never lived in Russia in the 1990s, could claim Russia was worse off in 2015 than twenty years earlier.

Still, there were disturbing clouds on the horizon that even I, in my venture capitalist world, could see. There was a sense that the security structures of the Putin government had become insatiable monsters, even worse than the oligarchs in the 1990s. While some argued the measures were necessary to push the oligarchs out of the central corridors of power once and for all, the business environment was badly impacted whenever there was a takedown of a business figure who appeared innocent, or – perhaps more accurately – had been arbitrarily accused of crimes for some infraction that would usually be ignored. It was precisely the arbitrariness that most negatively impacted sentiment among local investors and the business community. But I still felt like these risks didn't relate to our business. Those who found themselves on the wrong end of things, I rationalised to myself, were usually either engaged in politics, or had somehow challenged the strategic interests of Russia's state-owned companies. I felt that as long as investors recognised the 'rules of the jungle', and especially if you invested mostly in knowledge-based sectors less likely to be targets of expropriation, you would be safe. We had endured few problems and always overcame them, which seemed to validate my view. Obviously, in hindsight, I was painfully wrong about this.

My optimism about our business was generally shared by the entire Baring Vostok team. The Russian internet was a particular driver of rapid growth in the 2010s. For instance, we invested in Avito, an online classifieds platform mostly for automobiles and apartments, which eventually became the number one player in Russia. We put money into other market-leading platforms like Ivi.ru, Profi, 2GIS, and Kazakhstan-based Kolesa. Financial services was also a successful arena for us, with investments in Europlan (number one in auto leasing) and CFT (number one in banking software and money transfer), as well as three banks: Kaspi (a consumer-focused bank that transformed to also become Kazakhstan's leading online shopping marketplace and dominant mobile app and payments platform); Tinkoff Credit Systems (Russia's leading online bank and credit card issuer, as well as an online financial supermarket for insurance and brokerage services, among other things); and Vostochny Bank (the deal that ultimately led to all my problems). In 2012, we were in good enough shape post-2008 downturn to raise our next fund, Fund V. We secured total capital commitments of $1.5 billion but this time it was a much slower and more difficult process, taking about a year in total.

My travel in this period was manic. I flew from London to Moscow and back almost every week. The Friday evening Aeroflot flight was like a commuter train journey that I eventually optimised down to the last minute. I'd walk out of my Moscow office with just a small backpack at 5.50 p.m. to catch the 6 p.m. fast train from Belorusskiy Vokzal to Sheremetyevo Airport, then quickly through fast-track passport control and straight to the boarding gate just before the doors closed and the aeroplane took off. Besides this regular weekly 'commute', I also travelled a few times each year to visit our investors in the USA and Middle East, or to join board meetings for companies in Brazil and Hong Kong. I'd spend about half the year away from my family, which took a toll and probably made me lose a sense of reality. Growing accustomed to non-stop, optimised business travel and on-demand support from our efficient team, I was highly productive but ceased being grounded in the real lives of normal people – something I had sworn to myself I would never do. Remarkably, my wife and kids remained steadfastly supportive and seemed sympathetic, if not exactly understanding, about my peripatetic travels. When I arrived home in the UK late on Friday evenings, Julia almost always arranged a cosy, candle-lit family dinner, where we all caught up on the week's events and I gratefully tried to reconnect with their lives.

Meanwhile, Fund V got off to a seemingly good start. We continued to invest in internet commerce, online marketplaces, and consumer businesses. As well as putting new money into existing investments, we backed companies providing ride sharing, off-price fashion retail, fresh food and education technology. In addition, we looked towards infrastructure projects as a sector for rapid growth and maybe even an entirely new fund within our group. But then, once again, another economic earthquake sent shockwaves through Russian markets. The crisis of 2014 shared a major common theme with those of 1998 and 2008 – a sharp drop in the oil price (this time mainly because of a steady rise in US shale production). As in those previous crises, there was another sharp devaluation of the rouble in 2014, triggering a spike in interest rates and wreaking havoc in the Russian banking sector. But this time, there was also an even more pronounced geopolitical component. Ukraine's Maidan Revolution in February 2014 saw the ousting of the pro-Russian government of Viktor Yanukovych. Putin, fearing that Ukraine was moving towards membership of NATO and the EU, responded by annexing Crimea and propping up separatist forces in Donbas.

International sanctions for the first time were applied to many top Russian officials, companies and business figures close to the Putin regime. These sanctions increased the perceived risk premium for all investments in Russia and therefore decreased the valuations for all Russian assets. I estimate that, after 2014, there was at least a 50 per cent discount in Russian company valuations compared to global peers. There was also concern in the business community that the FSB would use the heightened sense of Russian national security risks and the isolation of Russia from international markets as an excuse to launch more arbitrary criminal cases and end up expropriating more assets from local businesses. From 2014, these two factors already noticeably impacted sentiment and levels of new investment, but not enough to significantly damage the economy. Many Russian companies, including most of our portfolio companies, resumed growing after a brief drop in 2014, and seemed to prosper.

I sympathised very much with Ukraine's desire to be independent and to chart a European future for itself. But I still believed it was a strategic mistake for the US and European countries to put NATO membership on the table for Ukraine, and a double mistake to promise it 'in the future, but not now'. It was a move destined, I felt, to undermine Ukraine's security, not to enhance it. I favoured a 'Finland model' – a heavily fortified neutrality – as the best-case scenario for Ukraine, allowing alignment with Europe politically and even EU membership eventually. Ukraine, for understandable reasons, rejected the Finland model and wanted to be like their neighbour Poland, both in the EU and NATO. There was also a lot of scepticism in the West that Russia would honour a Finland-type arrangement. Nonetheless, in my view, it was worth a try, as I believed the alternative would almost certainly result in conflict.

The sharp deterioration in relations between my American motherland and my adopted home in Russia saddened me deeply. I felt by now a deep connection with Russia and had laid down roots. I was probably influenced too strongly by my friendships and daily interactions with the many bright, decent people who wanted Russia to be open to the world, and vice versa. Despite the sanctions, I still believed our investments in Russia would likely outperform most other global investment ideas, and I continued to promote the country to global investors. Between 2015 and 2018, Baring Vostok funds invested more than $500 million of fresh capital at a time when the direction of travel for most investors was out of, not into, Russia.

By 2018, Alexei Leonov had retired, and Alexey Kalinin was about to do the same. Mikhail Lomtadze, our most talented partner and a close friend, had left the firm to focus exclusively on Kaspi, the extremely promising company in Kazakhstan that he had already been leading 'temporarily' for a decade. Elena and I were co-senior partners of the firm. Like any two strong-minded individuals, our relationship could be tense sometimes, particularly over personnel matters and the approach to particular investments. But we shared a common vision and belief in the overall strategy for the firm and felt that our partnership was too valuable and too complementary to change anything major. Below us was a next layer of strong, capable and ambitious individuals driving the whole team forward. We were excited to explore new sectors and believed some of our companies had vast potential.

As 2019 started, I felt that the firm was in great shape, despite frequent market turbulence and negative political trends. With Elena proving herself not just a great investor but a strong manager, I began to envision a future role for myself as non-executive chairman or something similar. A position that would allow me more time to spend on other activities besides business. The funds' portfolio companies had recorded an average revenue rise of 31 per cent in 2018, and although the climate for selling assets was difficult, we believed that value inevitably followed revenue growth in the long term.

We looked to the future with a sober confidence and continued ambition. I could hardly imagine the devastating hurricane into which we were sailing.

12

Man Grows Accustomed to Anything

In *Crime and Punishment*, published in the 1860s, Fyodor Dostoevsky wrote: '*Chelovek ko vsemu privekaetsya, merzavets*' ('Man grows accustomed to anything, the scoundrel'). Dostoevsky had himself by then spent five years in a Siberian penal colony accused of subversive activities, so he spoke from some experience. And 150 years later, sitting in a Russian prison myself, I am starting to believe he was right in his sentiment.

Every morning, I watch in wonderment as the daily *progulka* – our walk outside – unfolds. Despite the miserable confines of the tiny open-air cell and the intimidating guards with machine guns marching above us, my cellmates of 604 are determined to take advantage of the almost-fresh air and ability to move. Doing so in such a tight space requires an inspiring demonstration of coordination, in which eight men perform their different exercise routines with zero friction or overlap. Sometimes there are two groups running circuits, a slower group around the edges and a faster group inside. Occasionally, a faster jogger or walker steps out of his 'lane' to pass a slower man in front, almost like cyclists in the Tour de France, drafting behind others and then in turns passing in front to take the lead. Amid the sophisticated clockwork of this drafting, passing, and jogging, one by one the guys take turns darting in between others to the bench in the middle, where they do a set of dips or push-ups, before seamlessly rejoining the circling throng on the edges. And then, just when you think this precise machine is working on auto-pilot, someone gives a barely noticeable signal, and the entire group instantly starts circling the opposite way. It is like how birds can fly in flocks and fish can swim in schools, silently but perfectly coordinated in one direction, and then suddenly – as if by an invisible signal – turn 90 degrees and head in an entirely different direction.

It has taken me a while before I could hope to get in sync with this complex choreography. It strikes me that Russians must have an inner signalling mechanism that we foreigners just can't comprehend. Several times, I have failed to notice the signal and bumped straight into the man in front of me, as he turned quickly to march or jog in the opposite direction. Then, suddenly, one day, it was me giving the signal and the others following my lead, their eyes smiling silently as if to show that I'm finally being accepted as one of the team. It was also evidence that I was becoming attuned to the rhythms of prison life that dictated our daily existence with monotonous predictability. Like Dostoevsky, I am growing accustomed.

The weary sense of familiarity is also reflected in the language and abbreviations we use. The casual response to almost any enquiry on progress on our cases: 'BZ' – *byez izmenenie*, 'no change'. Another common expression, usually accompanied by a deep sigh, is 'NTV' (*nyet takoe vozmozhnost*, roughly translated as 'there is no such possibility here'). 'Shall we have a vodka with dinner?' Ha ha, NTV.

A typical day starts at around 5.30 a.m. as I hear the first squawks of an assembly of crows in the prison courtyard, slowly rising to a cacophony. Around the same time, noises emerge of the first cars out on the streets, early commuters on their way to work, and the occasional train can be heard passing in the distance. There is also that bizarre laser-type sound that emanates from somewhere in the courtyard, still a mystery. I lie in bed most mornings, in the moments before arising, listening to this symphony of the outside world.

At 6.30 a.m., the lights are abruptly switched fully on in the cell and the TV bursts violently into life – often at full volume if nobody's turned it down before the corridor guards centrally switch off all the sets at about 10.30 p.m. The official end time for TV is ten o'clock in the evening but the guys always beg the guards for a bit longer. Some of the guards are decent guys and willing to occasionally accommodate such minor requests, but many are bastards who enjoy refusing every entreaty just because they can. But when the TV roars on first thing in the morning, somehow the other guys don't even turn in their sleep. Yet some days it startles me right out of bed, and I have to hunt down the remote, almost always on the floor beside Zhendos' bed, and set the volume to zero.

Besides me, Andrey and Sanych are always the first to rise. Andrey whispers some prayers alone by the cell's icons while Sanych dunks his head under the sink tap, dousing himself with cold water. He then combs his thick, wet mane straight back and dries his beard with a towel, before switching places with Andrey, who washes his face while Sanych prays. Meanwhile, I take two small square kneeling carpets and combine them into a pseudo-yoga mat on which to do fifteen minutes of stretching exercises. Ever since my hernia, this has become an essential part of my morning routine, saving me from becoming a hobbled old man. Then it's time for a quiet breakfast with Andrey and Sanych, passively watching the silent TV while the others sleep on.

Sasha Rostov and Grisha are the next to get up at 7.30 or 8. Around half an hour later come the metallic raps of the guard knocking with his keys on the door. Everyone stands to gather near the entrance for our morning check (*proverka*). Whoever is 'on duty' gives a simple report: '604, 7 people, all in order.' Most of us make the report without particular enthusiasm or effect, but when it is Sanych's turn, he delivers it in his own inimitable way, a true military man down to his bones. The words fire crisply from his mouth like bullets from a machine gun. It usually makes even the guards smile, and they probably have to stop themselves from snapping to attention at his authoritative tone. The guard then asks 'Any questions?' ('*Voprosy yest?*'). Some days there are, some days not, and never anything more than a query about a light that isn't working, or a leaky sink, or some such annoyance. The guard then collects our *zayavlenie*, reads them quickly to make sure they include nothing too unusual, and leaves. Sometimes Zhendos and Big Sasha will then return to their bunks for some more sleep, but now they have to slumber on top of their blankets, or else they will be seen by the Sauron Eye and receive a crackled warning over the cell's speaker. Zhendos is always the last to get up properly, sometime between 9 and 10.

The rest of the day follows a familiar schedule. *Progulka* from 10 until 11, then morning tea and snack at 11.30 (usually nuts and fruits, but sometimes something extra like cheese and dill wrapped in lavash, a sort of flatbread). Time for reading and/or work on legal papers follows until lunch at 2 (borscht or some other type of soup or cabbage salad, all bought from Matrosskaya Tishina's official supplier and heated up on the metal steaming pot). Everyone naps after lunch for about an hour, except for whoever's turn it is to clean the cell, deep-scrubbing the floor and toilet on hands and knees for a couple of hours. Then there's coffee at 4 p.m., and more reading or note-taking before dinner at 7, followed by communal TV until switch-off, and lights half-off at 10.30 p.m. There is a mid-evening *proverka* too, usually around 8 p.m.

The weekends have a slower pace than the weekdays, with no court hearings or visits from advocates and investigators. But Saturday is the day when prisoners who are willing to pay a small amount can go to the SIZO's fitness centre and take a shower. 'Fitness centre' is an extravagant description of what it just a single small, dimly lit room, about halfway in size between a three- and eight-man cell, with a few weights and barbells scattered about. All of us in 604 pay the equivalent of roughly $4 for an hour's access. The equipment is ancient, virtually identical in terms of brands and vintage to the stuff I used on my high school basketball team in Oklahoma in the 1980s. It's shiny – not like kit straight from the box, but more like an old threadbare jacket – with grips worn smooth by decades of constant usage. At least it's still functional. Some of the 604 guys – Andrey, Sasha Rostov, and Zhendos – are into interval training, while Sanych, Grisha and Big Sasha prefer heavy weightlifting, each of them able to bench press more than 250lb. I have joined the interval training group but I'm struggling to keep up with the young Turks. Andrey, who is probably fittest of us all, has told me his goal is 'cryotherapy' – he wants to try to 'freeze' his fitness in place so that, when he eventually regains his freedom, he will be in even better overall health than when he entered, and therefore won't 'lose' the time he has spent in prison permanently.

Part of the process of growing accustomed includes me getting my hair cut in the style of most of the other inmates of 604. One day I am standing at the sink in our cell, trying to cut my hair myself with an old pair of scissors, when Andrey looks me up and down. 'Don't even try it,' he says. 'It isn't going to work.' Later, the guards bring us an old electric hair clipper out of storage and I get a tight buzz cut like all the other guys, except for Sanych, who has a great thick head of hair along with his mighty beard. There are obvious practical reasons for a close army-style cut when you're allowed a shower only once or twice a week. Andrey shaves my head down to about an inch on all sides, the shortest my hair has been since I was 19 and at Officer Candidate School in the Marine Corps during a summer break from college. It feels strange to rub my hands over the top of my head, but the guys say I look ten years younger. Now I officially have the look of a real prisoner.

The patterns of institutionalised life imprint themselves upon me almost unnoticed. I am becoming numbed to indignities and hardships, my initial terror at what might happen to me giving way to different emotions – boredom, bleakness, and despair at 'the system'. The television plays an inordinately large part in my new day-to-day. One evening, we sit glued to a women's curling match. It's Russia versus Japan. I can think of few sports less likely to generate interest among a group of hardened men in prison, but astonishingly, everyone is engrossed. It's a close game and in the end, Russia wins, which provokes loud cheers and cries of '*Ura!!!*' and '*Malodtsi!*' (roughly, 'Good work!'). It is amazing how patriotic Russians remain even when detained in SIZO, seemingly betrayed by their country, and with little hope of returning to a life of freedom. And all channelled into a sport that most men wouldn't spend ten seconds watching if they had a free choice.

When no one is watching anything in particular, the TV tends to be left on 'Muz-TV', which shows endless music videos. As elsewhere, Russia has maybe eight or ten hit songs at any given time, and these are played over and over and over again. 'Psycho' by Lady Gaga, 'WTF' by Amber van Day, '*Molnya*' ('Lightning') by Dima Bilan, and '*Ya veru chudesa*' ('I Believe in Miracles') by Zvonkii are drilled relentlessly into my brain in cell 604, where I must have heard them each at least 200 times. Eventually, I train myself to ignore the music and concentrate on other distractions like reading, a job made easier because I learn to blend those same, monotonous songs into a kind of neutral background noise.

But every now and then, a song cuts through to me. Near the end of *progulka* one morning, Retro FM plays Chris Rea's 'Looking for the Summer'. All the 604 guys know the song and the words from its main refrain, but none of them understand what it's about. I like the song but confess that I have never really paid attention to the lyrics either. But now I listen carefully as it crackles from the old loudspeaker and translate the meaning for the guys. It's a song not only about the change of season and onset of summer, but also about coming of age, love, and heartbreak. We all contemplate these themes with a new appreciation as we plod through another repetitive exercise circuit on a crisp March morning. And then, as if on cue, the sun bursts through the clouds and beams bright rays down through the barbed wire. Andrey, Sasha Rostov and I all stop to face the sun, closing our eyes, and breathing deeply. The combination of sunshine, endorphins, music from my youth, and sudden nostalgia for my childhood make it an emotional moment. I fight back a tear in my eye and again resolve that, if I ever get out, I'll never again take for granted the beauty of nature and joy of music. I look over at Andrey and Sasha, and they nod silently to me, a shared moment of enlightenment. I can see that they, too, are momentarily transported to a different, happier place.

Other times, there are songs that prove memorable for different reasons. One such is 'Tequila!', made famous by The Champs. With its single-word lyrics, all seven of us from 604 shout it in unison as we pace in the usual synchronised way, punctuating the word 'Tequila!' by thrusting our fists into the air. The machine-gun-toting guard watching from above must wonder whether this is the beginning of some kind of prison insurrection.

Unlike the music speakers by the *progulka* rooms, the one in our room is used by the guards to give us orders from their central command post. All too often, what comes out of the speaker is completely incomprehensible to me. My conversational Russian is generally pretty fluent but I find myself almost always having to get one of the guys to repeat the orders coming through the raspy speaker. Typically, the commands are given in abbreviated form. 'Calvey. With documents' means I am to get ready for a meeting with my advocates. '604. Banya' is a warning that a guard will soon come to take us off to the shower rooms. I imagined a kind of central dispatcher sitting in a guard control room, working diligently through his complex schedule of prisoner movements, always ensuring none of us run into each other, just like the controller of some vast rail network.

The prison nurse does a round of visits to all the cells every evening, stopping by to drop off medication. I can see the sense of a system designed to prevent anyone from having so large a prescribed drug supply in hand that they might overdose, but it brings to mind Nurse Ratched of *One Flew Over the Cuckoo's Nest* and her 'medication time'. The Matrosskaya Tishina nurse never actually enters the cells, but knocks three times on the *karmyak* (the small window in the main metal door), opens it, barks out the prisoner names one by one, silently hands the medicine through the window, and leaves without further discussion.

Shortly after I arrived in cell 604, one evening after the other guys had already received their daily prescriptions, I strode over to the *karmyak*, leaned over to peer through it, and asked whether there had been any decision yet about the second mattress I'd requested for my bad back. 'In Guantanamo,' she says coldly, 'they don't give prisoners a second mattress.' I was struck to hear the stony Nurse Ratched complete an actual sentence but also by the unemotional harshness of her words. I was too stunned and amused to muster a reply. She was no doubt right about Guantanamo, but then again, I'm not a terrorist.

Occasionally, the order is given for us to gather our property and get ready to go to 'the Box'. This happens about once a month so that the authorities can carefully search our belongings, take a detailed inventory and make sure we have no forbidden material. It is a huge hassle to gather and organise our miserable belongings, so the guys try to negotiate with the guards to leave some things in the cell. They allow us to leave behind all our food and cleaning supplies, but everything else – clothes, shoes, towels, bedsheet, books, notebooks, etc. – has to be rolled up in our bulging mattresses and carried with us. The guards escort us to the Box, where we each place our belongings in separate piles on the floor before going to sit in the Box's tiny holding cell – seven men shoulder to shoulder in a dark, windowless space the size of a small closet.

One by one, the guards bring us out to collect our individual mattress bundle and place it on an examination table. Two guards go through each item, flipping through books to make sure there are no hidden papers, stretching and bending shoes in search of any dangerous items, and so on. The grand finale requires each prisoner to strip naked so his clothes can be searched, an intentional indignity of no obvious utility. Every detail from the search is painstakingly transcribed on a piece of faded yellowish paper, the kind that seems to circulate in all stifling bureaucracies. Of course, these exhaustive handwritten inventories are destined straight for a dusty archive somewhere, never to be seen again. When one prisoner's inventory is finished, he gets dressed again, places his bundle back on the floor, and goes back into the holding closet to await processing of all the other cellmates. Meanwhile, back in 604, other guards carry out a separate search for contraband. This entire routine is apparently an ancient procedure in Russian prisons, so everyone involved – the guards and my cellmates – approach it with an air of boredom and inevitability. In the miserable dark room where we sit, packed together like sardines in a tin can, with no watches or way to measure time, it seems to take an eternity. We exchange grim jokes and laugh at the Kafka-esque absurdity of it all.

Some things, though, you can't laugh off. The hardest part about being in prison is being separated entirely from my family. I miss the simple pleasures of togetherness. International Women's Day, 8 March, falls a few weeks into my incarceration, and it brings into sharp focus my sense of loss. Normally, I would be at home, cooking breakfast with my boys for Julia and my daughter Sasha. A few days later, it is the 17th birthday of my youngest son, Niko. It kills me to miss these milestone family moments. And the worst of it is being completely out of contact with them. I still have no idea what they really think about what is happening to me. To us. My biggest fear is that my kids might think I am actually guilty of fraud, too young to understand the absurdity of the accusations against me. Instead of being a role model for them, maybe they now have doubts about me. Maybe they are having to juggle awkward questions from their friends about me. Regardless, I am sure that they are worried terribly about their dad, and I hate the fact that I have no way to reassure them that I am OK and feeling strong. Teenagers shouldn't have to deal with this sort of anxiety, and I dread that the trauma of it all might knock them off their rails at a vital time in their school lives.

It's over a month after my arrest that the first letters from Julia – three of them – finally make it through the system to me. The way it works is like this: people on the outside can open a special account with Yandex (the company I myself helped to create, yet another great irony) and type a message to be sent to any prisoner via 'Yandex. FSIN'. All messages are reviewed by the prison censor in case they contain information relevant to a case. Only Russian-language text can be submitted, and one photo attachment per message is allowed. Prison letters prove the truth of the old cliché: a picture is worth a thousand words. One of Julia's notes includes a photo of her and Sasha visiting a university in the UK. Such a relief! It feels like a massive weight has been lifted from me, knowing finally what is happening with them and what they are feeling.

Julia's messages are drafted carefully, reflecting her knowledge of the censorship requirements, but contain enough for me to feel reassured that she and the kids are doing as well as can be expected under the circumstances. The main comfort I take is the knowledge that the kids are getting on well at school, keeping up friendships, and making plans for the future. Also tremendously encouraging are the messages of support that Julia passes on from hundreds of friends. If there is a silver lining to my nightmarish predicament, it's that I really learn who my true friends are. It is humbling and wonderful to know how many people there are on whom I can truly count.

I stare at the photo of my wife and daughter for hours. The eager smile on Sasha's face seems to carry with it a slight twinge of apprehension. I guess and hope this is down to her nervousness about the approaching next stage of her life, away from home and at university, rather than because of my circumstances. I wish so much that I could be there, to give her a hug, and to tell her that we all went through the same thing, and that she is going to be just fine. I lie on my bunk most of the day with a bittersweet feeling: happy to see my family's faces and to know they are OK, but resentful at being denied my right to help guide my kids at this important time in their lives. But I know I'm so fortunate to have a wife and life partner like Julia, who is rock solid in her inner strength, a truly wise woman, despite her choice of husband. She must feel 'stress tested' in the extreme just now, and I know we have more traumatic days ahead of us, but I also know she will be the pillar of stability that the entire family can cling to for support. She is my foundation.

Not long after I get this first batch of letters comes a second – more from Julia and one from Sasha, along with more photos. Sasha definitely speaks Russian worse than me, so getting a letter from her in Russian is especially surprising. I'm guessing she's used Google Translate, since the text is like a literal translation from English and not natural Russian. But it is great to hear her words unmistakably in her own 'voice', commenting on the trivial but precious stuff of daily life and addressing me as 'King Padre', her own term of endearment.

I find it hard to write a reply in Russian. I almost always speak Russian with my wife and with my colleagues in the office, and can understand most of what I read (slowly) in Russian. But I rarely text or write in Russian, as I never learned to touch-type on a Cyrillic key-board and it takes me too long. The language skills I do have are not school taught but gained by immersion over twenty-five years, and my grammar is still embarrassingly poor. The guys in cell 604 help me with writing *zayavlenie* and other documents when needed, but I don't feel comfortable leaning on them for support in drafting very personal letters to my family. Besides, it feels awkward and strange to communicate with my kids in Russian. To help them become bilingual, we decided early on that Julia would speak to them always in her mother tongue, while I would speak to them only in English, except for some words that are just perfect in one or the other language (like '*Malodyets!*' or 'Don't forget to be awesome!', our playful family motto). But the system demands I respond in Russian, so that is what I must do. It is a small price to pay for the comfort of being in regular contact. Just another thing to get accustomed to.

13

Dark and Light

Most time in prison is characterised by dull tedium, accented by occasional troughs and peaks of heightened emotion – the troughs, sadly, far more common than the peaks. My own situation is enough of a roller coaster but I also get to see up close the toll that navigating the system has on one of my cellmates. The final stages of Andrey's long, drawn-out criminal prosecution are playing out, as gripping as a television drama. But the stakes are monstrously higher, his entire future on the line. I am getting an insider's glimpse of someone going through hell.

He rises early one morning to ready himself for the start of his long-awaited trial in court. He looks nervously through his papers, running one more time through the handwritten speech he plans to deliver. When the guards come around 8 a.m. to collect him, we all give him fist bumps and wish him '*S bogom!*' ('God be with you!'). He doesn't get back until midnight, famished and parched with thirst. He wolfs down some food and drinks an entire bottle of water, before lying down and trying to rest. It turns out that the prosecutor is pushing for a sentence of almost twenty years – outrageously long for the crimes that Andrey is accused of. He is alleged to have committed financial offences, although his advocates have significant evidence showing his innocence. Some press commentators describe the case simply as fallout from a bitter feud between two rival local government officials. Andrey seems to still have adrenaline pumping through his body after his long day at court, and he finds it hard to wind down with another few days of hearings to come. He must feel like an astronaut in outer space, desperately grasping with one hand the cable of an orbiting space-ship, knowing if he loses his grip, he will float away irretrievably into the abyss.

The next morning, he and I are the first to awake. By the time I get up, he is already fully dressed and ready for court, his folders of papers organised and neatly packed. He has eaten breakfast and now stands next to the TV, watching intently while the others sleep. The TV is tuned to a nature programme, one that's regularly on for half an hour in the mornings. Today, it shows a sunset near a rocky beach somewhere unrecognisable. Waves lap gently on the rocks, seagulls fly overhead, and the sun peacefully comes to rest over the distant sea. Though Andrey's jaw is granite like a boxer's, I detect a faint trace of a tear in his eye as he takes in this simple but beautiful scene. I imagine him thinking that if he is ever to be free again, he'll never take for granted the simple things in life that all free men can enjoy.

The moment is interrupted by a sharp metallic rap on the cell door, and a pair of guards take him away to court. The rest of us watch the Russia 24 news channel that afternoon. More than half of its hour-long programme is devoted to ongoing criminal cases involving various Russian officials and business figures. One features a Gazprom distributor in the Caucasus, another is concerned with food safety violations in the Urals. The 604 guys monitor the reporting on criminal cases avidly – unsurprisingly given they are all under investigation themselves. But I wonder if this stuff really represents the most pressing news of the day. I doubt it, given the civil war still raging in Syria, yet more disputes over North Korea's nuclear programme, and so many other things happening in the world. Eventually, even my cellmates grow weary of the non-stop coverage of what sometimes feels like pretty low-level criminal matters. 'Come on!' they yell at the TV. 'Isn't there any other news!?! Seems like half of Russia must be locked up by now!'

Around this time, we discover the TV in our cell is broken. I don't mind as it brings a few hours of blissful silence when I can get on with reading and doing some work on my case. But the guys are convinced the set has been knocked off its perch by guards rifling through our cell during *progulka*. It's quite possible that they were carrying out one of their unauthorised searches but they deny it, claiming the TV must have fallen by itself. It's true that it is often stacked precariously on a fruit bowl for the benefit of Zhendos, so that he can see it while lying on his bunk. But no one is sure what really happened.

I don't know if it has any influence on what follows, but later that night there is a huge argument in our cell after the regular 604 dominoes match. Almost every evening, Grisha and Big Sasha team up against Sasha Rostov and Zhendos, and it's usually pretty evenly matched. Whoever wins, of course, gloats mercilessly over the losers. But tonight, it seems Zhendos makes a simple mistake near the end, causing his team to throw away a certain victory and fall to a shameful defeat. Zhendos is a smart guy, but he just doesn't care as much about the game and isn't as hyper competitive as the others, so he relaxes and loses concentration. Sasha Rostov explodes at him, cursing and calling him every name you can imagine. It carries on, bitterly, for about an hour and I feel sympathy for Zhendos. After a while, I eventually distract Sasha Rostov by discussing with him some English slang words to add to his notebook. Peace is restored but it's clear that the pressures we're all under are taking their toll.

Grisha plays a special role in the life of cell 604, with his deep knowledge and experience of the legal system. Some mornings at *progulka*, it feels like he's running his own advocate's bureau. He stands solemnly in the corner, smoking his cigarettes, occasionally flicking ash down towards an ashtray on the ground, while the others sidle over one by one to seek his wise counsel. Later in the day, it's reported on the now repaired TV that the prosecutors in his case have added an additional charge to his preliminary indictment – 'participation in a criminal group', a classification that gives prosecutors extra procedural advantages and limits some scope for defence. The news comes as a shock to Grisha and his discouragement is obvious as he contemplates a still longer potential prison sentence. Somehow, though, he finds it in himself to quickly rally, and he spends several hours writing down detailed notes to give to his advocate team.

Later that evening, we gather to watch a Russian reality TV show, *The Last Hero*, which is similar in concept to *Survivor* in the US and UK. A group of people are dropped on a remote island, separated into two 'tribes', and given a physical challenge of some kind to contest every episode. A lot of mini-dramas play out within the tribes, and at the end of each episode, one person is voted off the island, triggering even more intrigue among the contestants. All of us in cell 604 ridicule the contestants mercilessly, but somehow they fascinate us and we faithfully watch each new instalment. In order to create drama, the producers portray an exaggerated sense of terrible hardship and suffering the contestants face, when in fact they are living in a carefully monitored island paradise. For those of us locked up in prison, we can't even imagine the happiness we'd feel if we were to be sent to such a place. This week, one of the contestants cries on camera, overwhelmed by the sadness of being separated from her family. It turns out that she has only been away from them for sixteen days! When she says this, all of 604 erupts in unison, cursing at the TV and throwing newspapers or pillows in disgust at the screen. Some of my cellmates have already been in here, away from their families, for three years.

Andrey, meanwhile, is summoned to his final day of hearings, expecting to receive his sentence. He remains grimly silent as he waits to leave, although his eyes betray his profound nervousness. We give him the usual fist bumps and 'God be with you!' before he is taken away; we all hope for a good result for him, but none of us is optimistic. His wife has given birth to a daughter since his arrest, whom Andrey has only ever seen through a prison phone-booth window.

When Andrey returns that evening, he confirms the bad news: he was sentenced to sixteen years in a penal colony, 'harsh regime'. He never hoped to be acquitted, since Russian criminal cases always result in a conviction, but he did hope the strength of evidence in his favour might influence the judge to reduce the sentence, perhaps to just seven or eight years. Having already been held in SIZO for three years, he might then soon be able to apply for early parole after a couple more years. But the sentence of sixteen years is utterly devastating. Breathing hard, unable to speak, he collapses on his bed, silent tears in his eyes. I imagine him thinking of his daughters growing up without a father, and only being able to embrace them – for the first time, in the case of his youngest girl – when they are almost grown women. The rest of us try to be supportive, but we all know there's nothing we can say to comfort him in this situation. We spend the evening in quiet but impotent solidarity.

Andrey's case highlights the arbitrary and unfair nature of the process in which we all find ourselves trapped. We have recently seen news reports of the case of a Russian man convicted of multiple homicides to which he finally confessed, yet for which he has been sentenced to just eight years, while Andrey was given double that for alleged, and possibly spurious, economic offences. It is impossible to reconcile and brings into sharp focus my own personal situation. I am already devastated to be missing milestones in my family's life yet hardly dare to imagine the years of confinement potentially stretching ahead.

On one of the days Andrey is away from the cell, the rest of us watch a broadcast on the TV news about Britain's departure from the European Union, after the UK Parliament has again refused to pass a Brexit Bill. I'm surprised and impressed that Russian prisoners, firstly, care at all about events in far-off Britain, but also that they have at least some knowledge of what Brexit means. I doubt many in US prisons would have a similar awareness. We end up having a discussion in 604 about the various perspectives of the 'pro' and 'anti' Brexit camps. The Russian guys are naturally resistant to the idea of control by any 'foreign' or 'international' parliament: 'Since we finally kicked out the Tatars, we defended our lands, and we will always defend our lands.' On the other hand, the idea of free movement around Europe seems to them like a fantasy of prosperity, pleasant weather and honest judges – who wouldn't want that? Naturally, as often happens, the conversation turns to Russia's own domestic issues: sick children, corrupt oligarchs and officials, a government that fails to help ordinary people. I listen silently, having long ago learned that if I contribute a critical comment – even in support of their own words – they will take offence at an outsider attacking their motherland. More than any other nationality I have ever known, Russians can be hyper-critical of their own country yet deeply patriotic at the same time.

When I do join the conversation, it's to point out that the USA and Europe have their own problems, from chronic inequality to obesity and opioid epidemics, and much more besides. I point out that I have met thousands of Russian entrepreneurs and innovators doing incredible things, no less impressive than in the West. So, it can't be all bad in Russia, I suggest. There must be something about the education system, the culture, and the economy that allow for these success stories. But the guys in cell 604 grumble that I have a distortedly optimistic view, too Moscow-centric, and not reflective of reality in most of the country. It's a standard and valid refrain, but not entirely true, since I have travelled and worked across almost all of Russia. Still, I don't press the point. Sitting in a cell around our *dubok*, drinking tea from plastic cups, 'marinating' while the immovable Russian criminal justice system crushingly determines our fate, it is impossible to try to convince anyone to be an optimist.

★ ★ ★

Andrey's plight is casting a huge shadow over all of us. Yet still we all carry on, our collective solidarity and resilience a source of comfort. Even in such a dark place, we manage to find ways to get through the days, to fight back as best we can against the constant threats marshalled against us. And, indeed, to continue finding pleasures in small things – in our little commune, in memories of our loved ones, and in the games and entertainment we share. Exploring the joys – and strangeness – of each other's language, and telling riotous jokes brings us laughter even in the most difficult times. When you don't know whether to laugh or to cry, it's better to laugh.

I have some personal epiphanies along the way, too. On one glorious, crisp sunny day that follows a period of depressingly bad weather, I hear joyful birdsong through the 6in opening in our cell window, perhaps a sign that spring is coming. I make yet another resolution that when I taste freedom again I will 'smell all the flowers' and enjoy every sunset, making sure never to ignore the simple stuff that makes life beautiful. In important ways, my time in the cell is an uplifting one, in which we band of brothers face down adversity.

As I navigate my way through the labyrinth, I come to realise that I rely not only on the powerful camaraderie with my fellow inmates but also the ability to mine my own internal resources. With so much time to pass, a lot of it is inevitably spent in introspective contemplation. And, of course, being in prison forces upon me a sort of detox – from alcohol, of course, but more importantly from the digital world. I know my liver will be fresh as a daisy if/when I ever get out, and a few weeks without either phone or internet raises my consciousness of just how much of daily life outside is wasted on low-value digital activity on phones and laptops. I employ much of my newly available time on reading – up to ten hours a day. As I lie on my prison bunk for endless hours, my body may be trapped but I feel that my mind is radically free.

To read in Russian is a slow and arduous process for me, with little of the enjoyment I feel when speaking the language. Unfortunately, the English-language selection in the Matrosskaya Tishina library is restricted to only about twenty or thirty titles, mostly well-worn copies of contemporary bestsellers. My office has sought permission to send me a few books of my choice, but it's been a tortuous wait to get them cleared by the censor. Absurdly, even the English translations of Tolstoy, Gogol and other classic Russian authors need to be checked by the censors for secret messages they fear could be encoded within them.

I am by no means the only reader in 604. Almost all of us pore over the newspapers that are delivered each afternoon. And when we have finished with them, they are usefully employed as, for instance, floor mats down by the trash can, to line baskets of fruit, and as liners for sandals, apparently to prevent fungal infection. A valuable double life. Andrey tells me that the books he loves best are humorous stories like those of Mark Twain. But he is currently reading *The Two Captains*, a Soviet-era novel by Veniamin Kaverin, as his daughter is studying it at school and he wants to be able to discuss it with her in one of their monthly phone calls. Sanych, in contrast, is reading a book on project financing, with a view to eventually building a career in the private sector when he gets out of here. Big Sasha is engrossed in a book about the personal lives of the Russian Czars, Sasha Rostov is reading up on the writings and teachings of the Russian monk Siluan Afonsii, and Grisha favours the classics like Dostoevsky and Turgenev. I'm sure 604 is an outlier in terms of its literary tastes, and that reading must play a less significant part of life in the wider prison community. Even in our cell, Zhendos is much more devoted to the television than the written word. But the rest of us bookworms of 604 cherish the intellectual escape.

Among the first books that eventually find their way to me from the prison library is Michael Crichton's *Andromeda Strain*. I race through it in two days, gripped by its depiction of a deadly virus outbreak. I follow it up with an abridged version, probably intended for children, of Dumas' *The Count of Monte Cristo*, and another Crichton, *Timeline* – a time travel tale that cleverly examines the endless permutations that could happen if time travel were possible. I don't typically like airport novels, but Crichton is really good. Perfect to consume in a single day or two while stuck in a Russian SIZO cell.

While I'm waiting for more books in English, I am also trying to improve my Russian-language skills, working my way through copies of *National Geographic* in Russian, noting all the words I don't understand, which are many. Andrey lends me his Russian–English dictionary for the purpose of self-education. It's a great way to pass the time, as I am fearful that I'll get through the prison library's English titles long before I receive anything from outside. As the censor takes his time, I read some Agatha Christie, and then make a start on *Contact* by Carl Sagan, the renowned astronomer, who effortlessly brings to life the known and unknown vastness of the cosmos. *Contact* is about some astrophysicists who discover radio signals from outer space, proving that we are not alone in the universe and, indeed, that there is a civilisation out there far more advanced than our own. It's a book fundamentally about the conflict between faith and science, ultimately exploring how they might be reconciled. I find it entertaining and thought-provoking; it makes the intrigues of men on our tiny planet seem petty in comparison – a big idea that is comforting in my current predicament.

It takes several weeks, but eventually some of the titles I asked my office to send make it past the censor. First to arrive are Dickens'

Great Expectations and Dostoevsky's *House of the Dead*. I start reading the latter, a semi-autobiographical work based on the author's own imprisonment and exile in Siberia in the 1850s. In those days, there were thirty prisoners housed in a single room, all types of criminals mixed together and condemned to hard labour. It's a stark contrast to the 'sorting' system that seems to exist today, separating inmates into groups based on the types of crimes they've committed. Prisoners in Dostoevsky's time were allowed to work in the local community and even earn money for doing jobs like shoe repairing and fixing garments, which they could spend on vodka or cigarettes in a thriving black market (even though vodka was formally forbidden in the prison). This cash economy caused tensions of its own inside the prison, while books were prohibited, which must have been a particular torture for Dostoevsky. Today's conditions, especially in SIZO #1 in Matrosskaya Tishina, are unquestionably better in this respect.

I am struck by Dostoevsky's description of a stray dog, Sharik, who lived inside the prison walls, and became an object of the author's love – an unexpected connection that helped him to retain his sense of humanity. I am also surprised and impressed by the description of the prisoners' attitude to work. According to Dostoevsky, the convicts loathed meaningless work, finding all kinds of clever ways to thwart assignments obviously without a useful purpose. But they actively enjoyed work that produced visible results, even brutal chores like shovelling snow on a frozen Siberian winter day. Amid the misery of a nineteenth-century prison, Dostoevsky shows us there was still undeniably a link between a man's work and his dignity. Although it is fascinating to compare the novel with my own experiences, I decide to put on hold finishing it until I am out of prison. It just hits too close to home at the moment, causing more anxiety. Instead, I start *Great Expectations*, a captivating story into which I can escape and get away from my own troubles for a while. In fact, I enjoy it so much that I convince Big Sasha to order a copy in Russian to read.

After Dickens, I move on to Somerset Maugham's *The Razor's Edge*. I loved the film, an uncharacteristically serious dramatic outing for the actor Bill Murray, but I have heard the novel is even better and I hungrily consume it. Perhaps it's because my emotions are amplified by life as a prisoner, but I'm simply overwhelmed by the novel's core message and how much I relate to its hero, Larry Darrell. Encountering tragedy as a pilot in the First World War, he rejects the superficial, staid career path he had planned, and embraces a non-conventional life in search of understanding and purpose. The book is really about the unconquerable human spirit, and the process of seeking enlightenment — something 'harder than walking on a Razor's Edge' but ultimately available to anyone who lives according to their own values and inner yardstick. Maugham's prose is entrancing, and after finishing the book, I lie on my bunk, contentedly alone with my thoughts. It has been a long time since I read something that so perfectly chimes with my own ideas about spirituality, enlightenment, and the true path to happiness. It makes me determined to reject superficiality in all its pervasive guises, and to try to make a positive impact on the lives of everyone around me. To create good karma, and to appreciate every day how blessed and fortunate I am.

From Maugham, it's back to Dostoevsky and *The Brothers Karamazov* — the favourite book of my brother, Kevin, one of the smartest men I have ever known. I have read and loved other of Dostoevsky's works, including *Crime and Punishment* (how relevant now!), but never this one, considered by many to be his greatest. I was meant to have read it in my senior year at high school, but somehow managed to wriggle out of it, much to my teacher's annoyance. As almost all Russians know, the novel tells the story of a troubled family full of strong-willed characters, including the eponymous three brothers with their diametrically opposed personalities, and a despicable father. It is a murder mystery, and the nineteenth-century trial that Dostoevsky describes is particularly fascinating to me reading in my prison bunk 150 years later. The hot-tempered but big-hearted Dmitry Karamazov, with a hearty appetite for all things but especially for vodka and the voluptuous Grusha, reminds me of some of my closest Russian friends.

One of Dostoevsky's side themes is about 'habit' and 'routine', which he describes as the most powerful motive force in the world. How easy it is to fall into routine, for better or worse. In prison, the daily routine can help to overcome one's sense of hopelessness, and to recover some dignity. In the outside world, it can help you become more productive. But too much routine and an overdose of monotonous daily rituals causes us incrementally to lose a bit of our souls.

Prisoners, I think, have a tendency to become more religious, especially when confronted with an immovable criminal justice system that apparently requires a miracle to overcome it. Praying for help from a higher power can seem the only source of hope. Moreover, as a prisoner you have a lot of spare time in which to contemplate spiritual matters. But it does seem to be an incredible coincidence that I have picked almost at random a few books to read here that explore similar thought-provoking, inspiring themes. Consuming *Contact*, *The Razor's Edge*, and *The Brothers Karamazov* in such close succession has had a huge impact on me. I feel more than ever that we can't find lasting happiness through objects and superficial things, nor solely in an intellectual world of ideas where we become isolated from real people. The key to happiness is to be grounded and genuine, to leave a positive footprint in your wake, and to enjoy the simple things, like a child's laughter or the beauty of a mountain sunrise. But I think I need to stop now, before I become like Jerry Maguire reading aloud his lofty statement of ideals while his colleagues laugh uproariously in the background.

A typical middle-class American family, circa 1970: me with parents (Harry and Mary Jane), brother (Kevin) and sister (Cathy). Our youngest sister Beth would arrive a year later.

Me at age 5, badly in need of an orthodontist but already an optimist.

Me as a new Oklahoma University graduate, aged 21. Full of energy and heading to Wall Street.

Julia, my wife, an unsinkable ship. The luckiest day of my life was when she said yes.

Me with a rambunctious Nikosha (Niko) on Red Square, Moscow. Julia and I worked hard to make our kids proud of their dual Russian–American heritage.

My adventurous daughter, Sasha, comfortable and at home in her cowgirl attire.

My eldest son, Mishuta (Michael Jr), with his 99-year-old Russian great-grandmother. A priceless conversation for both of them.

The cover of *Forbes* in 2016. I was still confident of the future even though dark geopolitical clouds were forming on the horizon. (*Forbes* Kazakhstan)

The Baring Vostok team circa 2015. We didn't always agree on everything, but we had a legendary partnership and achieved amazing results together over more than twenty-five years.

Press conference in Yekaterinburg with my colleague and dear friend Alexei Leonov. A legendary cosmonaut and national hero, he was a beloved figure to all Russians.

What I admired most about Leonov was his ability to connect emotionally with anyone – from presidents to bus drivers, and everyone in between. Here he's sharing a tender hug and ageless wisdom with Mishuta.

The inner courtyard of Matrosskaya Tishina, the infamous Russian prison where I was held in 2019. It is nicknamed 'Kremlin Central' since detainees' cases are under direct supervision of Russia's FSB. (Sovfoto/Universal Images Group/Shutterstock)

Morning inspection in a typical cell (not mine) in Matrosskaya Tishina prison. (STRINGER /AFP via Getty Images)

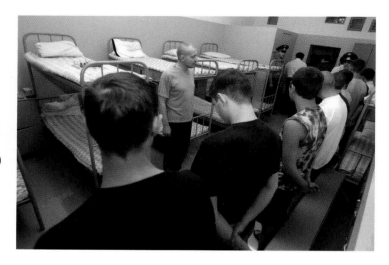

An early court hearing on my detention conditions, when I was still held in prison. I can barely be seen on the TV screen, participating in the farce remotely while behind bars. (Maxim Shipenkov/ EPA-EFE/ Shutterstock)

In a Russian courtroom's typical glass cage for prisoners under investigation — guilty until proven innocent. A familiar backdrop to anyone who watches Russian TV. (Kirill Kudryavtsev/AFP via Getty Images)

Leaving Moscow City Court for the umpteenth time, frustrated and deep in concentration about our next moves. (Maxim Shipenkov/EPA-EFE/Shutterstock)

Leaving Meshansky Court on Verdict Day in August 2021. My American friends texted condolences about being convicted for a crime that never happened. My Russian friends texted 'Congratulations!', knowing that my suspended sentence was a rare victory in the cynical Russian system. (Yuri Kochetkov/EPA-EFE/Shutterstock)

14 January 2022: The Aeroflot flight when I finally left Russia after three long and stressful years. When we finally started accelerating to take-off, I sent this photo to my wife, who was nervously waiting for me at home.

SECTION 3
1–12 APRIL 2019

14

The Bad Deal

My determination to live meaningfully doesn't mean I can lose focus on fighting the accusations against me. Reading offers a temporary escape, but I need to work intensely to defend myself across all aspects of my case. I minutely analyse the Vostochny investment and its chequered history that got me into this mess – a sadly typical Russian case study in how good intentions rarely go unpunished. Although I can hold my head high knowing that I have done nothing wrong, I am bitterly aware now that it is the costliest deal I have ever made.

The story, which has a lot of moving parts, begins back in the early 2010s. Our team at Baring Vostok had identified Russia's retail banking sector as ripe for growth and under-invested. We knew we couldn't match the state-owned banks with their heft in the corporate banking arena, but we had better hopes for consumer lending. Retail deposits in Russia were growing steadily and we believed they would increase by something like five times over the coming decade – an estimate that proved prescient. We were confident that there would be substantial returns for backing the right banks who focused on consumers, similar to Capital One in the US. We believed it was an almost sure-fire way to benefit from the expansion of Russia's middle class and the maturation of Russia's millennial generation, who seemed intent on banking with different institutions to those of their parents.

We searched the market for opportunities and ended up making investments into three banks: Tinkoff and Vostochny in Russia, and Kaspi in Kazakhstan. Kaspi and Tinkoff became huge successes for us, generating billions in profits for our funds. This validated our sector strategy but mainly served as testament to the extraordinary entrepreneurs and management teams behind them – people like Mikhail Lomtadze and Vyacheslav Kim at Kaspi, and Oleg Tinkov and Oliver Hughes at Tinkoff. These individuals proved to be among the world's top fintech visionaries and had the talent to build massive, unique businesses.

Vostochny also initially seemed to have great potential. It was led by a strong CEO and founding shareholder, Sergei Vlasov. Its headquarters were in Khabarovsk in Russia's Far East, a region we believed was attractive for retail banking since its local population had above-average incomes, but banking competition was lower than average. Vostochny's model was to attract deposits through a nationwide branch network but lend mostly to customers in Siberia and the Far East, where it was already well known and had reliable customers for repeat business.

Between 2010 and 2012, Baring Vostok funds invested some $150 million into Vostochny, alongside other investors, in order to increase the bank's capital base and promote steady growth. Initial results were encouraging. Net profit doubled in the first two years of our investment and deposits grew strongly, giving it an advantage over many of its peers. These strong initial results made the bank over-optimistic, and it decided to expand from its Far Eastern base into the European regions of Russia, where it was way behind other banks. In hindsight it grew too rapidly, and the new customers it acquired outside its home regions had lower incomes and excessive debt compared to Vostochny's older customers.

CEO Vlasov had many positive characteristics, including decisiveness, a deep knowledge of the sector, and the type of personality that could bulldoze through most obstacles. But he was such a strong micro-manager that he didn't listen to colleagues or create the kind of teamwork necessary for success in a complex, cyclical industry. He wasn't fast enough at responding to new data or signals from the market. We pushed for the recruitment of new specialists able to highlight problem areas and head off trouble, but it was not enough to reverse the downward trend under Vlasov.

There was another problem, too. In the period 2010–11, the bank repurchased a portion of its own shares from an existing shareholder. The intention was to re-sell them at a profit to new investors in 2012, when the bank planned to raise its next round of new capital. But the sale was postponed in 2012 due to market conditions, so management needed an alternative plan to avoid losing the value of the shares from its capital and falling into regulatory problems. Their solution was to agree a sale-repurchase arrangement (REPO), a common financing mechanism in the banking industry globally. Vostochny would sell the shares it had previously re-acquired to the independent bank in return for cash. Meanwhile, the independent bank had a guarantee that Vostochny would buy back the shares in the future at an agreed price. At that stage, Vostochny could then sell them on, as originally planned, to new investors.

However, more trouble was brewing. By 2013, economic conditions had taken a turn for the worse, and many of the bank's loans were showing losses. Vlasov decided to refocus business back to the familiar Far East, but even here the quality of new loans worsened. The bank's planned share sale was repeatedly postponed, requiring new REPO arrangements to be made. The last of these, in late 2014, was with Broker Credit Service (BCS), a leading Russian brokerage firm. That November, we and other Vostochny shareholders decided the only solution to the bank's ills was to fire Vlasov and fundamentally change the management. He was replaced by Alexey Kordichev, a risk management specialist, who quickly grasped the scope of the problems and seemed to have the right approach to solving them. Now burdened by substantial losses, the bank needed to raise capital urgently. With too little time to attract new investors, Vostochny launched a share offering targeted at existing shareholders. But Baring Vostok ended up as almost the only shareholder willing and able to invest, and so in 2015 our funds became the bank's majority shareholder.

We now learned more about the arrangement with BCS, as none of Baring Vostok's staff had been involved in negotiating the original deal. Plans were in place to arrange a sale of the shares that would see BCS paid off in a two-year time frame, allowing for the bank's capital requirements to be met. But more bad luck dogged Vostochny. In the summer of 2015, the Russian Central Bank announced a change in regulations regarding securities holdings that resulted in BCS demanding early repayment of 2.5 billion roubles – equal to about $35 million at the time – from Vostochny under the share repurchase agreement. That November, BCS instructed Vostochny that the money was to be paid by 11 December, or else Vostochny would lose the collateral put up for the deal, Eurobonds worth more than 5 billion roubles, or two times more than the amount to be repaid. At this point, Baring Vostok was well within its rights to simply walk away and leave Vostochny's management to sort out the mess, but the likely consequences of losing the collateral would be bankruptcy and a loss of the bank's licence. A disaster for shareholders, bondholders, depositors and other stakeholders alike. So, we stayed and committed to the battle to keep Vostochny afloat.

Attempts to renegotiate the deal with BCS got nowhere. Our funds had already reached their exposure limit to a single company, so we had no ability to invest further in Vostochny without additional investor approvals, which would be very time-consuming. We were also involved in productive negotiations with several investors interested in buying Vostochny outright, but none of these discussions could be concluded in time. So, Kordichev and his chief financial officer, Konstantin Rogov, came up with a Plan B. Would PKB, one of our fund's other portfolio companies, be willing to borrow funds from the bank on a temporary basis, using them to repay the bank's obligations to BCS? PKB had a long-standing commercial relationship with Vostochny as both an active buyer of loan portfolios and a partner helping with loan collections. If Vostochny made a loan to a creditworthy third party like PKB, that in turn paid the money to BCS, the amount lent to PKB would remain an asset until it was repaid. This would buy time to either sell Vostochny to a deeper-pocketed buyer, or to secure new capital that would then be used to settle the PKB loan.

The deal was okayed by the PKB board. Meanwhile, talks were under way with J&T, a bank from Czech Republic, and Sovcom, a larger Russian bank, about buying out Vostochny. We expected that this would see the PKB loan repaid in 2016.

The bank went ahead with the 2.5-billion-rouble loan to PKB, which used the proceeds to repay BCS, who then returned to the bank the 5 billion roubles of Eurobonds held as collateral. Disaster had been averted, for the time being at least. Negotiations with J&T, Sovcom and other buyers continued in 2016, with the PKB loan disclosed as a debt that needed to be repaid as part of any sale agreement. It was around now, as talks dragged on, that a new potential bidder appeared. Uniastrum (UNI) was a small Russian corporate and retail bank, about half the size of Vostochny by assets, that had until recently been owned by Bank of Cyprus. In 2015, Bank of Cyprus had sold Uniastrum to Artem Avetisyan, a young but well-connected Russian businessman. When I met him in May 2016, he initially came across as a charming, confident, persuasive character who made decisions quickly. His right-hand man and junior partner was Sherzod Yusupov, a details guy who structured all the transactions and led most negotiations.

As we had done with everyone else, we proposed a simple transaction to sell part or all of Vostochny to UNI for cash, and made sure to specifically disclose details of the PKB loan and its need to be repaid within the terms of any deal. But after a few meetings, UNI suggested a different deal structure: a merger of Vostochny and UNI, with repayment of the PKB loan by receipt of shares in a brokerage and fund management company. Given Vostochny's branch network and huge retail customer base, Yusupov argued that the bank could sell mutual funds and other brokerage products to Vostochny's customers and immediately increase the scale, and value, of any fund management company it acquired. This would also generate valuable commission income for the bank. It was a plausible idea and we agreed to consider it, if an attractive target company could be identified.

We understood the obvious motivation for Avetisyan and Yusupov to want a merger: they could secure a stake in the combined company without needing to invest more cash. But we could see a logic from our perspective, too. Assuming UNI's reported capital figures – which showed a surplus of approximately 8 billion roubles – were accurate, Vostochny's capital adequacy problems would be solved at a stroke. If we could stay as a shareholder in the combined bank instead of exiting immediately, the rising profits of Vostochny's new consumer loan portfolio would eventually enable us to sell the combined bank at a higher price, probably recouping our fund's huge costs, and perhaps even earning a profit. Moreover, there was obvious synergy for Vostochny in acquiring a business in the Russian fund management sector. With all this in mind, we decided to explore the merger idea seriously. Yusupov took the lead in searching for potential acquisitions in the fund management and brokerage sectors, in order to settle the PKB loan in-kind.

Ahead of the merger, Baring Vostok appointed KPMG and Uniastrum appointed Ernst & Young to analyse each bank based on its detailed list of assets and liabilities as of 31 May 2016. As a result of this process, we agreed on a shareholding split for the combined bank in which Vostochny's shareholders would have 60 per cent of the total, and UNI's 40 per cent. We agreed that UNI would have an option to buy an additional 10 per cent of the bank, subject to some other conditions, including UNI's help in raising further capital for the bank.

During these negotiations, Avetisyan presented us with a letter that he had sent, on behalf of UNI, to President Putin outlining the need for a large new bank in Russia to focus on small and medium-sized enterprises (SMEs). He emphasized that UNI was seeking merger and acquisition partners to fill this gap, and at the bottom of the letter, Putin had scribbled: 'I support.' Rather than making us more enthusiastic about the merger, as Avetisyan intended, this letter only added to our nerves. Having presidential support might seem like a good thing in an authoritarian country like Russia, but it created risks of negative consequences if the new bank failed to deliver on what was promised. Small business lending is always risky and requires specialised expertise. We simply didn't believe our combined bank would have the competence to successfully lend money to small businesses, regardless of the level of state support. Avetisyan was very reassuring, saying that he agreed that lending money to SMEs was too hazardous, but that providing other banking services to them was still attractive. Avetisyan also claimed that with such high-level state support, the Central Bank would surely take a kindly view of our newly combined bank and perhaps ease the pressure on capital requirements. But, in fact, our team was hearing quite the reverse – that the Central Bank, with its reputation as one of the few truly independent regulators in Russia, took a dim view of UNI's balance sheet and lending practices.

A colleague and I met with Avetisyan and Yusupov for lunch at Madame Wong, a Chinese restaurant near our office. We sat outside on the terrace, with trendy young Muscovites walking cheerfully past us on the street, enjoying Moscow's warm summer weather at its finest. Our concerns about UNI's loan portfolio needed to be addressed before we would agree to go ahead with the merger. We wanted an assurance that if the Central Bank demanded further capital increases due to bad loans or asset write-downs on UNI's balance sheet, then both sides would commit to renegotiate the merger terms. Avetisyan agreed to this and our general counsel noted it in writing.

Still, not everyone at Baring Vostok was convinced about the merger and it fell to me to make the final decision. We were under intense time pressure from the Central Bank. Based on the latest trends, I was confident that Vostochny's new loan portfolios would generate big profits in a year or two, more than enough to fully recapitalise the bank on its own. But in the meantime, the need to increase Vostochny's capital was pressing, and we had no authority to invest further capital into Vostochny from the funds ourselves. A deal with someone was unavoidable. Taking all these factors into account, I decided to go ahead with the merger.

Of all the decisions I made in my thirty-year career, this merger had by far the most disastrous consequences.

15

Red Flags

Doing nothing wasn't an option if the bank was to remain solvent. In truth, all we really wanted from the deal was time. We believed that Vostochny was a sound business on an upward trajectory. We just needed breathing room to see the full fruits of this success. We didn't need UNI's business to deliver massive profits, just as long as it didn't start immediately producing big losses. We'd gone into the merger knowing that one of their major assets, a land holding in the town of Stupino in the Moscow region, was over-valued. But we were confident we could weather that being written down even to zero, if necessary.

Alexey Kordichev was made CEO of the newly merged bank, and a necessary streamlining of staff and branches was negotiated between Vostochny and UNI. We also agreed a broad division of labour among shareholders, with Baring Vostok's team taking the lead on monitoring the bank's retail portfolio, and Finvision (as Avetisyan's holding company was now known) monitoring the bank's corporate and small business loan portfolio. Despite all the obstacles Vostochny had faced up to that point, it felt like we had stabilised the situation and I looked forward to a period of relative quiet. For a few blissful months, until roughly mid-2017, this is what happened.

Sadly, though, it was all too good to be true. That summer, my colleagues started to hear from the bank's management that there were problems in UNI's corporate loan portfolio, much worse than had been disclosed or expected. We already knew about Stupino, but we'd entered into the merger believing that all the loans and investments made by UNI were at least genuine. Now, we discovered that many of their corporate loans or investments involved fundamental conflicts of interest, often to the benefit of Avetisyan, Modulbank (another bank affiliated to him), and Avetisyan's friends.

For a few months, we hoped to negotiate compensation for our funds for the damage caused by these undisclosed deals. But talks soon fell apart. Yusupov insisted each loan and investment made by UNI was high quality and argued that any overdue loan repayments were caused by Vostochny's decision to cease lending new money to those borrowers after they had defaulted. That's a common refrain, of course, from borrowers who don't repay their debts on time. But eventually, even Yusupov had to concede that adjustments to our original merger deal were needed to achieve fairness. After several meetings, an agreement in principle was struck with Yusupov that Baring Vostok Funds would receive a payment of between 2 to 4 billion roubles, payable from the proceeds of a future sale of the bank.

That October, I celebrated my 50th birthday with a big party at my UK home in Surrey, outside of London. Friends and business partners from Russia joined together with many of my friends from Britain, America, and elsewhere. Avetisyan and his wife were among them; I had invited him several months earlier, before we knew that he had deceived us about UNI. We anyway still viewed the situation as redeemable, as long as the performance of the bank's core retail business continued to improve, and shareholders would not be required to pump in further capital.

Meanwhile, Finvision served notice that Avetisyan wanted to exercise his call option for 10 per cent of the bank, only to then withdraw the notice. This happened a couple of times, for reasons we didn't fully understand, but most likely related to trouble obtaining Central Bank approval for him to become Vostochny's majority shareholder.

Then, in January 2018, the Central Bank took matters out of our hands and initiated steps to revoke Vostochny's licence, mainly because of the losses from UNI's weak loan portfolio. Avetisyan reached out to me and my colleagues, urging us to take immediate steps to avert this disaster. There was no doubt this was an existential threat to the bank. He and Yusupov pleaded that Baring Vostok send a letter to the Central Bank indicating our willingness to invest 5 billion roubles of new capital into Vostochny. We promptly did this, which was enough to persuade the Central Bank to halt the licence revocation. But, as part of this decision, the Central Bank demanded a detailed audit of the combined bank that would conclude, once and for all, how much of the loan portfolio, and which loans specifically, needed to be written off.

As soon as the immediate threat of losing our licence receded, Avetisyan changed tack yet again. He told me that the share issue we'd promised the Central Bank was 'just PR' and we didn't actually need to go through with it. Instead, Finvision submitted a new notice to exercise its 10 per cent option and take control of the bank. Obviously, we viewed the situation very differently. Firstly, you don't give a direct undertaking to a regulator unless you intend to fulfil it. But we were also convinced that the Central Bank audit would result in an increased capital requirement for our bank, entirely because of undisclosed problems with UNI's old loan portfolio. I told Avetisyan that we needed a fundamental renegotiation to reflect this, solving how best to secure the bank's future and how Baring Vostok's funds should be compensated. The question of the 10 per cent option also needed reviewing, but he was insistent that he be allowed to purchase his additional 10 per cent on exactly the same terms before sitting down to discuss the other issues.

Several of my colleagues were by now pushing to let the London Court of International Arbitration (LCIA) sort things out, but I hesitated. It would inevitably be costly and would bring our problems into the public sphere, which could cause a rush of customers to withdraw their deposits. In March 2018, I attended a meeting of Vostochny's management board, hopeful that perhaps my colleagues were exaggerating the scale of the problems faced by the bank. I was soon disabused of that notion. The UNI portfolio was full of loans that were either already in default or within days of going into default – many of them involving associates of Avetisyan. Looking at the numbers, I was staggered. Roughly 50 per cent of UNI's entire corporate loan portfolio appeared irredeemably impaired. Even in times of severe economic crisis and recession, rarely do banks suffer losses on more than 20 per cent of their corporate loans, and there was no economic crisis in Russia at that time. We had used KPMG to check UNI's corporate loan portfolio carefully prior to the merger, and we didn't have big surprises from their loans made prior to June 2016. But the total size of UNI's corporate loan and investment assets had increased one-and-a-half-fold from June to August 2016 – precisely the three-month window between our due diligence cut-off date and the signing of the merger. Such a dramatic expansion was not only in breach of our legal agreements, it was also irrational and logistically impossible in such a short space of time – unless it was part of a carefully orchestrated scheme. Almost 100 per cent of these loans and investments were now described by members of the bank's management board as essentially hopeless. There was an unmistakable conclusion: many of these transactions were designed specifically to transfer cash out of UNI right before the merger.

I am told by friends and colleagues that I have extraordinary patience, probably to a fault. But sitting through that management board meeting, I finally 'lost it'. I was sure now that we had been deceived on a massive scale by Avetisyan and Yusupov. When I asked how it was possible for any bank to make so many bad loans in such a short time, I was met only with shrugs. I instructed my colleagues to go ahead with filing a claim with the LCIA to invalidate Finvision's call option and to seek damages over the UNI transactions.

When the notice of our LCIA claim reached his team, there was radio silence for several days. I think they were shocked that we were actually going to take action to enforce our rights. Their strategy was immediately to look at how they might counter-claim – a means, I believe, simply to create leverage so we would drop our claims. They began by seeking 9 billion roubles in damages arising from the post-merger firing of UNI employees. Not a transaction at all, and not an event from which we derived any benefit. But Yusupov argued that the problems in UNI's former corporate loan portfolio arose solely because 'competent employees from UNI' had been made redundant. In fact, the process had been entirely consensual and agreed with

UNI's top management, including by Yusupov himself. The UNI redundancies were only in their retail banking division, so as not to double up in an area where Vostochny had a stronger existing team. The corporate banking group of UNI, which was the source of all the problem loans, was untouched after the merger, even though in hindsight we should have sacked them all immediately. In any event, it is a borrower's obligation to repay a loan from a bank, even if the bank had no employees. To blame us for the failure of UNI's borrowers to make good on their debts was absurd.

There were other smaller transactions that they professed to have suddenly 'discovered', despite them having been included in our Disclosure Letter prior to merger, suitably accounted for in the official merger calculations, and having never been questioned until the filing of our LCIA claim. One of these transactions concerned the PKB–IFTG settlement, even though Yusupov himself proposed IFTG as an acquisition target, and participated in negotiating the acquisition. Like the French police captain in the classic film, *Casablanca*, he now claimed to be 'shocked ... shocked!' about IFTG.

That summer was tense as the conflict raged on, though mostly out of public sight as both sides wanted to avoid bad press for the bank. There were attempts by the Finvision board members to call meetings without us, and Yusupov and his henchmen tried to persuade the Russian Interior Ministry (MVD) to initiate a criminal investigation into the PKB–IFTG transactions. After a couple of months of looking into it, the MVD decided that there was no criminality and abandoned the case. I remember talking to Baring Vostok's head of security, an ex-colonel in the FSO, the influential entity responsible for security of the President and presidential offices. I asked whether he thought there was a risk of an all-out raid against us or something similar. He replied: 'This isn't 1937,' referring to the infamous year of Stalin's Soviet terror. He said that in Russia in 2018 he didn't think it was conceivable that representatives of a reputable foreign investor could be arrested without an opportunity to put their side of the story first. Some of my contacts in the Russian government separately described Avetisyan as a minor figure, and encouraged us to stand our ground and not be intimidated.

Even so, we continued attempts to reach a compromise, mainly because we didn't want a loud public conflict that would cause further problems for the Bank. Along with my colleague, Vagan Abgaryan, I agreed to meet Avetisyan and Yusupov at the high-end Selfie Restaurant on Novinsky Boulevard. It proved to be a disconcerting experience. Some workers were meant to be carrying out repairs that day to the roof insulation of my apartment building. Instead, the roof caught fire, just above my apartment. When I heard about it, I raced to the building, watching in horror as flames engulfed the top two floors, exactly where my apartment was. Firefighters were still struggling to contain the inferno when I had to leave the scene to go to our meeting. The two contractors, both hailing from Belarus, promptly fled the country, making good their escape before the police had a chance to question them. When I got to the restaurant, still flustered, Yusupov was quick to say, 'That had nothing to do with us.'

With my nerves frayed, the discussion that followed was both tense and surreal. Sat amid a sea of blissfully happy diners in one of Moscow's trendiest restaurants, Avetisyan held to his line that he either wanted control of the bank, or he wanted out. He suggested a 'two-envelope divorce' procedure, where one of us names a price at which he is willing to buy out the other, and the other side can either sell, or buy, at that price. I told him that I would be very happy to divorce, but I didn't believe he had the money to buy us out. While we waited for him to prove otherwise, I favoured a new share issue, as promised to the Central Bank, and shared control of the bank until it could be sold. Avetisyan still had no appetite for such an issue, since it would result in him permanently losing the ability to obtain a controlling stake.

The discussion got increasingly heated, and I told him that we had reached an unresolvable impasse. As things were going, I thought it likely that the Central Bank would put the bank into bankruptcy. While that would be bad for all the shareholders, I pointed out that he had the most to lose. 'For our fund,' I reminded him, 'this investment is less than 10 per cent of our assets, so we will survive. It is a much bigger asset for you, so you should think carefully before exposing the bank to this potential disaster.'

He was visibly enraged by my words, his face red as he snarled across the table: 'I will destroy your entire fund! You think this will just affect your investment in the bank, but you're wrong! I will use all my resources to destroy your entire fund!'

I looked him in the eye. 'Artem, once your friends in government see what you did at UNI, none of them will support you.'

Vagan Abgaryan tried to get us back on track. He suggested that we defer any decision about the share issue and Finvision's option until the Central Bank had completed its audit, and suggested some adjustments to the potential exit mechanisms for our fund. None of us were entirely convinced by what was on offer, but after an hour or so we were at least closer to an agreement than we had been. Vagan ordered four glasses of whiskey and proposed a toast. The rest of us drank sullenly as, around us, cheerful young Moscovites enjoyed their dinners. Then, when I turned in my chair to say something to the waiter, out of the corner of my eye I saw Avetisyan pouring some of his whiskey into my glass, so he wouldn't have to drink it. Only a truly slippery person would do that, I thought.

That July and August, there were further discussions to hammer out terms, but there was always some reason or another to prevent agreement. Then the Central Bank concluded its audit that August, and its conclusions were damning. It demanded the bank create an additional 19.5 billion roubles of reserves for loan losses, of which 17 billion were related to former UNI loans and investments. Moreover, the report categorised several UNI loans as 'schemes for asset stripping' from the bank. The 1,000-plus-page document almost entirely validated the claims we had made against Finvision and Avetisyan in our LCIA filings. Although we still felt very strongly about the damages caused by UNI, saving the bank was our top priority. We managed to negotiate a deal with the Central Bank that they would allow the 19.5 billion in reserves to be absorbed over a couple years, rather than immediately, on the condition that the bank raised 5 billion rouble of capital from shareholders. In September, a 'peace agreement' among all the warring parties was signed, calling for this 5 billion increase to be completed not later than December 2018. Various other disputed provisions were also ironed out, and it could be considered a true compromise, since both sides felt disappointed with the overall outcome. We remained on alert but it seemed, finally, like the big crisis was averted.

The ink was barely dry on the peace agreement when Avetisyan tried to renegotiate again. In November 2018, he asked to meet me for breakfast at Coffeemania on Kutuzovsky Prospect. He told me everything was still agreed and going according to plan, except for 'one final issue'. His ability to pay his 2.5 billion rouble share of the capital increase depended on him selling Modulbank, which was taking longer than expected. He asked for my support to persuade the Central Bank to extend the share issue deadline by four months, until April 2019. If we could agree this one final revision, he assured me, then it was full-steam ahead. I was angry and frustrated by yet another renegotiation, but it seemed like a minor concession, so I reluctantly agreed.

We met once more with the Central Bank's top management, including chairwoman Elvira Nabiullina, at their headquarters on Neglinnaya Street, an imposing nineteenth-century building in the centre of Moscow. Nabiullina and her colleagues were, understandably, very suspicious and opposed any postponement of the capital increase. I explained that the peace agreement was fragile and the consequences would be disastrous for everyone, including the Central Bank, if conflict resumed and Vostochny had to be nationalised. I suggested that Baring Vostok funds could deposit 5 billion roubles in cash with the Central Bank by December, and this 5 billion would automatically be applied in full to Vostochny's capital increase in April in the event that Avetisyan wasn't able to come up with his 2.5 billion. The Central Bank could rest assured that the capital increase was fully funded and 100 per cent certain. Nabiullina looked Avetisyan squarely in the eye and asked him, 'If you don't come up with your share of the money, you agree it goes ahead anyway and you will be diluted?' Avetisyan nodded his assent. It was just enough to convince the sceptical Central Bank, and Avetisyan left elated. We went for tea at the Bosco café in Petrovsky Passage, just across the street from the Central Bank building, to discuss the next steps. He thanked me repeatedly for saving the situation, and said that I had acted like a real partner. I was still very cautious and deeply distrusted our 'partners', but for once, we all left in good spirits.

Just two days later, Avetisyan and Yusupov asked to meet for lunch, back at Madame Wong. There were more expressions of gratitude, but before the appetizers arrived at our table, they made yet another attempt to renegotiate what had just been agreed. This time, they objected to the proposed share price of the capital increase. Rather than 1 kopek per share, as had been agreed in writing and was in line with previous share issues, they wanted it set two times higher. Their motivation was obvious – to make sure their holding was diluted as little as possible. My blood started to boil. Even in the face of an extra 19.5 billion roubles in losses for problems that *they* had mostly created, they wanted to tip the deal even further in their favour. It had been hard enough to convince our fund's investors to put any more money into Vostochny as it was. Besides, just how many more 'final issues' would there be?

Yusupov responded that he still wasn't sure that the share issue was needed at all. If we didn't keep pressing the matter, he said, it was possible that the Central Bank wouldn't insist on it. I almost choked on my food. 'What planet are you on!?!' I asked. 'Weren't you at the same meeting that I was two days ago?' My patience entirely spent, I simply got up and left, telling them that they were the most unreliable negotiating partners I had worked with in my twenty-five years of investing. I had better things to do, I told them, than to waste my time on people who can't stick to their agreements. I walked out of the restaurant as they continued shouting threats in my direction.

There was an exchange of letters in December, proposing different paths forward, but no progress and no direct contact. After the long Russian New Year holidays, Yusupov and I both attended a routine Vostochny board meeting at the end of January, but Avetisyan did not. Afterwards, Yusupov reluctantly agreed to a brief chat. We walked to his spacious office, and sat at his ornate wood conference table. He seemed nervous and didn't make eye contact. I said that we still wanted to avoid a shareholder conflict that would inevitably damage us both. Yusupov listened, but said that he couldn't respond without Avetisyan. I asked when Avetisyan would be available, Yusupov told me he wasn't in Moscow, but would be back in a couple of weeks. OK, I said, let me know when he returns.

Shortly afterwards, Yusupov confirmed by WhatsApp that Avetisyan would be in Moscow on 14 February. He suggested dinner that evening, and I changed my plans to ensure I could fly to Moscow specifically for the meeting. On the 12th, he reached out again, asking if I was already in town. I replied that I had just arrived, and reconfirmed for dinner on the 14th.

I had no idea of the treachery that was to be unleashed against me in a little over twenty-four hours' time.

16

Dropped Keys

The boardroom antics of my enemies continue while I am stuck here in cell 604. On Monday, 1 April – April Fool's Day, no less! – I get news that my accusers are taking court action to block the Vostochny Bank's share release and to seize the disputed option shares. It is an outrageous violation of all our merger agreements and breaks the promises we made to the Central Bank. They have filed their papers with a court in Blagoveshchensk in the Russian Far East, and judging from the court's speedy response, it looks like it has predetermined to side with them. Meanwhile, we have our complaint going through the London Court of International Arbitration and our main hope rests with getting a High Court injunction in the UK. Even if we are granted one, I expect the Russian court will probably ignore it, but there's a reasonable chance that Avetisyan and Yusupov won't want to put themselves in contempt of a British court and therefore subject to European arrest orders. On instructions from my advocates, I fill out some detailed voting instructions for an upcoming Vostochny board meeting regarding the pair's attempt at a company takeover, even though I know they will likely refuse to recognise the instructions as valid. But by submitting the paperwork, we will at least have grounds for a future challenge.

Tuesday brings better news, or rather rumours of better things to come. My advocate has heard whispers that I might be released from SIZO to 'house arrest' at my next custody extension hearing next week. He cautions me several times that it is just a rumour, and could easily be false. He even raises the prospect that it may be a psychological warfare tactic aimed at lifting my hopes, only to shatter them on the day of the hearing. He doesn't really need to temper my expectations. Given everything that has happened already, including yesterday's news from the court in Blagoveshchensk, it takes a lot for me to feel any optimism about our case. I have no idea what might be going on in the higher circles of power where this type of decision is likely be made. I am certainly not counting any chickens. But I am buoyed by a letter I receive from my great and loyal friend Oleg Tinkov, head of the eponymous bank. He's a truly unique individual – crazy, brilliant, emotional and full of zest for life. Reading his letter of support gave me a boost of energy.

Wednesday comes around, with its regular routine. But then something curious happens. I am on my way back from the *banya* with the other inmates of 604, when one of the *prodolni* (corridor guards) drops his keys as he is escorting us back to the cell. They hit the floor with a resounding clang, and I notice Big Sasha immediately freeze. He looks straight at me, signalling with his fingers to be silent. Then he nods with his eyes closed, as if to say, wait a minute and I will tell you something important. We get back to the cell and the guards leave, at which point he excitedly regales me with an old superstition among Russian prisons: when a prisoner is going to be freed, one of the guards drops his keys on the ground as a sort of secret signal. I would have thought he was totally crazy had I not heard the same rumour from my advocate just this morning. It is certainly enough to make me think.

This evening at dinner, someone jokes about how cool it would be to open a prison-themed restaurant in the middle of Moscow. It could be called *Hata* (Russian slang for a prison cell) and we'd decorate it like 604, with towels and clothes drying everywhere on ropes made from our stretched-out trash bags. There'd be a *dubok* for the dining table, while the food would be cooked on a copy of our quirky steaming device, and served in rubber dishes and cups. A sort of nod to the dacha-themed *Mari Vanna* restaurants, but catering more for ex-convicts! Sanych volunteers to be head chef. The human Swiss Army knife would be perfect for the job, and could double as the technical repairman for all the restaurant's equipment. The idea delights us. Today has been a much better day than yesterday, I think to myself, capped by my receiving five new letters – two from my friends Leonid Boguslavsky and Oliver Hughes, two from Julia, and one from my boy Mishuta. In his note, written in Russian, he updates me on his university progress, and then tells me his views about some of my favourite books that he is now reading. He says how much he misses our conversations and how much only now he appreciates the values I always talked to him about. The letter concludes simply, '*Ti moi geroi*' ('You are my hero'). The pride I feel reading his words brings tears to my eyes.

★ ★ ★

My detention hearing is scheduled for the 10th, and the day before I have a meeting in the late afternoon with one of my advocates. He tells me that the Investigative Committee has formally confirmed their recommendation that I be moved out of prison and put under house arrest. But there is not such good news for my Baring Vostok colleagues, who are still to be kept in SIZO. I have mixed emotions for the rest of the day. Of course, I am overjoyed by the prospect of getting out and being able to see my family again, but I am still suspicious that this may yet be a psychological ruse, and that tomorrow the court will rule that I am to continue to be detained. I wonder how my status as an American and as the central figure in what has become a *cause célèbre* might influence the court's decisions as well. Are these my trump cards that ensure I avoid a fate similar to the one I have witnessed Andrey so recently suffer? Or does being a high-profile Westerner up the stakes? Could I be entirely unaware of other sub-plots playing out? Doubt wracks me, but the 604 guys are much more confident. Big Sasha references the dropped keys in the corridor again, as if it is irrefutable proof that I will be leaving prison. I am worried that some of them might be jealous of my potential good fortune, or that it will highlight their own grim prospects of long sentences. But I detect no signs of bitterness; they seem genuinely happy for me.

My thoughts turn to the other Baring Vostok prisoners. I wonder whether I should refuse my release unless they are granted theirs, too. But my advocates strongly advise against taking such a stance. They say it would likely backfire, serving as a provocation to the authorities, whereas my release might serve as a signal that the 'system' wants to de-escalate the dispute and find a negotiated solution for all of us. An opportunity, they argue, that I shouldn't refuse. They point out too that to refuse may well discourage our many Russian supporters who have lobbied on our behalf. What would be their reason to continue to put themselves out for us if we don't accept such hard-won concessions? There is a practical consideration in all this, as well. If I really am released to house arrest, I will have much more scope to help prepare a comprehensive and truly robust legal defence for us all. The logic is unimpeachable. In my mind, I am convinced by their arguments. But in my heart, all of this still does not sit quite right.

As well as seeing my advocates, I also meet with the Ombudsman, Boris Titov. He has been one of our biggest allies since the beginning, and he reiterates today how we have the support of the entire business community. He also confirms that he too has received the same encouraging signals about tomorrow's decision. But he, like me, is reluctant to assume anything, crossing his fingers and rolling his eyes to emphasise that it's not yet a done deal. For my part, I reassure him that I will do nothing to undermine the Russian investment climate as a result of my arrest, not least because it is not in my own interests to do so. This conflict is, or at least should be, a purely commercial dispute, and I have no desire to be an enemy of the Russian system forever.

Altogether, it has been an extraordinary day, and tomorrow may be even more so. My nerves are in a heightened state of tension as I ponder the different scenarios that may yet play out. I do not sleep well, and I get up early. I wash myself in the sink with a hand towel, and shave with a brutal prison-issue 'disposable' razor. The Russian term for these is *odno-razovi*, which translates as 'one-time' razors – a considered description since after you've used it once, you'll have so many nicks and cuts on your face that you'll never willingly use it again. I know I will likely run the gauntlet of photo-journalists at court in a few hours, so I take my time and use all my concentration so as to lose as little blood and flesh as possible.

Then, while the rest of the cell are still asleep, I sit at the *dubok* and write them a note in Russian:

Dear friends from the 604 team!

I came to you seven weeks ago as a 'golyak', with nothing besides the shirt on my back. You fed me, clothed me, embraced me. At a time when I was scared and alone, your basic decency and generosity was incredibly moving. Every one of you is a real 'human human-being'. I will never forget your support for each other, your courage, and your invincible spirit in the face of an unjust system. I hope to meet each of you in freedom, sit together at a dubok in the fresh air, and to drink, laugh, and remember this time we spent together. If I can ever do anything to help you or your families, let me know.

Yours,
Mike

The prison nurse comes by our cell one last time before I leave – the same one who'd told me that they don't give prisoners extra mattresses in Guantanamo. Through the *karmyak*, she leans in and asks after my health. I tell her I have no complaints, and she almost smiles with her eyes, as if to say goodbye. Even Nurse Ratched has a soft side, apparently. Not long afterwards, a voice announces over the speaker that I am to be collected in ten minutes. As I gather my papers, the 604 guys all come to me, giving the usual fist bumps and exclamations of 'God be with you!' But each of them also embraces me with a manly hug. This is not just 'Good luck', but 'Goodbye'. Realising it might be many years before we see each other again, they read my note, and I think they are touched by it.

Before the guards arrive, I remember Pascal's wager – the one that says a rational man is best served by believing in God because he has nothing to lose if God doesn't exist, but everything to gain if he does – and cross myself in front of the icons in the corner of the cell. Then I am handcuffed by the guards and taken into the corridor. The door of cell 604 clangs shut with an emphatic finality. With three rusty metallic twists of his giant keys, the guard locks the thick steel door and marks an ending. But the end of exactly what remains to be seen.

17

Day of Reckoning

I am halfway down the *Psycho*-stairs before I even notice the siren. I recall how its horrible shriek scared me almost to death the first few times I heard it. But now it hardly registers. Another example of man growing accustomed to anything.

The guards lead me outside and I climb into the convoy truck waiting in the courtyard. There are already four prisoners inside, and they all nod towards me, as if they know or recognise me. We wait another ten or fifteen minutes to collect a few others, the last of whom is a Russian billionaire businessman, one of the Magomedov brothers. He has been in Matrosskaya Tishina for a long time already, and knows several of the other guys in the truck from having shared cells with them. He apparently recognises me from TV, saying in English, 'Ah, Calvey! Nice to meet you!'

There is a lot of banter on the truck, the usual mixture of grumbles and jokes, as we make our way to various courts spread throughout Moscow. It's a major logistical exercise. First, we are taken to some kind of central hub, through which hundreds of convoy trucks from all of Moscow's prisons apparently come throughout the day, dropping off prisoners to be loaded on to other trucks, each going directly to one specific court. A Clapham Junction or Frankfurt Airport for those accused of criminality. The next truck on to which I am loaded has a whole new cast of characters. There is just a single cage with two long benches to sit five or six men on either side, all in handcuffs, so close that our knees overlap in the middle. As the cage fills up, we are scrunched into a tight mass, knees and shoulders pressed together. I look around and see that most of these men are not suspects of 'economic crimes' of the type I have been used to. Among them are a couple of tough-looking, heavily tattooed Central Asian men in tracksuits in the far corner, taking up more than their fair share of room, but no one is rushing to sit close to them. What I notice most is the stench that gathers powerfully over the cage. These guys clearly operate to a different standard of prison hygiene.

Then, in this most unlikely of mobile dungeons, someone recognises me. In fact, he introduces himself and proceeds to pitch an investment idea! Like any venture capital investor, I get approaches all the time from aspiring entrepreneurs, but this one is truly hilarious. He earnestly delivers his sixty-second elevator pitch, determined not to miss his chance regardless of the setting, being one of a dozen prisoners handcuffed in a dimly lit cage. I can't stop myself from laughing at the incongruity of it all, but I don't want to discourage a determined young guy with so much chutzpah. So, I tell him that it sounds like a great idea, but it's really not the best place to discuss it. He apologises for his lack of business cards, and expresses his hope that we can speak again 'in freedom'. What a great country, I think! Such spirited people never cease to amaze me.

At Basmanny Court, I hear the sound of dozens of cameras furiously clicking away as I get off the truck and am led into the building. It's a bright, sunny spring day, but I am quickly deposited into one of the dreary underground holding cells, where another prisoner already lies asleep on the bench. It's obviously been a busy day at Basmanny already, and they are having to double up in the cells. The sleeping man wears an old, frayed Adidas tracksuit, with his hood pulled over his eyes, so I cannot see his face. He doesn't notice my arrival and shows no signs of stirring. After about an hour, I am led up to the courtroom, and this time I am better prepared for the overwhelming assault of camera lights and whirring shutters that capture the moment. The guards take off my handcuffs and lock me in a glass bubble cage, from where I will learn the direction of the next phase of my life.

The hearing is short. The investigator stands and announces that they have revised their recommendation. Instead of detention in SIZO, they are happy for me to be detained under house arrest. This change of heart apparently stems from unexpected intelligence they have received in recent weeks about my 'extensive ties to Russia', including ownership of an apartment in Moscow, about my 'social connections' in the country, and my 'charitable activities'. I want to ask, but of course do not, how it is possible that they didn't know all of this before I was arrested. Instead, I make a short statement, reconfirming my innocence, restating that the charges against me are motivated by a shareholder conflict, and promising to abide by any court restrictions so that my release to house arrest poses no risks to the ongoing investigation. My final words are to confirm that, despite my personal situation, I still believe in the investment potential of Russia. The judge calls for a recess, and retires to his chambers to prepare his decision. It feels like a well-rehearsed performance with a pre-determined outcome, but I am still suspicious and make sure to keep my mental 'suit of armour' on.

Even before the judge returns, a couple of new guards in different uniforms appear in the courtroom. These are officers from the FSIN, the 'federal service for implementation of punishment' – basically, officers from the Russian prison services who are a hybrid of court marshals and parole officers. Then the judge returns and, after the usual preliminaries, bluntly announces his verdict. Sure enough, I am to be released to house arrest. There is no nasty last-minute surprise. The guards unlock my cage and I am led, uncuffed, out of the court by FSIN officers. There is a loud buzz of energy in the crowded corridor outside. I can make out scattered applause and shouts of '*Malodyets!*' ('Good job!') and 'We are with you!' As the journalists' cameras snap their images, I raise one arm in the air as a gesture of gratitude for the support I have received, and as a signal of my determination to keep fighting to prove my innocence. The FSIN officers briefly take me downstairs into the holding area, where I wait to be processed. I ask a guard if it is like this often. He thinks for a moment, then says: 'Yes, in terms of journalists, but no, in terms of anyone getting released to go home.'

Before leaving, we have to go back upstairs to collect the paperwork confirming the court's decision. Only a few people remain in the corridor, but among them are a couple of Baring Vostok colleagues, who smile and rush to greet me. I hug them but immediately caution that today is not a cause for celebration. Victory will only be when all of our colleagues are home with their families. That's when I hear a woman sobbing nearby. I turn to her and see it's Nina, the wife of my colleague, Ivan Zyuzin, who is still being detained. Nina and Ivan have four young children, the youngest just an infant. I hadn't seen her earlier, but she is relieved to hear my words about victory not yet secured. I tell her that we will do everything possible to reunite all of our colleagues with their families, and that none of us will rest until it's achieved.

I am now taken to the car of one of the FSIN officers and he drives me to my apartment. I learn that he is from Dagestan in Russia's Caucasus region. He's a decent guy, and we talk about our families and other ordinary things. Only, none of it feels ordinary. To be back in the outside world, with no handcuffs, sitting in the front seat of a regular car, listening to the radio while driving to my apartment – it is completely extraordinary.

I have not actually ever properly lived in my apartment. I was about to move in back in 2018 when it mysteriously caught fire just prior to my meeting with Avetisyan and Yusupov. The inferno had destroyed the entire roof and top floor, including my apartment, and the resulting refit was finished just weeks ago. When I arrive at the apartment building, there are two FSB *operativniks* there to greet me. I recognise one from the original search of my apartment on 14 February. They tell me they have already visited my new apartment a few days ago to check it out and install equipment. I barely hold back a sarcastic response, 'Thank you very much, I always wanted some FSB monitoring devices in my apartment.' Now they escort me to my front door and open it. I am at once thrilled and slightly embarrassed (especially in front of the *operativniks*) to discover that my Baring Vostok colleagues arrived a few hours earlier to fill the place with hundreds of 'Welcome home!' balloons.

The FSB and FSIN guys fit me with an ankle bracelet and run through the rules of my house arrest. The equipment they have already put into place will monitor me in both video and audio formats. I have to sign a document confirming that I do not object to such surveillance, which rather takes me aback. I am not surprised to learn that I will be so comprehensively monitored – I have been fully expecting it – but the openness with which they discuss it and their request for written consent comes as a shock. They also explain that I am not allowed any form of internet in the apartment, and no communication is permitted with anyone besides my advocates and my family. One of my advocates, Dmitry Savochkin, arrives and asks if I can have a mobile telephone to make calls to those on my approved list, but he is told that this must be approved by the investigator – usually, we are led to believe, a formality. In the meantime, the FSB *operativnik* allows me to use Savochkin's phone to make one call to my family right now, which is an unexpectedly humane gesture. Maybe it's his way – just like with the investigator-major I talked to in prison – of saying: 'Sorry for almost destroying your life, but it isn't anything personal.'

I call Julia, who is currently in the USA with my mom and our youngest son, Niko, touring universities. When she hears my voice, she screams with excitement. I imagine the rest of their tour group cowering, scared half to death. The joy of hearing her, and the voices of Niko and Mom, is indescribable. I want to tell Julia so much, and yet so much is understood even without words. We agree that she will continue the tour with Niko, and then come to Moscow with him straight afterwards. They should be here in six days. The presence of FSB agents definitely stifles conversation, but it cannot diminish the elation of being back in contact with the people I love.

Eventually, the FSB and FSIN guys leave, and I pour a whiskey for me and Savochkin. Not to celebrate, but just to mark the moment. A chance to at last exhale and decompress after eight weeks of extreme stress and confusion. When Savochkin leaves around 8.30 p.m., I go up to my bed and collapse face down in the pillows. A wave of complete mental and physical exhaustion sweeps over me and I am asleep within seconds.

* * *

I rise early the next day. There is yet another procedural hearing in court to attend, to address the question of whether to extend the investigation until 14 July. The outcome is, of course, a foregone conclusion, but I do get my first opportunity to speak to the lead investigator on my case. She is a tough, unemotional woman, quick to anger, and instinctively harsh towards her targets. But there are glimpses of occasional kindness and even a sense of humour. In her packed office at the Investigative Committee, amid overwhelming stacks of paper and several items of Zenit football paraphernalia, a small banner on the wall reads 'Sentence myself ... to Bali' with a painting of a beach and palm tree. Although very experienced and senior in rank (she is a lieutenant colonel), it is obvious that ultimately she is still just a loyal foot soldier and decidedly not the final decision-maker on our case.

After the hearing, she pulls out a transparent folder full of documents. Among the paperwork, I can see my blue US passport. She catches my eyes growing wider, sighs deeply, and flashes a rare smile. It is as if she is coming to terms with the fact that she is about to do something with which she deeply disagrees. In accordance with her instructions, she unzips the folder, takes out my passport, and presses it into my hand. She keeps a grip on it for an extra couple of seconds longer than she needs to, looking me straight in the eye, as if to say: you are a lucky man, but you better not do anything to make me regret this.

Later, she approves a telephone for me but insists that the Investigative Committee check that it isn't internet enabled. She also commands that it must be registered properly in their system, which I understand to mean that it is to be fully monitored. One of my advocates has already purchased an old-style analogue-only phone for me – a vintage one from fifteen or twenty years ago – and hands it over for their approval. It is cleared almost immediately, and when it is given to me, I call my daughter, Sasha. She answers in a hesitant voice, not recognising the caller phone number. I respond by singing the 'Sasha Calvey song', a ditty I made up when she was an infant, which involves repetition of her name in various tones and verses. It's one that I have continued to use through the years, creating a special bond between us. The ice immediately breaks and we both end up crying and laughing, as I catch up with what's been going on in her life and what plans she has for the future. I then call my son, Mishuta, and we also embark on a long, deeply satisfying conversation. He has already heard the news of my release from his mother, so has been expecting my call. He's reached a level of maturity that makes me feel like I can talk to him about anything. I tell him about cell 604, and we ponder the truly invincible spirit of the Russians, especially in the bleakest of circumstances. Then I try to explain the unexpected sense of 'groundedness' and enlightenment I gained from the books I read in prison. Mishuta updates me on his friends, his academic progress, and his plans for the next year. It is so great, an almost unbelievable joy, to simply talk to my family and to be a part of their lives – and they mine – again. It is the wonder of sharing both the grand and small stuff that makes life special.

When I wake up the next day, I am struck by the absolute quiet and stillness in the apartment. It feels so strange. In cell 604, even when everyone else was asleep, there was still that ever-present feeling generated by a mass of human beings trapped in a confined space. There were constant muffled sounds of movement, and noises from the courtyard and the streets beyond. Now, I find the utter silence deafening. Lying alone in bed, I just breathe deeply and take some time to observe my new environs.

I find myself contemplating not only the past two months, but the last fifty years, and marvel at life's strange twists that have brought me to this time and place. Right here, now. Life under house arrest has begun.

SECTION 4

13 APRIL 2019–
14 JANUARY 2022

18

House Arrest

What I quickly come to realise is that living under house arrest is akin to being in Purgatory. An intermediate state that is neither heaven nor hell. Paradise is there, but just barely visible on the horizon and always out of grasp.

Of course, there are positives to being out of prison. My apartment is a comfortable split-level loft, with high ceilings and expansive views of the centre of Moscow on both sides. There is a long, narrow balcony where I stand and fill my lungs with air – not exactly fresh as it hovers above the busy city streets, but still invigorating. Compared to anyone condemned to detention in a Russian SIZO, including my four tormented Baring Vostok colleagues, I am now in unimaginable heaven. But looks can be deceptive.

I had assumed that once I could get out of prison, I would have somehow unlocked the door to real freedom. It is entirely logical to assume that this whole sorry story will come to an end soon. But no matter what I do – whatever compelling new evidence my advocates provide, however many scurrilous allegations we decisively disprove, no matter which new testimonies of support from leading figures in Russian society we receive – none of it seems to bring us closer to liberation. All the while, the prospect of a trial and potential conviction hangs like a Sword of Damocles above not only my head, but above those of my colleagues, too. Truth, facts and justice feel like mere impediments to 'the process'. I may not be incarcerated in 604 any longer, but I am far from being a free man. I am like a goldfish in a small glass bowl, able to swim only in tiny, repetitive circles, and constantly watched on from the outside.

The house arrest restrictions imposed by the Russian criminal justice system are more severe than in many other countries. The sense of isolation is overpowering. I am enormously frustrated by the lack of internet access, and I long for the opportunity to stay in touch with friends via FaceTime, or even just through regular phone calls. I am not allowed to go out even to the supermarket by myself, and the FSB's surveillance devices leave me feeling exposed and paranoid.

By far the best part of house arrest is reuniting with my family. They come in waves, like cavalry reinforcing an embattled garrison. First, direct from the college tour of the States with our oldest son, is Julia, whose arrival prompts tears of joy from both of us, together with my youngest, Nikosha, who nearly breaks my ribs when he hugs me so tightly and for so long. Then a couple of days later, Sasha and Mishka. Too filled with emotion to be able express ourselves in words, we embrace one another, our heads tight together for several powerful moments. Eventually, we have deep and wonderful conversations, not only reconnecting but trying to process, absorb and learn from everything that has happened to me.

After a few weeks together, we decide that the kids should go back to their schools or colleges in the UK and USA. We agree that it is better all round if they just visit during their school holidays. We agree that Julia will stay mostly with them during the regular school terms, because the last thing I want is for my situation to dramatically impact their last years before university. But the result is that I am spending about half of my time under house arrest by myself. I start to feel a bit like Bill Murray's character in *Groundhog Day*. Almost every day starts and ends the same way. Upon waking, I open the curtains and pause for a moment to stare outside, taking in the silent, unchanging Moscow skyline and noticing the slow, inevitable changes of season. Then every night just before bed, I switch off all the lights and stand in silence for five or ten minutes, looking at the familiar twinkling lights of Moscow's old centre. I think back to the opaque windows of 604 that opened no more than 6in – not enough to see anything beyond a narrow slice of the courtyard and the exteriors of the prison buildings opposite. The views that I enjoy up here in my apartment help to give me some mental stability and a sense of normality. But the silence of these moments also makes me feel lonely. Their tranquillity a reminder of how much precious time I am losing in isolation. It is already weeks, and soon it will be months turning into years.

One of the most painful moments comes when I have to miss the college graduation of my oldest son, Mishka, in the USA. Julia is there, of course, and I love seeing the photos of the raucous graduation parties with his friends, but I am deeply bitter about being unable to congratulate him in person. Yet another irreplaceable life moment missed. Around this time, as he is about to embark on his career, he adopts a Twitter handle, '@Telemachus'. It refers to the son of Odysseus, who Homer tells us fought to defend his family from persistent enemies during his father's long absence from their home in Ithaca. The fact that Mishka would make such a reference, and thinks of himself in these terms, makes me cry with pride.

Despite its many challenges, I always keep in mind that house arrest signals a new stage in the case. I am well aware that I would still be in prison if there was not recognition at the highest levels of government that the case against us is a mess. It is a nod to the fact that the Baring Vostok team are 'useful people' who have done a lot of positive things for Russia's economy, and that the accusations levelled at us are manifestly unjust, brought by accusers with serious questions to answer about their own conduct. Nonetheless, the investigators evidently still firmly believe that we are guilty of *something*, even if it's not the thing we are actually accused of. They continue their determined search for some damning evidence of wrongdoing that will allow them to conclude that our arrests were justified all along. They pore over the documents and devices seized in their searches, pressuring witnesses to testify against us in search of something – anything – upon which they can hang their hats.

I decide to retain a new legal advocate, Timofey Gridnev, for the battles to come. He comes recommended by a close American friend and Julia has mentioned him in her letters, too. He is well known as one of Russia's leading criminal defence lawyers, representing clients in many of Russia's most high-profile cases. I am grateful for the work my other advocates have done for me since I've been in SIZO, but Timofey is truly at a different level. I soon come to trust his advice completely and over the many hundreds of hours we spend together, I come to consider him a good friend.

In June, the two of us are preparing documents and evidence for my testimony, as Russia holds its annual St Petersburg International Forum. The SPIEF is a gathering of thousands of businesspeople, journalists and government officials for a three-day conference to promote investment in the country. Long before my arrest, I had registered to attend, as I have done every year, and no one from my office has yet unregistered me. While I remain hidden from public view, a journalist notices my name on the invitation list. At a routine press conference a few days before SPIEF, the journalist asks Dmitry Peskov, Putin's presidential spokesman, if this means that I will be attending. Peskov, whom I have met a couple of times, has clearly not been briefed on the matter. He answers simply that he knows me well and that he will be happy to see me there. His words cause a media sensation, and speculation is rife that Putin himself has approved my attendance. It feels like an important moment.

Coincidentally, we are also marking Baring Vostok's twenty-fifth anniversary this month. Our PR firm, the canny EM Advisors, come up with an idea to hand out 'Baring Vostok 25 Years' lapel pins to anyone at SPIEF willing to wear them. It becomes a viral sign of the support that exists for us, and it's worn by hundreds of attendees, including several of Russia's most prominent business figures and even a couple of government ministers. As SPIEF opens, rumours continue to swirl that I might be attending. Ironically, I am stuck sitting in my apartment, able only to watch coverage of the event on RBC-TV, the twenty-four-hour business news channel. It's surreal to watch a TV programme on which my name is mentioned every ten or fifteen minutes. Putin himself is asked a question about my attendance during the plenary panel of the conference. He answers: 'As long as there is no guilty verdict, everyone is considered innocent, including Mr Calvey.' Then he lays into the security services for their 'unreasonable and sometimes simply illegal interference in the work of businesses'. It's strong stuff, although I understand Peskov has got into trouble with the FSB for his unguarded comments, which have prompted a surge in public support for us and embarrassment for them.

By now, I finally have access to all the emails, files and documents to prepare a full and accurate testimony. It is a revelation, given that I hadn't been directly involved in most of the negotiations about the disputed deals. I had never seen for myself all the underlying source documents and, therefore, hadn't known all the facts. But after a month or so of reviewing thousands of Baring Vostok emails and Vostochny Bank documents, we have a mountain of evidence to support our innocence.

This, however, does not stop the investigators trying every tactic possible to gain an advantage over us. One of my legal team warns me to expect a call to another routine interrogation – not an unusual occurrence. Trips to be probed by the investigators or for preliminary court hearings at least offer the rare opportunity for interaction with the outside world. I forge a particular bond with one of my parole officers. I can tell he is rather disgruntled with his lot in life and sympathetic to my plight. After hearings, he will sometimes park the car we travel in a mile or so from my apartment so that we have an excuse to walk back together, breathing the fresh air. I appreciate his gesture. But when I get to the Investigative Committee headquarters today, I am startled to see Sherzod Yusupov waiting there in the interrogation room, together with the investigator. I am told that we are to have a cross-interrogation, in which both sides get to ask questions of the other. Yusupov is wearing a fashionable Italian jacket and holds a cup from Coffeemania. He shakes my hand and flashes me a smug and passive-aggressive smile.

Yusupov and his lawyer, a cynical fellow called Teplyashin, fire out their questions first, all carefully prepared beforehand. The lead investigator sits to one side of the table, recording the conversation. I think I answer their questions reasonably well, pointing out that Yusupov himself had proposed and approved the deal about which he now accuses us of criminal malpractice. He keeps repeating his claim about flaws in IFTG's articles of association that he says meant their shares were of far less value for the Vostochny Bank than they should have been. He ignores the fact that I wasn't involved in negotiating the deal at all, but that *he* was. That being so, I counter by demanding to know why he proposed and approved the deal in the first place. If there are genuine questions about these articles, why are we being held responsible instead of the companies and individuals actually responsible for them? Not to mention the fact that the articles were immediately amended to remove any questions about the bank's ownership anyway. And if he doubts what the IFTG shares are worth today, why not instruct the bank to try to sell them and see what the market value really is? He tosses this proposal aside, knowing of course that this would prove how profitable the IFTG shares really are for the bank. The sparring continues, even though only one of us knew we were heading into a bout today.

It is a few weeks later when we discover a bombshell hidden in the case materials. Back in 2018, when things were turning nasty at Vostochny, one of my Baring Vostok colleagues started carrying a recording device to some of his meetings with Yusupov. I didn't know about this at the time, but apparently my colleague thought they might someday be useful – and how right he was! That October, we had been immersed in meetings with the Central Bank to finalise agreement on the Vostochny Bank's so-called 'financial recovery plan'. It was at one of our pre-meeting get-togethers that Yusupov admitted to my colleague that he had raised questions with the Central Bank about IFTG 'only because of the shareholder conflict'. Regarding the valuation of the Bank's IFTG shares, he said: 'Neither we nor the auditors ever had concerns about the actual valuation, there was only a legal concern about potential restrictions in the IFTG charter.' The issues he raised were based on a legal opinion he now described as being 'not complete', admitting that 'deeper legal analysis confirmed that there were no restrictions on the bank's shares'. 'Based on a full analysis,' he concluded, 'there is no problem.' It was an astonishing acknowledgement that the accusations ranged against us are baseless. And we had it all caught on an audio recording. The recording device was seized by investigators when they searched my colleague's home, and now, to my utter surprise, a transcript of its contents will become part of the official case files. A smoking gun revealing Yusupov's utter cynicism. A depth charge, too, that blows out of the water his testimony during our recent cross-interrogation.

Then another breakthrough. The investigating authorities have retained an 'independent valuation expert' to appraise the IFTG assets. The job falls to Svetlana Tabakova, head of the Russian Association of Independent Appraisers – a very experienced, and famously haughty, woman who has frequently appeared as a witness in Russian criminal cases. We have not been allowed to meet with her or give any supporting documents to assist her valuation, so we assume she will reach a conclusion that 100 per cent supports our opponents. When she releases her report, she does refer to a flaw in IFTG's charter that was later corrected, but then concludes that the IFTG shares acquired by the bank have a value more than double what was needed to settle the loan. In other words, based on Tabakova's valuation, the bank made a huge profit, not a loss, on the transaction. *Kommersant*, a leading Russian business newspaper, covers the story, putting a photo of me smiling on the front cover with the headline: 'Calvey's Innocence is Proven'.

It is after yet another interrogation that I share a candid moment with one of the investigators. We are walking down a corridor in their HQ when the investigator quietly admits that they know I am telling the truth, and that they have tried to get their superiors to agree to reduce the charges to a misdemeanour and reach a settlement. It would have been a face-saving way to end the story, but the rules say that you can't detain people in SIZO for misdemeanours, only for felonies. So, the investigators' bosses were predictably cold on the idea. 'Are you going to go to the President and say that it was a mistake to arrest them?' they'd demanded to know. And of course, no one was prepared to do that. By the rules of 'the system', such an admission of failure would demand that the investigators are themselves investigated and they'd likely face prison time of their own. That's why it could never happen. And why the investigation drags mercilessly on.

In the end, the investigators are scrambling to complete their indictment against us within the time limits imposed by the law. They decide to charge me and the others with 'misappropriation of funds', rather than the more serious charge of fraud that had been on the table. This is presumably because of the recording that has Yusupov admitting that he never was 'deceived' and didn't believe there was any actual damage done by the IFTG deal. In light of this, the claim of fraud would have been laughed out of court. But the new charge of misappropriation requires a sleight of hand of its own. The date of our 'crime' now moves back a couple years to 2015, when Vostochny initially loaned the funds to PKB to pay off the Vostochny Bank's obligations to the Russian brokerage firm, BCS. This occurred fully two years before Yusupov and Avetisyan even became shareholders in the bank, which should instantly destroy their status as alleged victims. But misappropriation of funds is still a felony under the law, and the text of the indictment is a word-for-word, copy-and-paste job lifted from a document based on Yusupov's original allegations that was used to justify our initial arrest.

It's 24 December 2019 – Christmas Eve – when I am called in to the Investigative Committee headquarters to formally receive the indictment. It has clearly been drafted at the very last minute, since they haven't had time to translate it into English, as required under the law. One of my advocates thinks we might be able to delay acceptance of it for this reason, potentially giving us some procedural advantage. But the investigator shrugs and calls our bluff. We wait about three hours for one of their translators to join us. It is an attractive blonde woman I recognise from several earlier court appearances and interrogations. Since I have never needed to call on her to translate anything, I have never actually heard her speak English before. Now she looks hesitantly at the thick pile of papers in front of her, grabs her purse and pulls out an English–Russian dictionary. Apparently, she doesn't know how to translate even the word 'indictment'. I look at the lead investigator as if to say, 'Do you really want to go through with this brain damage?' But she just laughs and tells the translator to do the best she can.

The translator plods on haltingly for hours, with frequent breaks to consult her dictionary. There are now seven of us crammed in the stuffy and cluttered investigator's office, and my mind numbs as I listen to the endless drone of the translator's voice. I notice that the investigators aren't listening at all. Instead, they scroll on their mobile phones, yawning lazily and checking the latest football scores or finding something else to amuse them. Having started this performance at around midday, it is already evening and we are less than halfway through the document. Someone has unfortunately mentioned that today is a big holiday for Americans, and that my family are all in Moscow waiting for me to get home. Julia has planned a grand family dinner and has already texted several times to find out when I will be done. But this only makes the investigator more determined to keep me there – all night if necessary. She expects me to capitulate and sign to confirm that I had reviewed the entire document.

But finally, at about 10.30 p.m., even the investigator is too exhausted to continue. 'That's enough for one day,' she says. We agree to take the rest of the night off and to reconvene the next afternoon. Driving back home under escort in an FSIN vehicle, and weary from the endless hours of pointless boredom I've just had to endure, I text Julia to say I am at last on my way. I morosely assume that dinner is long over, and the kids will be asleep when I arrive. Our Christmas Eve ruined by the investigator's caprice. But when I open the door of the apartment, I am greeted by a roar of 'Merry Christmas!' from the whole family. Julia had rallied the Calvey team, as she always does. She has a festive meal laid on a candle-lit table, a Christmas tree sparkles with lights, and cheerful Christmas music fills the air. I well up momentarily with happiness, overwhelmed by the contrast with the pitiless environment in which I have just spent the day. My oldest son hands me a cold bottle of champagne, and I pop it open right above the box that contains some of the FSB audio monitoring equipment. '*Uraaa!!!* Merry Christmas!' my boys and I shout, flipping our middle fingers towards the box and the system that it represents. Julia disapproves of such gestures, but we all know right then that we won't let our family be defeated.

19

Chess

There is some good news that comes our way early in the new year. In February, the court decides to release my colleagues Vagan Abgaryan, Ivan Zyuzin, and Maxim Vladimirov to house arrest. They have spent an entire miserable year in SIZO, separated from their families and kept in isolation. Every day a new nightmare. But, however belatedly, they are at last reunited with their loved ones.

It's a positive start to 2020, but just a few weeks later I am side-swiped unexpectedly. You think you know your enemies, then a new one comes out of nowhere. It is early spring when I am finally allowed to visit a doctor for an overdue health check-up. The investigator has refused my requests for almost a year, and then tried to insist I attend a state hospital, instead of Moscow's European Medical Centre (EMC), where I have received routine medical care since the 1990s. But eventually, the investigator relents and author-ises an appointment at EMC, as it is my right under Russian law. All the results for my blood and heart tests come back fine, but there is another problem. My doctor notices a disturbing lump on my leg – what I thought was simply a lipoma that had been there for years. Over the last few months, it has grown larger, and the doctor orders some X-rays and ultrasounds. These come back inconclusive, so he recommends an MRI scan. But the investigator rejects that idea, refusing to authorise even a momentary removal of my metallic leg bracelet, making it impossible for me to have the procedure. But based on the ultrasounds, the doctor is concerned enough to insist that I have an operation straight away.

A surgeon at EMC removes the growth, which is the size of a pear, and a biopsy confirms that it is a malignant liposarcoma, a form of cancer. As the doctor relays the news, it is as if he is speaking at me from far away and in slow motion, every sound coming from his mouth magnified in the deafening silence. My body feels occupied by unwanted aliens, no longer entirely my own. It is possible, he explains, for stress to cause a benign lipoma to transform into a malignant one, and this seems to be what has happened in my case. More positively, it's a Grade 1 malignancy, the first level, so there is a good chance that it hasn't yet spread elsewhere. The surgeon who operated on me noted that the tissues surrounding the growth are clean and appear healthy, a view backed up by lab analysis that shows no signs of malignancy in those samples. The signs are good that the cancer is confined, but because it wasn't possible to do the MRI before the operation, my oncologists recommend a ten-day course of radiation therapy. Soon enough, I find myself lying on a cold, raised platform at EMC as a grand-piano-sized radiation machine hums, whirrs and spins in a 360-degree circle around me. Not for the first time in recent years, I find myself meditating on life's bizarre and unexpected twists.

I am now fighting on two fronts – my battle against cancer, and my conflict with the Russian authorities, which rumbles inexorably on. And Covid has arrived to turn the world upside down, too. Ironically, with billions across the planet suddenly confined to their homes, there ought to be a new sort of solidarity with prisoners of the state. But, of course, the truth is that for most people the hardships of Covid isolation are very different to those endured by those living under punishments imposed by Russian courts. I can just imagine my former cellmates from 604 erupting in curses and throwing their crumpled newspapers at the TV as they watch endless interviews with whiners complaining about spending a few months at home with their families during the Covid lockdowns, keeping up with their friends over Zoom, and having times outdoors every day for exercise.

The Covid response from the Russian investigators and courts is a mixed bag. Social-distancing guidelines are observed in the court hearings I attend after the Russian lockdown is declared in April 2020 but not once do I see an investigator wearing a mask in any of the fifteen or twenty visits I make to the Investigative Committee head office during those quarantine months. They do, however, have a man on the front door with a laser device to temperature check all visitors. But whenever I look to see my result, the device always gives some bizarre reading: 27.4 one day, 18.6 the next, 46.1 after that. Never a number even remotely associated with a regular human temperature in either Celsius or Fahrenheit. Once, I ask the guy taking the readings: 'Does that thing actually work?' He laughs and tells me: 'Apparently not.' A classic case of Russian bureaucratic form over substance.

The periodic court hearings about the detention conditions for myself and my colleagues have become a ritualistic circus. It is said that the definition of insanity is to repeat the same exercise over and over expecting a different result each time, despite nothing ever changing. There is undoubtedly a Sisyphean quality to Russian criminal court hearings that makes you feel like you are going mad. When one among us accused, or else one of our advocates, stands to make a statement, the investigator and prosecution representatives routinely stare disinterestedly at their mobile phones, paying absolutely no heed to what we say or whatever evidence we are presenting. We point out the most obvious facts that prove our innocence, and highlight how our accusers want us isolated to facilitate their takeover of the bank. But we are simply ignored. And when it's their turn to speak, they deliver their arguments in brief and simplistic terms, always on the same theme: 'The defendants are guilty of crimes and therefore must be isolated to prevent them from interfering with the investigation.' They stick to the same argument even after the investigation is formally completed, when there can no longer be even a possibility of us somehow interfering with evidence or witnesses. Despite pretences to the contrary, there is no presumption of innocence, but the opposite – a presumption of guilt. This is the most basic and obvious of the justice system's many structural flaws.

Sometimes the cracks in the veneer are easy to spot. Frequently, the judge announces a brief recess after listening to our statements, returning ten minutes later to deliver a fifteen-page ruling that has obviously been prepared in advance. On one occasion, a journalist spies a copy of that day's final ruling on the desk of the judge's secretary *before the hearing has even started*. Although we know the outcome is always a foregone conclusion, we attend each one in person and take the opportunity to get the facts about the shareholder dispute out to any journalists in attendance. If we cannot win in the court of law, we can at least make our case in the court of public opinion.

The investigator does authorise several visits from the US ambassador and US consular officers to my apartment. The ambassadors – first, Jon Huntsman, and then John Sullivan – have understood from the beginning that my case springs from an internal shareholder dispute, and not any criminal activity. But knowing that my apartment is bugged, we are always guarded in our conversations. In addition to being a heavyweight in diplomatic circles and a stalwart defender of American interests, Ambassador Sullivan is an experienced lawyer and has taken an interest in the legal substance (or lack thereof) of the case against us. Although he is clear that it is not the role of the Embassy or State Department to opine on the merits of the allegations, he is clearly angry about the absurdity of our situation.

All the way through, I have asked the Embassy to avoid making any public ultimatum or demands about my release. It seems obvious – and my lawyers all confirm – that it would be counter-productive to do so in the current geopolitical situation. Two other Americans, Paul Whelan and Trevor Reed, have been arrested in Russia under different circumstances, and are widely reported to be the subjects of negotiations for a 'trade' involving Russian prisoners held in the USA. I discover that there has been a suggestion by Russian negotiators that I might be swapped for Viktor Bout, a notorious arms dealer. His illicit international arms trade saw him convicted to twenty-five years in prison by a US court in 2011 for conspiring to sell weapons to a US-designated foreign terrorist group. But I want to avoid becoming a pawn in this sort of diplomatic chess, as I believe it will make the path to freedom longer, and almost certainly worsen the prospects for my detained Russian colleagues. I am relieved that Ambassador Sullivan and other US officials agree to keep me out of any hostage swap talks.

But I do want them to raise my wrongful detention as often as possible in bilateral discussions, and I deeply appreciate the nuance and sophistication they show in doing so. My plight is discussed on many occasions, including in a phone conversation between Presidents Trump and Putin, and several times between secretaries and ministers. Rather than linking my release to prisoner swaps, instead I am mostly discussed in the context of economic and investment cooperation between the US and Russia, something that could unlock billions in investment into the country if I am freed. Without ultimatums, this approach reminds the Russians of the importance of my case and that removing it from the agenda will clear the way for more productive things. On one occasion, my case is even raised by the US National Security Advisor with his Russian counterpart in a Geneva meeting on bilateral nuclear arms negotiations.

At this Helsinki summit with Putin, President Trump proposes to create a US–Russia Business Captain's dialogue that would include fifteen to twenty top CEOs from corporations on both sides. Such dialogues in other countries have ultimately resulted in billions of dollars of new investment in the countries involved. But in the case of the dialogue with Russia, the US Ambassadors – backed by various US trade associations – insist on my freedom first. Any country other than Russia would leap at such an invitation, but in Russia it's the security services calling the shots. They don't care a bit about the economy, but they do care about saving face. Even if Russia loses billions in investment, they won't end the case and release me until they decide it can be done without admitting fault – which in reality means a trial and a guilty conviction.

However much I wish the case to be judged on its merits, it is apparent that I am, after all, a pawn in this game of global politics. To America and the West, I am a symbol of all that is wrong in Putin's Russia: an unfree market where the law and due process are secondary to personal or political considerations. There are many in Russia who share this opinion and consider me a victim of overreach by unaccountable state forces, even as the prosecution stubbornly continues to characterise me as a 'shark' representing my own 'mercenary commercial interests'. This is a case that long ago became something much bigger than a bruising fallout among businessmen. And I understand that while my name may appear as the lead actor in this particular international drama, it is others who get to direct it.

As the months pass by frustratingly, I try to spend my time – all those long hours cooped up – productively. A way to distract myself from everything I am missing, like all those once-in-a-lifetime events in the lives of my children and other cherished friends and family that leave my heart heavy with regret with each one I miss. One of the most painful instances comes in October 2019. I am at the Investigative Committee headquarters, undergoing yet another round of interrogation, when terrible news comes across the wires. Alexei Leonov is dead. Cosmonaut and national icon, but most importantly to me, an extraordinary friend. By now, I have got to know well many of the investigators, prosecutors, and FSIN officers I interact with so regularly. Some of them are 'true believers' who never crack a smile or show a human side. But several of them, during unguarded moments, complain to me about their dissatisfaction with their jobs and with the cynical system in which they operate. A few even ask if they can get a job with Baring Vostok. So, I hopefully ask the investigator if I can have permission to attend Alexei's funeral, a chance to pay my respects. She looks at me and sighs. 'Probably not,' she says, crushingly. 'Imagine the PR for us if the news media is reminded of your friendship with such a hero.' I am bitterly sad not to be able to say goodbye to my friend, nor to be able to comfort the great man's wife and family. But this is my reality, and I have to find ways to deal with it.

Just as in SIZO, I continue to read a lot. I make my way through thirty or forty books in a year, covering a wide range of subjects and genres. But in contrast to prison, I am also able to watch international TV news stations like BBC World and CNN, and to watch films and documentaries on DVDs. I consume entire box sets from beginning to end, from *Game of Thrones* and *Downton Abbey* to *Silicon Valley* and *The Last Dance*. I also gorge on old sports matches sent to me by friends and relatives, especially vintage Oklahoma Sooners football games. I get through literally hundreds of them – so many that I'm sure the FSB agents monitoring my apartment must be convinced these old games contain secretly encoded messages!

Despite never being artistically inclined, I take a DVD course on urban sketching and painting. After learning and practising a few simple techniques – like one- and two-point perspectives, volume, and texture – I realise that anyone can achieve a sufficient level of proficiency to enjoy art. I manage to overcome the usual barrier that everyone first experiences – being worried about how something might look to others – and embrace it solely for my own enjoyment. Drawing and painting become a joy and a much-needed way to release stress, engaging seldom-used (for me, anyway) parts of the brain. I evolve a Sunday afternoon routine involving drinking wine, blasting out my favourite music – Ray Charles, the Rolling Stones and Johnny Cash – and happily sketching and painting, often until well after midnight. Losing track of time, eventually I retire to bed happy and exhausted.

On 16 April my hopes are dashed that my case might be resolved early through a creative diplomatic avenue. Russia celebrates Victory Day every 9 May, a commemoration of the Soviet victory over Hitler's Germany in 1945. These days, it is a celebration of Russian nationhood and an opportunity for Putin to rally popular support for the governing regime. This year marks the seventy-fifth anniversary of the end of the Second World War, and plans are in place for a major celebration in Moscow. The event is scheduled to be attended by President Trump and a host of other foreign leaders and dignitaries. It would be a typical PR tactic by the Kremlin to prelude such an auspicious and high-profile occasion with a symbolic gesture of goodwill. A few months before the 2014 Winter Olympics in Sochi, for instance, Putin surprised the world by pardoning his old oligarch foe, Mikhail Khodorkovsky, and freeing him from his incarceration in a penal colony near the Arctic Circle. It has crossed my mind that I might now be a good subject for such presidential 'benevolence', and some high-level Russian friends have encouraged discussions about this exact idea with the Russian Presidential Administration. But then Covid casts its gloomy shadow once more. With less than a month to go until the celebrations, Putin calls them off after several foreign leaders, including Trump, cancel their attendance. With no value to be obtained from a goodwill gesture, the prospect of his direct intervention dies. The case grinds on.

We keep searching for a knockout blow, some piece of evidence so powerful and undeniable that even the cynical prosecutors won't be able to proceed with their pretence at justice. One of my final hopes lies in obtaining the documents from the original transactions with the brokerage firm, BCS. These will provide incontrovertible proof that the subsequent economic arrangements that have been called into question were necessary, legal and undertaken for the benefit of the bank — at no personal profit to ourselves. I know that investigators interrogated the management at BCS shortly after our arrests, when presumably they would have been horrified to learn the truth: that we had committed no crime. But BCS has since flatly refused to hand over the relevant paperwork to our lawyers, despite repeated official requests. I suspect that they are themselves under threat of arrest by the investigators if they do.

It is only in 2021, long after the original indictment against me was issued, that we finally obtain a subpoena against BCS from the US Federal Court in the Southern District of New York. We are helped to get it by the US Department of Justice, which issues a letter of interest in the application, backed by Ambassador Sullivan's argument that resolution of our case is in the interests of US–Russian bilateral relations. In the face of a US federal subpoena, a firm like BCS active in the securities markets has no choice but to comply, so we finally received the documents. It's another bombshell moment. The BCS documents completely exonerate us, more decisively that I had dared hope. There should be no question that the charges against us be immediately dismissed. But when we submit them to the investigators, they just shrug us off. They knew we would eventually get hold of them, they explain, but it's too late to change course now. The case is going to trial whatever, and will be decided there. Anyway, they suggest, why the worry, since I probably won't get any more jail time? The cynicism of the system and its refusal to ever admit a mistake never fails to amaze. Their only way to save face is to push on with the trial, and gain a conviction. Instead of celebrating a checkmate, the game of chess drags on.

20

The Trial

From my apartment's bedroom window, I look down at a dilapidated old building next door in which Lev Tolstoy once lived. He was there between 1860 and 1866, the years when he started writing *War and Peace*, which I have re-read with deeper appreciation during house arrest. Alongside the building, there is a giant old beech tree, its massive branches now almost attached to the decrepit metal rooftop. I come to think of it as Lev Tolstoy's tree. I imagine him sitting quietly, looking at it out of his window, as he conjures the characters and plot of one of the greatest novels of all time. One night, when there are unusually high winds, I hear an inhuman noise coming from that direction, like a lost soul groaning with melancholy. When I get out of bed to check it out, I can see it is the branches of this tree swaying violently in the gale, pressing up and down on the roof, seemingly enraged with the universe.

To finally break the logjam of the legal process and hasten the route to freedom, my team and I are agreed that we need to seek some kind of commercial settlement with our opponents. Paying them off financially is an easy decision to make, as the amount of damages they are claiming is dwarfed by the costs of the ongoing case to me, Baring Vostok and everyone associated with the firm. It is the pragmatic option, no matter how much it might grate – and one we put on the table shortly after our arrests. The challenge is how to structure a settlement without admitting guilt. Our opponents have long insisted that we admit to what they accuse us of doing, perhaps under pressure themselves for having instigated an FSB investigation on such misleading evidence. But we're not going to take the fall for a crime that never happened. I have told the investigators since my first interrogation that I would rather be sentenced to a penal colony than falsely admit to being a criminal. Now, after almost two years, we have some movement. I put this down to a combination of factors, but especially pressure from the Russian Central Bank that makes it impossible for Avetisyan to remain as Vostochny's majority shareholder. In 2021, they finally agree to the settlement we have proposed from the beginning: compensating Vostochny Bank for alleged 'damages' without admitting any guilt. They at last waive their absurd claims against Baring Vostok, although they insist we approve a PR statement in which we confirm that the criminal case has nothing to do with our commercial dispute. It is hilarious, even ridiculous, but we sign it anyway, satisfied that the truth of the matter is obvious enough to everyone.

However, resolution of this commercial dispute does not mean an end to criminal proceedings. The authorities need to show that their investigations have not been in vain. It's not long afterwards that the Russian Supreme Court schedules a hearing to decide whether to extend our house arrests. It's a cold and rainy day in November 2020 as I stand outside Moscow's massive Supreme Court building on Povarskaya Street, waiting for my advocates to arrive. I am distracted by a statue outside the main entrance, a classic depiction of Justice as a female figure of a type you see at courthouses around the world. But this one is a little different. Typically, she is shown with the scales of justice in one hand, a sword in the other and a blindfold over her eyes – a symbol that she is impartial. But Moscow's version has no such blindfold. I laugh to myself, wondering whether this is an intentional omission by some mischievous Russian or Soviet sculptor, or simply an ironic oversight.

Blindfolded or not, the Supreme Court justice who hears our case over three brief sessions rules that we are to be released from house arrest. It is what we expected in light of the recent settlement, but still we are not entirely free. The court imposes an 8 p.m.

curfew, and insists we continue to wear ankle bracelets for monitoring. Still, the judgement comes as a massive relief, like a ray of sunlight piercing through dark and stormy clouds. After the ruling, I make some brief comments to journalists and then call my wife, who happens to be in Moscow at the moment. I decide to walk to where she is, instead of going by car. It is only about a mile away and I have desperately missed being able to stroll the city streets like any other normal human being. For the first time in two years, I wander by myself along Russia's boulevard ring, no FSIN escort tracking me. I look at the ordinary, cheerful people as they make their way home or head off for an evening out. Even amid a damp, dark winter Moscow evening, it is wonderful, and my heart leaps with joy. When I finally catch up with Julia, she almost tackles me as she engulfs me in a huge embrace. We laugh and together shout a big Russian '*Uraaa!*', to the astonishment of passers-by clueless about the source of our sheer happiness.

Unshackled from house arrest, I look forward to meeting friends and colleagues again. At first, I feel awkward. How much do people know about what has happened? What do they think about it all? How do I even start a conversation with them after everything? My greatest worry is that people I respect might wonder if there is at least some truth in the accusations. But I soon learn that I need not concern myself with this. Everyone who matters to me understands the absurdity of the case and where guilt really lies.

I meet with several important figures who have supported me during my detention to offer my personal thanks. Through them, I gain a clearer understanding of how and why the case was initiated. What most strikes me is the absence of any surprise among them that the 'system' can foster such injustice. Each of them has known other people wrongfully arrested. But in lieu of shock, they are regretful and maybe even ashamed that a foreigner has fallen foul of the system, especially one who had done so much for Russia. Through one of my friends, I also encounter someone who used to work at a senior level – a general – within the Russian security services. 'Even a good machine occasionally malfunctions,' he tells me. 'I'm sorry it happened to you.' I make no comment.

I have a group of friends who every Sunday go to Moscow's famous Sanduny Banya, a legendary sauna and bathhouse built in 1808. They invite me to join them, but I am not sure. What about my ankle bracelet? 'Don't worry,' they tell me. 'Half the people there have worn one of those at some point in their lives. It's like a badge of honour.' And so it proves. Whether because of the bracelet, or because they recognise me from TV, I notice several people nod to me in a sign of respect, and a few of them come up to shake my hand. Afterwards, I go with my friends to the Uzbek restaurant across the street, Beloye Solntse Pustini, named after the famous Soviet-era film. There, other patrons of the *banya* bring me vodka shots and introduce themselves. One Russian billionaire even hails me over to share a beer.

I visit the Baring Vostok office most weekdays. It is in some ways a bit uncomfortable, since the company and team had changed a lot during the last two years. I can see that everything has been well managed in my absence. In fact, despite the losses emanating from Vostochny, our funds have almost tripled in value since I've been away. My colleagues seem happy to have me back, and frequently ask my advice on different projects. But I don't want to reinsert myself into decision-making and management the way I have been in the past. I sense that it will be disruptive, even counter-productive, especially to junior partners who have recently assumed greater responsibility. However, I still love to join team discussions on potential investments, and the performance of existing companies. After twenty-five years of building muscle memory, my brain approaches investment challenges instinctively, the way others tackle crosswords or Sudoku puzzles.

Release from house arrest leaves me desperate for the trial to go ahead. I want a final, definitive end to the story. But the system seems to have an instinct for doing the opposite of whatever its victims desire. Various bureaucratic arguments are advanced to justify why the court cannot schedule its start. Then at last, at the start of February 2021, the trial gets under way at Meshansky Court in Moscow.

Our advocates warn us to expect a conviction, but predict only a suspended, or probationary, sentence. In other words, no more jail time. Just enough for the system to save face and avoid admitting that it has made a mistake. Even once the hearings are scheduled, sessions are infrequent and painfully slow. Numerous official requests from our lawyers to step up the pace are ignored. Instead of waiting until the end of the trial to give my own testimony, which is what defence lawyers normally advise their clients, my lead advocate, Timofey Gridnev, advises that I take the stand at the very beginning. The motivation is two-fold. Firstly, because we have nothing to hide, but also because we hope to educate the judge in what are admittedly a set of financially complex charges. I know I will be cross-examined afterwards, so I prep with my advocates over two lengthy sessions to anticipate the prosecutor's aggressive questions. But all the preparation proves unnecessary. I give my testimony, reciting the facts as simply as possible, and referencing the bullet-proof evidence in the investigator's own case files that support us – including the BCS documents and the valuation report from the independent expert, Svetlana Tabakova. I conclude by doing the maths for the judge, explaining how not only was there no loss or damage to the Vostochny Bank from the transactions for which we have been charged, the bank has actually made 9 billion roubles profit from them. 'If this constitutes embezzlement,' I say, 'it is the most profitable embezzlement for an alleged victim in history.'

When the prosecutor rises to cross-examine, he asks me the usual routine questions. What is my official employment status? What's my address? How many children do I have? Then he asks a single tentative question about the bank itself, which I answer directly and simply, illustrating that he does not understand even now the basic facts of the case. He quickly says, 'No further questions, your honour,' at which point the assembled journalists in the courtroom quietly laugh together. Everyone now understands that the rest of the trial is mere formality.

With the prosecution showing no interest in trying to prove our guilt, I am increasingly hopeful that we can achieve a better result than the advocates anticipate. There is still high-level attention on the case. In June 2021, the new US President, Joe Biden, meets Putin for a summit in Geneva and my case is high up the agenda. Afterwards, Biden tells the media: 'American businessmen, they are not ready to show up. They don't want to hang around in Moscow.'

The slow pace of the trial leaves me with a lot of downtime between sessions. On weekends, as summer arrives, I often go on long walks for five or six hours across Moscow, exploring neighbourhoods where I hardly spent any time over the last ten or fifteen years. I'm impressed with the improvements in housing quality and the vibrancy of city street life, with its teeming cafes and young people enjoying the good weather. The contrast of this encouraging atmosphere with the brutal and cynical reality of the country's courts and governing system makes me sad for the Russian people, who are its main victims and who could otherwise be among the world's most prosperous people. But I often feel solidarity with them: one day when walking in Moscow's wonderful Gorky Park, a young family recognise me, whisper to themselves, and then the man – a husband and father – raises his hand and shouts out, 'Mr Calvey, we are with you!'

Eventually, we reach the point in the trial when Yusupov comes to give his testimony, and it is almost comedic. He is visibly nervous and insists on presenting what he calls a 'new independent valuation report' for the IFTG deal, which claims to show that it has been only worth a few million roubles to Vostochny. This, despite the fact that the bank had already earned 1 billion roubles in commission income from these very same IFTG companies in 2020 alone. The judge refuses to accept Yusupov's report, since the one by Tabakova is unimpeachable. Our advocates then proceed to cross-examine Yusupov, with Timofey's colleague, Dmitry Kharatonin, leading the charge. It is brilliantly satisfying to watch him destroy Yusupov so comprehensively.

Witness after witness gives testimony proving our innocence, and even those for the prosecution end up confirming that no crime was ever committed. Surely, I think to myself, even if we're denied a full acquittal, there's a strong chance they will reclassify the 'crime' to a misdemeanour. But Timofey, more battle-hardened than me in the system, urges me not to get my hopes up. Still, I cannot altogether bury occasional flutters of hope as the trial reaches its conclusion. One of the prosecutors, in her closing remarks, admits that no witnesses have testified to any crime being committed. Her words cause me to snap to attention, imagining some kind of belated breakthrough. But then she continues: 'And that just proves what a well-organised criminal group we are dealing with here.' The entire courtroom laughs out loud. I shouldn't be shocked at anything by now, but this is truly Kafkaesque.

There is one final twist to the prosecutor's statement. At its end, she requests none of us be given any further jail time, on the grounds that Baring Vostok has done important work for the Russian economy, and because we have already 'compensated for the damage caused by our crimes'. After she says this, she catches my eye, smiling smugly as if to say: 'I have just done something highly unusual. I hope you appreciate it.' Timofey then makes his own closing remarks, their irrefutable logic delivered in a tone at once powerful and reasonable. It is a perfect performance, I think, reminding me of Gregory Peck in *To Kill a Mockingbird*. But what a terrible waste that talented lawyers like him and Kharatonin have to work in a system where trial outcomes are determined outside the courtroom, where facts and arguments often don't matter to the people who decide.

It is now August. The judge takes several days before she is ready to deliver her decision. When she returns, she reads aloud all the facts that have informed her conclusions. Incredibly, it is a word-for-word recitation of the prosecutor's written charges before the trial, which are in turn a word-for-word copy of the preliminary indictment against us delivered in late 2019. It is as if all the witness testimony and evidence presented at trial never happened. When she announces her verdict, it is exactly what we were told to expect before the trial started, and what the prosecutor had requested: we are convicted of misappropriation of funds, for which we receive only a suspended sentence, with a probationary term of five years.

★ ★ ★

Once outside, I make a statement to a throng of journalists and TV crews on the steps of the courthouse. I highlight the prosecutor's own admission about the absence of evidence of any crime, as well as the absurd text of the verdict. I explain that I recognise getting a suspended sentence, with no jail time, is normally considered a victory in Russia, but it still feels like a terrible blow to be convicted of any crime after building a record of professional integrity over thirty years. It is emotional and spontaneous, and exactly what I feel.

On the drive back home, my phone is flooded with texts and emails as news spreads of the outcome. Those from my American and British friends all offer their condolences, focusing on the injustice. But those from my Russian friends have a different tone. Essentially, their message is: 'Congratulations! You made it!' They all know that I have come away with what amounts to the best possible result in the circumstances. Nonetheless, for tactical reasons, we decide to appeal the decision, which means the terms of the verdict cannot come into force immediately. I remain subject to the same conditions imposed almost a year earlier by the Russian Supreme Court. I must stick to the 8 p.m. curfew and I am not allowed to leave Moscow.

Meanwhile, my advocates file a claim to the State Cassation Court, arguing that it is unlawful to continue to hold me under any restrictions now that the trial is over, since there are no restrictions attached to the verdict itself. Unlike all the applications and requests made prior to trial, which were on behalf of all the accused parties, Timofey decides to make this one alone. It is the only way to do it discreetly, away from press attention and free from gossip that is rarely productive. But I know that a positive decision for me will set a precedent that immediately benefits my colleagues, too. The weeks drag by as we await a decision, my state of limbo continuing.

As another autumn comes and goes, I often look down from my apartment window at Lev Tolstoy's tree. Day by day, its green leaves slowly transform to a magnificent gold colour, reigning majestically over the entire courtyard in the crisp October sunlight. But as the skies darken, and the autumn rain begins in earnest, its foliage becomes damp and lifeless. By late November, those once magnificent golden leaves lay sodden and trampled on the ground below. Yet I know that in about four months, green shoots will emerge on the branches and birds will return to sing their joyful spring song. This cycle of life makes me painfully aware of my own ageing and of the years lost under my arrest, but also gives me hope of personal renewal. It reminds me of the new life ahead, which for now remains only in my dreams.

When the Cassation Court finally meets to hear my claim in early January 2022, there are no journalists in attendance, no representatives of our opponents, no official translators. Just me, my advocate (Timofey's colleague, Larisa Kashtanova), and one prosecutor (one of the two who carried out the main trial against us). It is a brief hearing, with familiar arguments presented by both sides — an echo of every other hearing I have been a part of these last two years. But this time, after a brief recess, the judges return with a positive decision. A ruling that it is unlawful to continue to hold me under any restrictions, when the trial verdict itself hasn't imposed any. Afterwards, the prosecutor shakes my hand, smiles weakly and says, 'That's what I expected.' What he really seems to mean is, 'No hard feelings, and good luck.'

I am free.

21

Home

On 14 January 2022 it is icy cold in Moscow. I feel as if I'm embarking on a special operation as I am driven the route to Sheremetyevo Airport, my boarding pass for today's Aeroflot flight to Geneva clutched in my hand. The once-familiar Leningradskoye Highway now feels foreign to me. It has been almost three years since I last left the city. Igor, my loyal driver, makes a joke as we speed along, but he can sense that I'm nervous and absorbed in my own thoughts – and worries. We stay mostly silent, which seems to amplify the crunch of the car's tyres through the snow.

Arriving at the airport four hours before the scheduled flight departure, I'm unsure what to expect. Larisa Kashtanova and Grigory Zhdanov, two of my advocates, are with me, armed with documentation from the court, in case I face questioning or interrogation. Besides Timofey, Igor, and my wife, they are the only people who know about my plan to leave today. And no one besides them, the prosecutor, and a few FSIN officials seem to know about the recent ruling, which I have kept quiet to avoid the risk of my enemies taking counter-measures. Not even my colleagues in Baring Vostok are aware of what is under way. There are many competing agencies and bureaucracies in Russia who could easily put a spanner in the works, blocking my right to actually depart, if they are alerted to my plans to leave. 'Happiness loves quiet,' as the expression goes in Russia.

In my entire life, I have never before been so early for a flight. To
kill some time, I go to a small cafe near the airport entrance and have
a coffee with Larisa and Grisha. They are smiling and trying to get me
to relax, but my nerves are taut and anxiety courses through my body.
After what fells like an age, but in reality is about three hours before
departure, I head to passport control. Larisa and Grisha are on high
alert, trailing about 15ft behind. There's a young woman on duty. I
hand her my boarding pass and passport, which she opens and places
face down on the scanner. I'm expecting a red light to start flashing
on her monitor. Or for her to get a phone call from the FSB minders
who work at the airport, telling her to lead me off to some nearby
windowless cell to await further questioning. My heart is pounding in
my chest. But she only yawns and looks wearily at her mobile phone.
After a painfully long thirty seconds or so, I hear a 'beep' from her
monitor. She picks up my passport, lazily flips through it to find an
empty page, and stamps it. Never has that familiar thumping sound
given me so much relief.

But the ordeal isn't over yet. I wave goodbye to Larisa and Grisha,
who smile and wish me a safe flight, but now I face the security screen-
ing. I walk through to the security zone with my meagre luggage
of just one small backpack. The area seems unusually empty today,
which makes me suspicious. But again, my fears prove unfounded.
I breeze through in record time. Julia, who is waiting for me at our
home in Switzerland, is texting every ten minutes, asking what's
happening. She hasn't even told our kids yet about our plans for my
arrival later today. We are too afraid of crushing their hopes in case
it doesn't work out. But so far so good, I message her, adding a few
prayer emojis.

In the remaining hour or two before boarding starts, I nervously
walk in circuits around the terminal. In line with Covid rules, I'm
wearing a mask, like everyone else in the terminal. I try to avoid
eye contact and hope that nobody recognises me. When Aeroflot
announces the start of boarding for the Geneva flight, I'm the first
in line. This is where they will stop me, I think, unable to curb my
paranoia. Just when I think I'm safely on my way, they'll step in to
shatter it all. But again, it takes only a few seconds before I hear that

reassuring 'beep'. The gate attendant gives my passport the most cursory glance to check it matches the name on my boarding pass, hands me back my documents and welcomes me aboard.

As I take my seat near the front of the aeroplane, I watch the other masked passengers board, my heart still beating fast with adrenaline. Then, despite his mask, I recognise a familiar face boarding a few minutes after me. It's an old friend from the commercial world, Sergey Riabokobylko. His eyes widen as he spots me and processes what my presence means. Before he can call out a greeting, I signal to him to stay quiet, to avoid attracting attention. He nods, understanding immediately, and takes his seat a few rows behind.

Eventually, we start to taxi towards the runway, but then inexplicably come to a halt. We sit on the tarmac for what is about twenty minutes but which feels much longer. Then the aeroplane moves to some kind of holding area off to the side. This isn't normal, I think, panic rising within me. I imagine that someone from the FSB has got word that I am on the flight and has ordered take-off to be suspended. At any moment, I'm expecting a car with grey-suited men to drive out to the craft to haul me from my seat and back into custody. Julia keeps texting me to ask about my status, and about five or six times I have to respond 'Not clear yet'. I look back at Sergey, and I can see his eyes are also filled with tension.

I think about the three long years since this nightmare began. All the interrogations, stress, hopes and crushing disappointments. All the life moments that have been missed and which can never be replaced. I think about the brave Russians who stuck their necks out to help me, despite the consequences for themselves. I think about my colleagues, and how much their freedom depends on what happens with me, here today.

Sitting on that motionless plane, I get an idea of what eternity must feel like. But finally, and with no explanation, we resume taxiing towards the runway. The engines start to accelerate, and I get that familiar sensation in my stomach as we prepare to ascend. I text Julia 'Taking off' with a photo of me sitting on the aeroplane in my mask, giving a peace sign. I close my eyes and feel the moment when the wheels leave the ground, frictionless at last. When I open them, the aeroplane is still struggling to emerge from the thick, dark winter clouds above Moscow. I begin to think they will never disappear. But moments later, we break through into the crisp, bright sunlight above. The aeroplane stops shaking and suddenly becomes calm. I take a deep breath, and exhale.

As soon as the 'fasten seat belt' sign is switched off, Sergey and I both get to our feet, cheering loudly. We stride into the corridor to give each other a big hug. As we stand there, laughing, the other passengers look at us with fright, as if they have discovered there are madmen aboard.

Four hours later, and for the first time in three years, I am home – really at home, no longer a hostage. Sasha cries with happiness, unable to speak; the boys gear up for a festive reunion; and my beloved dog, Doby, barks non-stop with the excitement. Julia just smiles with the look of the wise, forever indestructible, and for which I will always love her.

Life begins again.

SECTION 5

AFTERMATH

22

Lessons Learned

Given the uncertainty and necessity for confidentiality around my exit from Russia, I haven't made any plans for what to do next. Now, finally back home in Switzerland, my only priority at first is simply reconnecting with my family. We spend a couple of blissful weeks together, enjoying the mountain air. When it's time for my kids to return to their jobs and schools, I travel with my sons to New York and Boston, where I get to meet many of their new friends. It feels like I am rejoining their regular lives again, and it's at once amazing and a bit scary to see how much they have all grown up during the past three years.

I also head for Oklahoma to visit my mom and siblings, who are overjoyed to see me on home soil, and to Washington, where I get to thank the people from the State Department who supported me throughout my ordeal. There are further trips to catch up with loyal friends and business partners around the world, but I intentionally keep a low profile, dodging journalists and staying off social media.

I am still in regular contact with my Russian advocate team, however. As I had hoped, the Cassation Court's decision to lift my restrictions is being used as a precedent by my other colleagues. The Meshansky Court quickly decides to follow suit and lifts all restrictions on them, too. It's a huge relief to me, but there is still a cloud on the horizon. Before I left Russia, I had promised my advocates that I would return at least once, to register with the FSIN as per the conditions of my probation sentence. When I mention this to my family and friends – and especially to people in Washington – they plead with me to reconsider. The last thing the State Department wants is for yet another American hostage to be added to Russia's bargaining list.

But I am concerned about the fate of my Russian colleagues. What will happen to them if I fail to show up? Theoretically, our verdicts are unconnected, but we are all aware that Russian prosecutors can do virtually anything they want. I worry that any refusal to return on my part might see their probation sentences converted to actual prison time. If that happens, I won't be able to live with myself.

So, suppressing profound nerves, I start planning a trip back for late February. My intention is to spend only forty-eight hours there – just long enough to register with the FSIN and get out again. As with my departure in January, I tell no one about the plan besides my Russian advocate team. They make various checks to ensure that there is currently no 'flag' against me on any state databases or any other unofficial barriers that would prevent me taking the same route out as last time. Still, I am suspicious and hesitant. I run through the pros and cons of the trip almost every day as I try to decide whether to go or not.

Finally, I buy a ticket and decide to go for it. Julia is booked on the same flight, and plans to visit her aged parents in Moscow. We are scheduled to fly out on 23 February 2022. As required, we take a Covid PCR test before we go, the kind that takes twenty-four hours to process. We time it to get the results shortly before take-off. In fact, we are in the taxi to Geneva airport when the email comes through. Julia's result is negative but I am Covid positive. It's the first time I have tested positive, and it takes me a minute to process what it all means. Obviously, there is no way I can fly today but, after a quick discussion, we decide that Julia should go as planned. We get the taxi to stop at the next nearest town, where we say our goodbyes and I take a train back home.

We have no idea that the next dramatic step in Russia's history is just around the corner. I wake up in Switzerland on the morning of 24 February to a phone call from Julia in Moscow. She asks if I have seen the news. I scroll through my phone and quickly grasp the disaster unfolding. Last night, Russian forces launched an invasion of Ukraine – a catastrophic act of aggression. We are both stunned but we don't share our true thoughts, since we know any phone discussion of the war will trigger monitoring by the FSB. I am completely unable to relax for the next two days, until her return flight has safely landed. The thought also haunts me that if I had gone back as intended, I might still be stuck there now.

★ ★ ★

I think often of the men from cell 604, the brave comrades who helped me survive my ordeal. I'm painfully aware how much my circumstances differ from theirs. I haven't been able to follow all of their fates, but I know of only one who was released from SIZO without a long-term sentence: Grisha, the former Deputy Minister of Culture, who was released to house arrest and was still detained at the time I left Russia. I bumped into him, coincidentally, in 2020 near the entrance of the Investigative Committee headquarters when we were both summoned there on the same day. We embraced in a hug, laughing and remembering briefly some moments we shared together, before the frowning investigators moved us along into the building for our separate interrogations. Two of the others – Andrey and Sanych – were sent to penal colonies with fifteen-year sentences. Some of the rest were still in SIZO at the time I left Russia.

When I was released from house arrest but still stuck in Moscow, I was contacted by the best friend of one of my cellmates, whom I won't name for reasons of anonymity. This friend asked for help with my former cellmate's legal bills and family, whose finances had become severely strained. I helped immediately, of course, paying his lawyers and meeting with his wife and son. I shared some stories about their husband/father and could tell from their mournful smiles that these stories rang true.

Since the war started, I haven't tried to reach out and contact most of my cellmates or their families, since a call from someone in Europe, and especially from me, might trigger unwanted attention from the authorities. I did, however, make one call to the wife of a cellmate with whom I shared a mutual friend. After getting her phone number, I called simply to tell her what a brave man her husband is, and the loving pride with which he talked about his family when we were together in SIZO. She sobbed when I told her and thanked me for sharing it.

Life is full of unexpected ironies. Growing up in Oklahoma, I never thought I would share a bond of camaraderie with a group of men from a Russian prison, with whom I intersected briefly for a miserable period in all of our lives. And yet, despite the misery and hopelessness, we somehow supported each other and retained a sense of humanity that helped us all survive it. I'm deeply grateful to them. I still hope to see them again in freedom someday.

★ ★ ★

Since 1994, I have experienced turmoil of almost every kind emanating from Russia: economic crises, currency collapses, hostile raids by ruthless competitors. And that was before my soul-crushing battle with its corrupt justice system. I'd thought these experiences had left me prepared for anything. But war is different altogether. The human impact of war is always terrible – battlefield deaths and mass displacement, atrocities and 'collateral damage'. The war in Ukraine will, I know, be no different. But it is soon clear that this conflict is having irreversible consequences at other levels, too.

During my various court appearances between 2019 and 2021, I said consistently that I continued to believe in Russia's investment potential. I truly did. My three years of detention coincided, ironically, with the most profitable years in Baring Vostok's history. Naturally, my arrest and the injustices I faced left me with a deep distrust of the people and system that rules the country. I knew I wouldn't be able to look investors in the eye anymore and tell them that I remained optimistic about Russia's future. But my Baring Vostok colleagues had remained bravely loyal to me during my ordeal, and our Russian companies were doing important work that I felt made Russia a better place. For all these reasons, I genuinely planned to remain involved with Baring Vostok, helping my Russian colleagues where I could while living outside of Russia and focusing personally on the fund's international projects.

But the war changes all of that. By April, it is clear that this going to be a long conflict, and that Russia will be subject to sanctions and international isolation long after it comes to an end. Overnight, our Russian portfolio companies have become toxic for the Funds, and our funds toxic for them. Banks close some of our fund's accounts and law firms threaten to drop us as a client because of our exposure to Russia, while on the Russian side, several of our portfolio companies are visited by the authorities asking suspicious questions about having foreigners from 'unfriendly' states as shareholders. There are rumoured risks of prosecution for Russian managers if they appear to be acting to comply with sanctions. All the while, we risk prosecution in the West if our funds fail to follow those laws. We conclude that we must make a clean break with Russia, selling the fund's Russian assets to our former colleagues and reaching a 'divorce' within our management company. The distressed exit causes a painful financial loss for our funds and for my family personally, but it is the only way to fully sever the Russian nexus and protect our non-Russian companies, which remain hugely valuable. After a few months, a basic deal is agreed with almost unanimous support from Baring Vostok's investors. Although we know there is a long road ahead to secure all the regulatory approvals, we are set on our path.

In parallel, I'm working quietly with my Russian advocates to manage an endgame in my case, while ensuring my Russian colleagues can travel freely and avoid problems with the FSIN. With skill and a lot of patience, Gridnev and his team pursue appeals of the verdict that delay the start of our probationary sentences and hold up the requirements for anyone to register with the FSIN in Moscow. They also manage to win a series of favourable court rulings that lighten my sentence, and those of my fellow defendants. Finally, on 5 April 2024, my probation period expires, and my conviction is automatically vacated and nullified. My colleagues mostly receive similar court decisions vacating their sentences shortly afterwards.

A couple of weeks later, we manage to complete the deal to sell Baring Vostok's Russian investments and separate fully from our former Russian colleagues. Some Russian conspiracy theorists will imagine a link between the sale of our fund's assets into Russian hands and my case becoming nullified. But it is indeed a coincidence, both events taking much longer to conclude than they should have, but for unrelated reasons. The decisions in each case lie in the hands of entirely different people.

It is a huge relief to be finally 'out' at every level. Freed from the massive weight that has lain on me for so long, I have more mental space to plan for the future. Time, too, to rethink all my views about Russia built over thirty years.

My own life experiences had made me an optimist about the country before 2019. Then, my arrest shattered many of those beliefs and assumptions. So long in isolation gave me a lot of time for introspection, even before the Ukraine invasion unleashed violence on a scale I hadn't imagined possible in our times. I realise now that I was wrong about Russia in many respects, especially where it mattered the most.

When Putin initially became President, I was among the many foreigners who welcomed the centralisation of power he imposed. After the chaos and corruption of the Yeltsin years, when the government was incapable of fulfilling basic obligations – and when Baring Vostok had to regularly defend our companies from hostile and arrogant oligarchs – I thought Russia was overdue a swing of the pendulum towards greater state control. This was a view shared at the time not only by investors, but by most Western governments, including the US.

The relative stability and prosperity of Putin's first two terms seemed to validate this belief. Now I can see that the system Putin was creating to subdue and control the oligarchs – his security and control apparatus, the *siloviki* – is a much bigger problem for Russia and its neighbours, and will be much harder to eliminate. The security forces will not willingly give up power now that they hold it absolutely. Even when their actions cause great damage to Russia overall, they will never admit a mistake and rarely, if ever, reverse gears. The Russian people themselves are the principal victims of this cynical and remorseless system.

Before the war, I was more optimistic about Russia than almost all my Russian friends. I thought this was because I was more exposed than most of them to the best side of Russia – hard-working entrepreneurs, great companies, creative young people. But perhaps my Russian friends' pessimism was grounded in a better appreciation of the country's history, and for the various forces that were leading to a conflict between Russia and the West.

I overestimated human rationality and underestimated the role of geopolitics and nationalism. I thought open military warfare between Russia and Ukraine was irrational and therefore unlikely. Even in the days just before 24 February 2022, like most people, I believed the Russian troops massed on the border were Putin's clumsy way of getting the world's attention and forcing real negotiations about NATO, Crimea and Donbas. Even once the invasion began, I had hope of a swift end to hostilities. In hindsight, I underestimated several key factors: the Ukrainian people's skill and tenacity in fighting to remain an independent state; the resolve of Western nations to support Ukraine with military equipment and financing; and, most significantly, Putin's capacity to make a huge strategic mistake with such damaging consequences for Russia itself. No matter how the war ends, Russia will be worse off strategically than it was beforehand.

As for my own case, I was never naïve about the depth of corruption in Russia, but wrongly assumed that it would never be applied against someone like me. I thought my funds were simply too useful to the economy. I had seen the brutal and arbitrary methods of the Russian security services in arresting and prosecuting various oligarchs and opposition figures, but rationalised those cases by labelling the figures involved as 'political'. Those were the rules of the jungle, as I saw it, and as a foreigner you couldn't change it, so you either accepted it or got out. As someone uninvolved in politics, I didn't think such types of arrest could ever apply to me, and probably also assumed that being a foreigner provided at least some additional protection. All those assumptions proved to be wrong.

I recall a meeting I had about ten years ago with a journalist, Arkady Ostrovsky, in which we argued whether Russia was getting better or worse. Based on the young people I worked with every day across dozens of companies and in many different cities, I held that this generation was much more productive, more empowered with information and with a vastly better standard of living than their parents', and, even more so, their grandparents', generations. Despite the corruption and increasing control of the *siloviki*, I believed Russia was taking two steps forward for every step back. But Arkady dismissed the significance of the younger business generation, predicting that the combination of eroding freedoms and nationalist fervour would eventually result in something terrible.

Neither of us convinced the other, and we agreed to disagree. I can see now that he was right, or at least more so than I was. It turned out that Russia was taking one step forward, two steps back, and not the other way around. But I still expect that in the very long term, looking forward another ten or twenty years, that young generation will be decisive for Russia. I continue to believe the seeds planted by the business community, including by foreign investors, have made a lasting difference to the perspective and outlook of millions of young Russians. They have seen first-hand the benefits and advantages of learning from global models that work elsewhere, and of playing by international rules in terms of contracts and governance. The innovative Russian companies like Yandex and Tinkoff that succeeded the most did so by embracing a culture that was anti-hierarchy, meritocratic, and willing to admit mistakes; in short, the exact opposite of the culture that exists in the Russian government and most state companies.

Eventually, when Putin is gone and the current generation of leaders no longer in the picture, the pendulum will swing and there will once again be an opportunity to pursue a new relationship with Russia. When that happens, today's young generation of Russians will hold the key. I hope the West will avoid closing doors (and minds) to them, starting with those who want to emigrate. If we remain open, I'm optimistic that they will help to establish a relationship that can deliver sustainable peace and prosperity for everyone.

★ ★ ★

As I plot the path of my new life outside of Russia, there are moments when I realise how my years over there have conditioned me in ways I had not grasped.

For years, Mastercard had a famous TV advertising campaign which it called 'Priceless'. A series of ads would start with someone purchasing an item – baseball tickets, in one example – and show the cost, $46. Then they'd purchase another item, like two hot dogs and two sodas, $22. Autographed baseball, $50. Then the camera shows the father and son watching the game, laughing and talking with great interest. 'Real conversation with 11-year-old son: Priceless'. There were many variations on the theme. It was a campaign that sprung to my mind around late 2022, several months after I had left Russia.

Russians have a paranoia about their mobile phones, for fear of someone monitoring them. This fear manifests in different ways. At meetings in Russia, it's not uncommon for people to leave their telephones outside a meeting room or away from the dinner table. Others will switch their devices off or turn them to aeroplane mode. When people mention President Putin, even in a neutral light, they sometimes only whisper his name, or refer to him as 'Mr Number One', or just point to the ceiling. It's as if he is Voldemort, the one who can't be named. I often thought such precautions were simply paranoia. But after my arrest, I too became paranoid about being monitored, for obvious reasons. Unconsciously, I adopted the approach of my Russian friends towards their phones.

There is a rational explanation for this behaviour. Since the rule of law in Russia is so arbitrary, a fragment of a phone conversation or a recording of someone speaking at a meeting has frequently been enough to justify an arrest. Even innocent comments may be taken out of context and used against an individual. It's a lot easier than proving someone's actual guilt. More importantly for the authorities, it's a means of ensuring obedience and keeping everyone constantly afraid of crossing lines. To have a telephone in your pocket in Russia is like staring at a billboard that says 'Big Brother is Watching You'. It's a symbol of their control over you, even if you don't recognise it.

When Edward Snowden fled the US and sought sanctuary in Russia after his revelations about surveillance by the US National Security

Agency, a Russian colleague of mine expressed outrage that the US government was monitoring phone and text conversations all over the world. I pushed back. 'In all my life,' I said to him, 'I never had a phone conversation in America where someone said "Let's not discuss that on the telephone." In Russia, I have heard that a thousand times. So don't try to pretend that America is the first or only country to do this.'

While true, what I should have said is that it matters less who is monitoring your phone than what they can do with the information. I never worried about American agencies monitoring my phone because I know I have rights to defend myself in America. I know I won't be arrested simply for expressing my opinions about politics or anything similar. In Russia, no one has that confidence. On the contrary, people know they are positively at risk if they are critical of Putin or his war.

For months after I left Russia, I continued to be apprehensive about my mobile phone, switching it to flight mode before certain meetings. I quickly got a new UK mobile phone and carried two devices for a while; but I still needed my Russian one as that was how my advocates and Moscow colleagues continued to stay in touch. I sometimes put my Russian phone in another room when having conversations on my UK model – and even on that one, I continued to be cautious to some extent. It takes a while to shake off paranoia.

I recall a meeting in May 2022 with a Russian friend, who had by then been living in Europe for ten years. He watched me glancing apprehensively at my phone when the conversation steered towards Putin and the war. He said, 'What are you afraid of? I'm free and in Europe. You're free, too. FUCK THEM ALL!!!'

It took several more months before I finally stopped fearing my phone altogether. It was a gradual process, but I recall a specific moment – a Zoom call, discussing the war and its consequences with a large, international group of people. Suddenly it hit me: I really am free and can say whatever I want. My phone, like those of most people lucky enough to live in free countries, returned to being *just* a useful device and not a tool for repression. It was a moment of enlightenment. I felt, at long last, like shouting, 'FUCK THEM ALL!!!'

Americans and Europeans take for granted the freedom in which they live. With some rare exceptions, they make decisions and express views without fear of unjust prosecution. They don't appreciate the cost of those freedoms or how lucky they are to live in countries with institutions that protect their rights.

But not me. I often think of that old Mastercard slogan. Not fearing your telephone: Priceless.

Epilogue

Brave New World

April 2024

It's a sunny spring Sunday in Mexico City and I'm in the festive and leafy Chapultepec Park with a group of young Russians. My company has recently invested in Plata, a start-up Mexican digital bank founded in 2022 by experienced managers from Tinkoff Bank in Russia. By now, there are already 1,000 people working for the company, including 300 Russians, of whom fifty work in Mexico City and the rest (IT developers and engineers) in Cyprus and Spain. The team has a wonderful mix of Russian and Mexican talent.

Oleg Tinkov, whose family also invested in the company, and I invite the company's Russian team members to join us for a walk in the park. It's a great opportunity to talk informally and get to know each other better. Most of them have left Russia since the start of the war, coming to Mexico in 2023.

My two-week visit to Mexico City has been personally intense and eventful. Working early in the mornings via Zoom and email with Baring Vostok colleagues in Europe, we have finally completed our fund's exit from Russia. Then, most afternoons, I'm at the Plata office for product review meetings and strategy updates, speaking in Russian for hours each day since the key managers in those areas are mostly from Moscow. These meetings are sometimes confrontational but also refreshingly direct, pragmatic and productive. Something I had grown used to with our successful companies of the past, like Yandex, Kaspi and Tinkoff.

I'm also out in the city every day with Mexican colleagues meeting local partners and visiting our operation centres. Mexico City, especially the central Reforma and Polanco districts, is buzzing with energy and has a fantastic vibe. Plata is running a popular TV ad and billboard campaign that is generating its own buzz. I can sense the excitement of the entire Plata team as they feel the interest growing in their brand and product. Applications to join the company are skyrocketing. We have the highest-rated Mexican financial app on the App Store and are attracting 3,000 new customers every day by word of mouth.

Amid all this activity, I get word from Moscow that my probation period has expired and my conviction is vacated. It's ironic to get this news when I'm more than 6,000 miles away yet surrounded by Russians. I mention the news to colleagues over tacos at lunch. In the usual Russian style, they hug me and erupt with congratulations, while simultaneously urging that all bastards of the world go fuck themselves.

About thirty of the Plata team show up for our Sunday walk, all young Russians and some with their families. Looking at this group, and especially their kids, reinforces my sense that we are living in truly historic times. Emigration from Russia since 2022 has reached almost a million people. The scale almost exceeds even the last great human exodus from Eastern Europe after the Russian revolution in 1917.

But the world is very different today, and these émigrés are different from their ancestors. There were many success stories among the Russians, Ukrainians, Armenians, Jews and other people who fled the Soviet Union after the 1917 revolution: composers or artists like Rachmaninoff and Chagall, and business titans like Sikorsky and Sarnoff, to name a few. But many more of today's wave of émigrés have the skills and mindset to thrive in a globally connected and digital world. As I listen to the team's questions and observations, I can't help but get excited about what this generation will achieve.

I also realise that I still have a lot to contribute. The young Russians on our team look up to me, and especially to Oleg, as role models who created unique businesses despite constant challenges. We both have the battle scars to prove it. Sharing jokes at each other's expense, we laugh out loud as we walk through the park. But we also get asked some serious questions, mainly about Plata but also about personal development and current events. I can see that our answers and advice make a difference as they pause and consider what we have to say. Of course, I also learn a lot from them as I ask my own questions back.

Lyudmila Bakatina, the wife of my friend and former colleague Vadim Bakatin, used to say that Vadim's time in our office rejuvenated him and made him feel younger. Lyudmila was a doctor herself and recalled lab experiments in which old mice were put into cages with young mice to test the impact. The results proved that the interaction resulted in renewal: the old mice became a bit faster and more agile as a result of the constant proximity with their younger peers. I'm convinced this is true for humans too, and our walk through the park with so many talented and ambitious young men and women reinforces it.

We complete a circuit in a couple of hours, but before we head for home, someone suggests a beer, a Russian *pasaschok* ('one for the road'). I wander over to a stall by the park entrance and buy a round of Modelos for everyone, cleaning out the inventory of the overjoyed vendor. We gather in a big circle, clinking our bottles together, and one of the Russians gives the classic toast: '*Za nas!*' ('To us!'). As I look into their eyes and see the sparkle of enthusiasm, I imagine them really thinking: 'To the future!'

Acknowledgements

I owe a debt of gratitude to many people who helped to make this book a reality, and even more people who helped me through the last five difficult years, the most trying ordeal of my life.

Odyssey Moscow would never have existed without the team from The History Press, who believed in my story from the beginning, especially Mark Benyon, Laura Perehinec and Jezz Palmer. I also received invaluable advice from Andrew Lownie, my literary agent. The talented Dan Smith helped tremendously as my editorial consultant, helping refine, reshape and reorder my drafts into what is now a much better (and shorter) book. I always appreciated Dan's tactfulness in delivering much-needed criticism of my ideas.

I also had invaluable advice and encouragement from many friends about the book. Big thanks to Mark and Lisa Pattis, Kate Brown, Kate Bucknell, Dudley Fishburn, David Bernstein, Charlie Ryan and Otto Pohl. And especially huge thanks to Liam Halligan, who was a constant supporter and sparring partner, encouraging me to keep going when I thought a few times of abandoning the project, and giving advice about all aspects of the book.

Zooming out and recognising the people to whom I owe my freedom, I start with Timofey Gridnev, my main Russian lawyer (advocate). I wouldn't be here, writing this in freedom, if not for Timofey. His reputation as Russia's top criminal law advocate is 100 per cent justified. But he also became a good friend through the hundreds of hours we spent together, and his wife and daughters are now friends of my family. I'd also like to recognise and thank my other advocates, Larisa Kashtanova, Dmitry Kletochkin and Dmitry Savochkin, all accomplished lawyers who helped me through dark times. And a special thanks also to Grigory Zhdanov, my lawyer from the former Baring Vostok team, who always provides wise counsel.

I have great respect and appreciation for my former colleagues from Baring Vostok. We didn't always agree about everything, but we had a legendary partnership and achieved amazing results together over more than twenty-five years. I'm grateful for the support they showed during my detention and I'm sorry for the enormous stress our case caused to the whole team, beginning with the raid on our office on 14 February 2019. Elena, Katya, Dmitry and Marina were under tremendous pressure, having to manage a huge legal team in a complex case about a project with which they had no involvement prior to our arrests: an almost impossible task. Yet somehow, they managed to do it successfully. Since the war in Ukraine and our fund's exit from Russia, we have now fully separated and have no common business interests, but I wish them success in their future paths. I would like to thank all former colleagues from the Baring Vostok team for our friendships and fun times over many years, with special thanks to Aleksey, Anatoly, Sasha, Anna, Jean-Michel, Tav, Volodya, Igor, Valera and Natalya. (The words and thoughts in this book are solely mine and don't reflect those of my former colleagues.)

I feel huge sympathy and solidarity with those colleagues who were caught up in the Vostochny case together with me: Vagan Abgaryan, Philippe Delpal and Ivan Zyuzin from Baring Vostok, as well as Maxim Vladimirov from PKB and Alexander Tsakunov from Vostochny. They all had a much harder experience than me, serving longer time in miserable Russian SIZOs for the same cynical, absurd case which targeted all of us. They are all honest men who faced the injustice and hardship with dignity and courage.

I am also very proud of the colleagues who form our core ongoing team at Baring Ventures focusing now on international investments:

David Bernstein, Alex Baumgaertner, Galia Maier, Holly Nielsen, and Nicki Marotta, as well as Julian Timms and Gillian Newton. This battle-hardened and deeply experienced team has enormous potential going forward, and it's an honour for me to work alongside all of you.

Eternal gratitude for Mikheil Lomtadze and Vyacheslav Kim, founders of the extraordinary company Kaspi, who have been my partners and friends for twenty years. It has been truly inspiring to watch Kaspi's growth from a vague idea into a world-class and -scale business; the company's culture is deservedly a Harvard case study for excellence in innovation. More personally, I always knew I could count on Misha and Slava, and I will be forever grateful for their support during my ordeal.

A big Siberian hug to my invincible (and irrepressible) friend, Oleg Tinkov. Oleg is one of the most unusual and talented people on our planet, and he never ceases to impress and surprise me. When I saw him after I finally got out in 2022, he noted the common destinies that bind us: born just a couple months apart, in the deep interiors of our countries, we rose to success beyond our dreams before each of us was humbled by arrest, prosecution and cancer. Now he is my biggest reminder every day to appreciate that we are alive and free. Thanks also to my friend Oliver Hughes, who was also a crucial part of the success of Tinkoff Bank before he left in 2022. The letters I received from them, as well as from Leonid Boguslavsky, the famous venture capital investor who is also my good friend, when I was in SIZO were a huge comfort and helped me endure that grim period of my life.

I was honoured to become close friends starting in the late 1990s with Alexei Leonov and Tom Stafford, two legendary space explorers and extraordinary individuals. To list their career accomplishments would take (and has taken) entire books. After the historic Apollo–Soyuz mission which they jointly commanded, they shared a friendship, mutual respect and camaraderie which spanned fifty years. It was touching to witness this friendship up close at a personal level, but it was also an inspiring example of what might have been achieved in bilateral relations if events were driven by normal people in both countries, and not by *siloviki* or geopolitics. Leonov and Stafford both recently passed away; I'd like to believe their heroic spirits live on in the eternal cosmos. They were my dear friends and will be missed by many, many admirers and friends worldwide.

There were several influential Russians who spoke up for me, and without whom I probably would never have achieved freedom: Boris Titov, Kirill Dmitriev, Pyotr Aven, Aleksei Kudrin, Andrey Kostin, Elvira Nabiullina, Valentin Yumashev and especially German Gref. It took courage for all of them to stand up for me against the powerful FSB. Some of them I have known for years, and some I never even met. Mentioning their names here with respect and gratitude will probably cause some people in the West to accuse me of excessive sympathy to sanctioned individuals. But only a coward would fail to recognise courageous actions from people who acted solely on principle. I will never forget that.

My friend Ruben Vardanyan was also among the influential figures who spoke up publicly on my behalf after my arrest. I was able to thank Ruben personally for his brave support. Ruben was himself later entangled in the tragic political conflict between his home country, Armenia, and Azerbaijan. He was detained by Azeri authorities in September 2023 and is now held in a prison in Baku. He is an honest man and I hope he will soon be free and reunited with his loving family.

The US government supported me constantly throughout the entire process, through two very different US administrations. I would like to thank Presidents Trump and Biden, Secretaries of State Pompeo and Blinken, Special Envoy for Hostage Affairs Roger Carstens, Ambassador Jon Huntsman and especially Ambassador John Sullivan. My wrongful detention was raised by them and others in almost every bilateral meeting held between US and Russian government officials from 2019 to 2022. The State Department showed a sophistication and nuance in their messaging about my case, being unfailingly supportive and keeping my name always on the agenda, but not (at my request) including me in the discussions about hostage swaps. They understood, like I did, that this was the best way to strengthen efforts of my Russian supporters and would get me out faster. At a time of bitter divisiveness in our American domestic politics, there is one fact of which we can all be proud: regardless of which party or individual is in power, when an American abroad is wrongfully detained, they know their government will work tirelessly until they are free. I deeply appreciate that.

I'm grateful to the many foreign journalists who covered my case, from the *Wall Street Journal* (Alan and Tom), *Financial Times* (Max and Henry), *New York Times*, Bloomberg, and BNE Intellinews (Ben). I also have respect and appreciation for the Russian journalists who bravely told the truth, or at least most of the truth, about my story despite what must have been intense pressure from the security services. Special thanks to *The Bell*, RBC, *Kommersant* and *Forbes Russia*.

The PR advisors of our fund played a big role in helping us, EM Advisors (until 2022) and now SnowHill. Thanks to Tom Blackwell, Denis Denisov, Sam VanDerlip and Maria Levitov. They were persistent and creative, keeping the story at the forefront of people's minds. That wasn't an easy task given short news cycles and attention spans in today's world.

Alexis Rodzianko of the American Chamber of Commerce and Dan Russell of the US–Russia Business Council worked actively behind the scenes to ensure that the US government and business communities were fully aligned about the case.

I'm humbled and still in awe of the friends in the US and UK who had my back and supported my family when I was away: Robert Luke, Joe Ferretti, Charlie Ryan, Andy Saperstein, Jon Duskin, John Karabelas, my OU college friends, the Aldro gang, Yulia Chupina and many others. And three cheers to my friends from the former Moscow expat community: Peter O'Brien, Dan Wolfe, Marcus Montenecourt, Mark Stiles, Avi Aliman, Drew Guff, Bob Foresman, Bernie Sucher, Mike White and many others. The pints of Guinness and darts competitions at Sally O'Briens are sorely missed. To all my friends, my main goal in the years ahead is to be just as good of a friend for you, whenever you need it most, as you were to me.

Big thanks to Joe Harroz, Joe Ferretti and Chad Bohanon for sending me USBs and DVDs of my beloved Oklahoma Sooners' football games, the full 2019 and 2020 seasons as they were happening but also some epic games from decades ago. I loved watching every minute of them; they helped me feel connected to my motherland and survive the maddening monotony of Russian house arrest.

The investors in Baring Vostok funds could have been excused for cutting and running immediately when the founder of their Russia fund was arrested in Moscow. Yet they stuck with us and remain to this day. Even after the fund's disappointing but unavoidable decision to exit Russia entirely after the war, their investments in our funds have been very profitable. This is due in large part to the exceptional entrepreneurs we backed. Besides those whom I already recognised above, I'd like to thank also Arkady Volozh (Yandex), Alexander Rodnyansky (CTC Media), and Finian O'Sullivan and Atul Gupta (Burren Energy). These companies were our fund's first breakout success stories; growing way beyond our initial expectations, they proved that the known unknowns of any investment can be joyful surprises when extraordinary teams come together.

To Neri Tollardo, Danil Anisimov and the entire Plata team in Mexico: working with you these last two years reminded me what I love so much about entrepreneurship. It will be a blast watching and helping you grow in the years ahead. *Ypa!* And *vamos!*

My bosses in my first jobs had a huge influence on me, especially Ron Freeman, John Dare, Terry English, Chris Brotchie, and Mike McMahon. I have been my own boss for twenty-seven years, but I will always be grateful to the people who trusted me at the beginning of my career. They all gave a chance to a boy from Oklahoma, and I hope I never gave them cause to regret it.

I can't describe without getting emotional how much gratitude I feel to the men for whom this book is dedicated: my comrades from cell 604. Andrei, Sanych, Grisha, Sasha Rostov, Big Sasha, and Zhendos – wherever you are, I hope you are free, safe, and surrounded by loved ones. If you're not yet free, I pray that you don't give up hope. Destiny is powerful and works in unexpected ways, and not only bad ones. *С Богом!* You deserve to live full lives and I hope our paths cross again one day.

I owe who I am, and much more, to my family in Oklahoma: Mom, Kevin, Cathy, Beth and their wonderful families. I'm sorry for the stress your distant son/brother may have caused. Wherever I am in the world, I cherish the roots which unite us.

Finally, the bedrock of my life, *La Familia*: Julia, Mishka (Michael), Sasha, and Niko. I still regret missing some key years of your lives, but I couldn't be prouder with how you handled it. Julia defended our family like a lioness, while making our Moscow apartment during house arrest a comforting sanctuary, and later becoming the most impactful reviewer of this book. I know my experience taught you kids the importance of integrity and reputation, without which I would have been doomed. I hope the book also teaches you the power of being optimistic, even in a world where bad things sometimes happen. Being optimistic is much more fun than the alternative. Together we are an unbeatable team, and I love you all very much.

Index